NEW AFRICAN THINKERS

AGENDA 2063
CULTURE
AT THE HEART OF
SUSTAINABLE
DEVELOPMENT

Edited by Olga Bialostocka

HSRC
PRESS

Published by HSRC Press
Private Bag X9182, Cape Town, 8000, South Africa
www.hsrcpress.ac.za

First published 2018

ISBN (soft cover) 978-0-7969-2565-7
ISBN (pdf) 978-0-7969-2566-4

© 2018 Human Sciences Research Council

The publishers have no responsibility for the continued existence or accuracy of URLs for external or third-party Internet websites referred to in this book and do not guarantee that any content on such websites is, or will remain, accurate or appropriate.

The publishers thank Titus Matiyane for permission to reproduce portions from two of his panoramas on the part opener pages.

Copy-edited by Linda Cilliers
Typeset by Karen Lilje
Cover design by Nic Jooste
Printed by Capitil Press, Paarden Eiland, South Africa

Distributed in Africa by Blue Weaver
Tel: +27 (021) 701 4477; Fax Local: (021) 701 7302; Fax International: 0927865242139
www.blueweaver.co.za

Distributed in Europe and the United Kingdom by Eurospan Distribution Services (EDS)
Tel: +44 (0) 17 6760 4972; Fax: +44 (0) 17 6760 1640
www.eurospanbookstore.com

Distributed in North America by River North Editions, from IPG
Call toll-free: (800) 888 4741; Fax: +1 (312) 337 5985
www.ipgbook.com

Contents

Figures

Tables

Preface

The 10th Africa Young Graduates and Scholars (AYGS) conference was held at the University of Limpopo from the 14th to the 17th of March 2016 under the theme 'The Africa we want'. The four-day conference gathered emerging scholars from varied African countries, among whom were representatives from some member states of the Southern African Development Community (Zimbabwe, Zambia, Botswana, South Africa and Swaziland), as well as nationals of Cameroon, Nigeria, Burundi and Kenya.

The theme of the symposium was a direct reference to the Agenda 2063 developed by the African Union (AU). Taking the Agenda's seven aspirations for Africa as a basis for all discussions, participants tried to emphasise specifically the role that culture, with its many aspects and dimensions, plays in sustainable development, peace, good governance and integration on the continent.

This book is a collection of papers presented at the symposium by their authors.

The conference was organised by the Africa Institute of South Africa at the Human Sciences Research Council (AISA-HSRC) in cooperation with the University of Limpopo (UL), and with assistance from the Department of Science and Technology (DST), the Academy of Science of South Africa (ASSAf) and the African World Heritage Fund (AWHF). The conference would not have been possible without the support of the Research and Impact Assessment (RIA) unit at the HSRC, particularly Sam Lekala, Lindiwe Mashologu, Adziliwi Nematandani, Ithuteng Sekaledi and Thulani Dlamini.

Introduction

Olga Bialostocka and Vuyo Mjimba

Culture at the heart of sustainable development

Africa's past and present classifications within the global labels of the First, Second and Third Worlds, the developed and developing countries, the industrialised and industrially lagging economies, and the Global North and South can be argued to derive from the dictates of the continent's history of being conquered and colonised by European nations. While direct colonialism has largely ended, its legacy lingers in the ideologies that dominate the continent's policies and practices. A notable and concerning entrenchment in this regard concerns the concept of development, habitually defined in economic terms and measured through indicators such as gross domestic product (GDP), per capita income, and access to electricity and education, among others (Dickson 2015). It is thus not surprising that all the previous and current systems of classification that divide the various regions of the world in terms of their state of development are predominantly based on finance-linked measures. However, such categorisation is misleading, because it reduces the importance of other human factors in discussions about development. This narrow view creates an image of a world built on the ideals of capitalism and modernisation, despite some ills associated with these principles. Todaro (1994) moves away from this constricted view by emphasising that economic development must, inter alia, include improvements in self-esteem needs, choice, and freedom from oppression. He argues that a wider view of the concept of development avoids and/ or prevents some of the shortcomings that are embedded in the narrow finance-based view of what it is to be developed.

While the gap in the simultaneous and equal consideration of the many aspects of development narrows globally, Africa remains trapped in the foreign *how* to develop and *what it means* to be developed. In the dominant view, development is considered as being driven by factors that include the rate and magnitude of domestic savings, innovation, improvements in the standard of living, and democracy. The implementation shows a bias towards neoliberal economic orthodoxy, and the expected outcomes are largely a Western vision of a 'developed' continent. While there are universalities in the formulation, implementation and outcomes of development, it is important to note that there are, and will always be, some fundamental differences too. Lall (1992: 7) captures these variances, stating that 'there are not only many roads to heaven but also many heavens'. The irony is that Africa remains largely bound to development arguments the merits of which, to some extent, are questionable. For example, positive trends in economic data are celebrated as a signal of economic progress. However, some of them do not necessarily indicate a change in the living conditions of the entire population. In addition, to date there is a paucity of evidence conclusively proving a strong and direct relationship between the highly publicised notion of democracy, as practised in the West, and positive economic development and growth. Equally, there is also limited evidence of an underlying relationship between the rule of law and economic development (Davis & Trebilcock 1999). These unsubstantiated correlations are persistently used and the concepts behind them promoted in public policy and practice spaces. This occurs despite a growing acknowledgement of the fact that development is a value-laden concept that is deeply founded on issues of power and culture, among others. This means that it is not politically and ideologically neutral; its meanings and interpretations are dependent on a context. Meanings and interpretations are constructed based on human modes of life and the different ways in which people adapt to various living conditions. As a result, the core of sustainable development, intra- and inter-generational equity, justice, participation and gender equity, as well as ecological quality, will differ between and within cultures (Dessein et al. 2015). Accordingly, the increasingly loud maxim of 'African solutions to African problems' is compelling (and should continue to compel) Africans to redefine their development objectives, means and ends, based on their own cultures and contexts. The question is: What space is available for the continent to exercise this right to free and minimally impeded practice and policy?

It is arguable that this space has opened under the international Sustainable Development Goals (SDGs) implementation policy regime. Proposals for the implementation of the SDGs emphasise the need for each country to mobilise domestic resources for the process. In principle, this mobilisation offers Africa the possibility of exercising its right to free and minimal external impediments in its practice and policy spaces. However, the desired freedom dictates the need for pragmatism that acknowledges local realities, capacity and capabilities. A big challenge in this journey is dislodging the deeply entrenched views of development that elevate economic wellbeing above all other wellbeing (such as social, cultural and environmental). The appropriate contextualisation of the state of being 'developed' is important in that the SDGs are explicit in the overarching imperative of 'leaving no one behind' not only during their 15-year tenure but, more importantly, at the end of it. The motto of 'leaving no one behind' entails that progress made under the SDGs' drive has to include considerations of the social, cultural, economic and environmental contexts of different global communities.

Within the sustainable development paradigm, and in a way responding to the call for the contextualisation of development strategies, is the continental Agenda 2063: The Africa We Want initiative. Prepared as a vision for Africa covering a 50-year period, Agenda 2063 lists political, economic, social and environmental ambitions of the continent that correspond to and complement the objectives of the SDGs, focusing on seven aspirations, namely:
1. A prosperous Africa based on inclusive growth and sustainable development.
2. An integrated continent, politically united and based on the ideal of Pan-Africanism and the vision of Africa's Renaissance.

3. An Africa of good governance, democracy, respect for human rights, justice and the rule of law.
4. A peaceful and secure Africa.
5. An Africa with a strong cultural identity, common heritage, shared values and ethics.
6. An Africa where development is people-driven, unleashing the potential of women and youth.
7. Africa as a strong, united and influential global player and partner.

The Agenda paints a picture of shared prosperity and improved socioeconomic wellbeing, unity and integration, self-determination and freedom that Africa should achieve by 2063. The aspirations address various challenges facing the continent. Of special interest to this book is the fifth aspiration of the Agenda, which directly and explicitly articulates the issue of culture as an integral component of the continent's development desire. This is an important consideration, given that culture directly and indirectly impacts on the deliverance of all the other aspirations. Harris (2010; 2005) posits that, instead of protecting cultures, religions, traditions and languages, the focus should be shifted to people. However, separating one from the other seems a daunting task. Accordingly, one needs to ask:

1. can human development be truly sustainable if it does not consider culture?
2. can we speak of Africa's Renaissance without reference to the plurality of cultures on the continent?
3. can human rights be rightly called human if they do not account for the cultural rights of indigenous people and cultural minorities?
4. can we envision a peaceful, strong and united Africa if we do not tackle the politicisation of cultural differences? and
5. will reducing an individual to their social role, forgetting about their cultural identity, be enough for the development of Africa to be considered people-driven?

South Africa declared its readiness to play a part in the realisation of the Agenda 2063 vision and, in line with it, launched the Charter for African Cultural Renaissance in May 2015. Thus far (2017), only 11 other African countries have ratified the Charter, which recognises the contribution of cultural diversity to the expression of national and regional identities. The launch of the Charter in South Africa was accompanied by the announcement of a festival of music, dance, film, crafts, and food culture planned for the month of May, traditionally celebrated as 'Africa month'.

But shouldn't every month of the year in Africa be 'Africa month'? Shouldn't Africans recognise their own identity, language and heritage, and celebrate these every day? Culture is much more than a demonstration of difference. We live our culture every day—through the language we speak, the behaviours we routinely and subconsciously exhibit, the means of production we choose, the values we live by and the communities we belong to, among other features.

Identity, belonging, nation-building and Pan-Africanism inform the way in which we live and relate to others. This means that the socioeconomic transformation on the continent—and, more broadly, the transformation of global relations—

should begin with changing the way we perceive our cultural background and heritage. These should be seen as assets, not liabilities. It is important to bring about a better understanding of what culture is as a component of our identity and a tenet of sustainable development. Not only does culture carry the potential of being a driver of sustainable development, it also enables that process. Therefore, culture must be understood in more than economic terms and be articulated with reference to all social, environmental and economic practices that characterise a society. In other words, culture needs to be acknowledged as a precept of sustainable development. Indeed, United Cities and Local Governments (UCLG) recognised at the United Nations (UN) Economic and Social Council (ECOSOC) meeting in 2013 that 'a three-pillar paradigm [of sustainable development[1]] fails because it lacks a soul, the values, practices and expressions providing coherence and meaning to development in cities, nations and in our existence as human beings: culture' (UCLG 2013).

Culture

Culture is a complex notion with multiple definitions and various approaches. Several levels (individual and collective), aspects (static and dynamic) and properties (for example, contextual—ecological, economical, sociopolitical; perceptual; and material elements) of culture can be distinguished, which makes the term so elusive that it is used differently in varied contexts.

The United Nations Educational, Scientific and Cultural Organisation's (UNESCO) Universal Declaration on Cultural Diversity (2001: 4) describes the term 'culture' as 'the set of distinctive spiritual, material, intellectual and emotional features of a social group'. These features can be perceived in two ways: as finite, historical phenomena that determine the individual (essentialist approach), or as socially constructed characteristics that are continually renegotiated (processual/dynamic approach). Cultural essentialism looks at aspects of culture as objective 'schemes'. Thus, it can easily lead to categorisation of people according to established patterns. Such a reified culture tends to give birth to stereotypes. Meanwhile, the non-essentialist approach to culture sees it as an outcome of a constantly dynamic process of change, in which people construct their identities rather than acquire them (Baumann 1999). None of the many identities 'created' in this process are ultimate, nor the values associated with them universal. Instead, they are all contextual.

Culture was neither included (explicitly) in the three-pillar sustainable development paradigm, as described in the *Brundtland Report* (1987) and many subsequent works, nor was it clearly present in the Millennium Development Goals (MDGs) (2000). The close relationship between culture and development has been emphasised by policymakers only in the last decade, when it was acknowledged that culture was not 'decorative' or secondary to sustainable development, but rather constituted a crucial element of the concept and the process. Consequently, the newest post-2015 sustainable development UN agenda (SDGs) speaks of the context-based approach to sustainable development and improved governance.

With the motto 'one size does not fit all', this new perspective can be argued to be human-centred compared with its predecessors, because it takes into account local contexts in designing development strategies.

Given that culture constitutes a foundation of one's identity and as such represents each person's frame of reference, it is contended that culture should be mainstreamed into all development policies. As a mediating force that regulates and shapes development, culture has a transformative power—either towards or against change. It can thus play different roles: *in*, *for*, and *as* sustainable development (Figure 1). Culture *in* sustainable development simply represents an additional, freestanding pillar linked to the other three tenets in the framework. Culture *for* sustainable development plays the role of a mediator, adding context to the existing paradigm. Culture *as* sustainable development is understood as the foundation and structure for achieving the aims of sustainable development. Being at the core of human thinking and decision-making, it represents a crosscutting dimension of all development initiatives.

Figure 1 *Culture and sustainable development*

The three roles of culture in sustainable development: culture added as a fourth pillar (left diagram), culture mediating between the three pillars (central diagram) and culture as the foundation for sustainable development. The arrows in the right diagram indicate the ever-changing dynamics of culture and sustainable development.

Source: Adapted from Dessein et al. 2015

It has been argued that culture has always been included in the sustainable development framework as part of its social pillar (Owosuyi 2015; Hawkes 2001). However, even though culture and social structure both represent social control systems, the two are significantly different in their scope and purpose. A cultural system deals with meanings, while a social one serves to link those meanings to conditions of particular behaviours within a specific milieu (Parsons 1972). Culture is therefore interwoven with and influenced by the social structure, but it does not have to be aligned with it.

Given the role of culture as a social control and value system that lies at the heart of one's identity and lifestyle, it is not surprising that only culture-sensitive development can be deemed truly sustainable. Accordingly, development strategies and policies should be aligned with the different ways people choose to live their lives and construct themselves, and consider knowledge produced within the many cultures to be more effective in responding to local realities.

> Acknowledgement of cultural diversity adds a crucial dimension to strategies that view sustainability as facilitating the integration of the economic pillar of development with its social and environmental pillars. In this sense, cultural diversity can be seen as a key crosscutting dimension of sustainable development.
>
> (UNESCO n.d.: 25)

The SDGs have acknowledged the importance of integrating cultural diversity and pluralism into development strategies against the 'one size fits all' model. By focusing on the needs and aspirations of people, and acknowledging the agency of local communities, this agenda has emphasised human wellbeing broadly and advocated for a bottom-up model of development. In terms of local responses to the new paradigm, the agenda should ideally translate into engaging local communities and empowering them through recognition of their culture-specific knowledge, and an appreciation of cultural norms and values. In seeking to improve people's living conditions, the freedom to choose their own 'road to heaven' in accordance with their systems of beliefs and values should be seen not only as a key to the sustainability of communities, but also as a basic human right.

Culture has a bearing on poverty and inequality, showing strong linkages to both the economic and the social dimensions of both. It plays a key role in enhancing the quality of education and making it more inclusive. Within this scope, intercultural communication, integration of cultural diversity into education systems, and consideration for gender dynamics are of special importance. Another key role that culture plays in sustainable development is the meaning it assigns to places and a sense of belonging that is born through that process. Accordingly, culture is critical to the sustainable planning and functioning of human settlements, particularly in building peaceful communities.

Finally, culture's intrinsic connection to nature should not be overlooked in matters of environmental sustainability. The more one considers the effects of climate change that are already experienced by communities worldwide, the more important culture becomes for managing the phenomenon. For instance, practices linked to choices of livelihood, food, energy sources and transport modes, among other preferences, can be changed, since they carry a cultural dimension that is dynamic, and thus mouldable. Differentiating between absolute needs and wants with the view to modifying behaviours is critical to meet the pressing dictates of the present (Mjimba 2016). In addition, as part of the effort to include local voices to the sustainable development space, the expertise of indigenous communities should pave the way for conservation, and the sustainable use of biological diversity and other natural assets. Created and tested through the centuries, local knowledge systems carry a greater capacity to adapt to changing local ecosystems in line with existing societal patterns.

The thematic areas covered in this book follow four of the seven aspirations of Agenda 2063, namely:

Part 1: A prosperous Africa based on inclusive growth and sustainable development (Aspiration 1).

Part 2: An Africa of good governance, democracy, respect for human rights, justice and the rule of law (Aspiration 3).

Part 3: An Africa with a strong cultural identity, common heritage, shared values and ethics (Aspiration 5).

Part 4: An Africa where development is people-driven, unleashing the potential of women and youth (Aspiration 6).

Within each of these, the authors analyse challenges faced by Africans on the continent, or particular matters of political, economic and social importance to Africa, and the significance of the sociocultural context in which these phenomena occur.

Part 1 relates directly to the sustainable development paradigm and the critical issue of contextualising development strategies and outcomes. It consists of three chapters in which authors tackle Aspiration 1 of Agenda 2063. James Ojochenemi David discusses the pervasive problem of systemic corruption in sub-Saharan Africa, trying to understand whether it is the 'culture of corruption' that undermines this part of the continent's developmental efforts or whether the 'corruption of Africa's culture' is to be blamed for the current state of affairs instead. The author suggests reimaging Africa's culture with regard to corruption with the view to achieving sustainable development and realising an Africa we want by 2063. Malatsi Seleka interrogates the integration of indigenous knowledge into development planning in Botswana and the sustainability of current practices. Given the limited research into integration, he suggests that a need exists to develop a framework to improve the sustainability of rural development projects through all-encompassing community participation. Dunia Prince Zongwe tells a story of contractual arrangements that three African nations have entered into with external stakeholders to trade natural resources for infrastructure projects. Using political culture as a lens, the author discusses contracts entered into with China by Angola, the Democratic Republic of the Congo, and Ghana, respectively, demonstrating risks associated with political and economic realities of each of these countries, and ways of mitigating them to protect the economic transactions. In his analysis of the three case studies, Zongwe shares lessons for other African nations.

In Part 2, three authors address Aspiration 3 of Agenda 2063. While describing different realities and developmental paths of African states, they argue for a context-specific definition of 'heaven'. Hlengiwe Dlamini discusses Swaziland's monarchical political system of *Tinkhundla* as a genuinely African response to the country's administrative system and local realities. She recognises the shortcomings of this traditional system of governance, while asserting that a refurbishment of *Tinkhundla* could see it adapt and become relevant to the contemporary political trends. Sabelo Wiseman

Ndwandwe examines international human rights and how these relate to African traditions in trying to come up with a framework that would guarantee the observance of law instruments while not relinquishing African moral and political philosophy. He suggests a rights-recognition theory as a model that endorses international human rights, while remaining true to African ethics and ontologies. Azubike Onuora-Oguno and Sigrid Shaanika interrogate the legal framework established to protect the rights of children who are victims of violence and abuse. Extending the traditional understanding of a healthy environment from the physical to encompass also the psychological, the authors explore the role of psychology in the post-conflict rehabilitation of children who have been exposed to abuse.

Part 3 focuses on the role of culture as an essential component of a community's identity and the recognition of cultural diversity as a key factor in achieving equality and inclusion. It comprises three chapters addressing Aspiration 5 of Agenda 2063. Natasha Katuta Mwila's contribution is a diachronic analysis of political leadership in Zambia, from the colonial era to the administration of Michael Chilufya Sata. She explores the relationship between different leadership styles of the successive leaders, and the cultural development Zambia experienced during their time in power, focusing on cultural features in politics, the economy, business and education. Pfunzo Sidogi exposes the limitations and pitfalls of Aspiration 5, juxtaposing its vision with contemporary visual artists' depictions of being African. Focusing on the artwork of South Africa's Titus Matiyane, the author debunks the myth of a homogeneous African identity he considers implicit in Aspiration 5, contending that the continent we want is a place where diversity of all types is unreservedly welcomed. Finally, Matheanoga Fana Rabatoko shares his musicological analysis of the indigenous songs of the Naro people of D'Kar in Botswana. The author's ethnographic research into the music world of this San group serves as a reminder of the need to protect intangible cultural aspects of an indigenous heritage. He argues that San music is suitable for contemporary education, and suggests the traditional songs of the Naro of D'Kar be included in school curricula to keep the indigenous music tradition alive.

Part 4 directly relates to the bottom-up approach premise of the sustainable development discourse as emphasised in Aspiration 6. Matshediso Joy Ndlovu analyses and evaluates stokvels (social groups formed around financial savings and lending) in the KwaZulu-Natal province of South Africa. She focuses on their role as microlenders to small businesses owned by women and the youth. Using a combination of qualitative and quantitative research methods, she demonstrates how stokvels can contribute to South Africa's economy and reveals challenges the microfinance sector faces when it comes to financing small businesses.

The book concludes with a message from two established researchers, who share lessons they have learnt on their scholarly journey. In '#Sowhat? Or a letter to new African thinkers', they disclose pitfalls and temptations emerging scholars may encounter on their career paths.

Notes

1   The three-pillar model of sustainable development consists of economic, environmental and social dimensions. It validated the links between people's economic development, their social context and the natural environment in which they function. It is used as a premise for designing developmental strategies attuned to the needs and capacities of the populations concerned.

References

Baumann G (1999) *The multicultural riddle: Rethinking national, ethnic, and religious identities.* New York: Routledge

Davis K and Trebilcock J (1999) *What role do legal institutions play in development?* Paper prepared for the International Monetary Fund's Conference on Second Generation Reforms, Washington DC, 8–9 November

Dessein J, Soinin K, Fairclough G and Horlings L (2015) *Culture in, for and as sustainable development: Conclusions from the COST action IS1007 investigating cultural sustainability.* Accessed September 2017, www.culturalsustainability.eu/conclusions.pdf

Dickson S (2015) Difference between economic development and economic growth. Accessed September 2017, www.academia.edu/7016400/DIFFERENCE_BETWEEN_ECONOMIC_DEVELOPMENT_AND_ECONOMIC_GROWTH

Harris S (2005) *The end of faith: Religion, terror, and the future of reason.* New York: Norton

Harris S (2010) *The moral landscape: How science can determine human values.* New York: Free Press

Hawkes J (2001) *The fourth pillar of sustainability: Culture's essential role in public planning.* Melbourne: Common Ground Publishing

Lall S (1992) *Selective industrial and trade policies in developing countries: Theoretical and empirical issues.* QEH Working Paper Series. Working Paper No 48

Mjimba V (2016) Relearning our wants and needs for sustainable development. In G Nhamo and V Mjimba (Eds) *Sustainability, climate change and the green economy.* Pretoria: Africa Institute of South Africa

Owosuyi IL (2015) The pursuit of sustainable development through cultural law and governance Frameworks: A South African Perspective. *PER / PELJ* 2015(18)5: 2011–2060

Parsons T (1972) Culture and Social System Revisited. *Social Science Quarterly* 53(2): 253–266.

Todaro MP (1994) *Economic development* (5th ed). New York, London: Longman

UCLG (United Cities and Local Governments) (2013) *ECOSOC 2013: The role of culture in sustainable development to be explicitly recognized.* Accessed September 2017, www.arsiv.uclgmewa. org/doc/kultur_vHYBe.pdf

UNESCO (United Nations Educational, Scientific and Cultural Organisation) (2001) Universal declaration on cultural diversity. Paris: UNESCO. Accessed September 2017, www.unesdoc.unesco.org/images/0012/001271/127162e.pdf

UNESCO (United Nations Educational, Scientific and Cultural Organisation) (n.d.) *World report: Investing in cultural diversity and intercultural dialogue.* Executive Summary. Paris: UNESCO

PART 1

A PROSPEROUS AFRICA BASED ON INCLUSIVE GROWTH AND SUSTAINABLE DEVELOPMENT

1 | Culture of corruption or corruption of culture? Sustainable development in sub-Saharan Africa

James Ojochenemi David

Africa's woes and wealth have been much debated and written about. Yet, only a handful of writers have acknowledged recent progress in economic growth in sub-Saharan Africa.[1] The most naturally endowed countries in the world can be found in Africa, and the continent is considered one of the richest on earth. One scholar observes that Africa has '50 per cent of the world's gold, most of the world's diamonds and chromium, 90 per cent of the cobalt, 40 per cent of world's potential hydro-electric power, 65 per cent of the manganese, millions of acres of untilled farmland' (Kwame 2006). However, at odds with these perceptions is the fact that Africa, especially the sub-Saharan region, still lags behind other regions of the world as far as living standards are concerned. Challenges like political conflict, disease, rampant poverty, inequality and staggering youth unemployment continue to loom despite the vast natural and human capital. These validate the persistent view that Africa is a rich continent with poor people (Berthoud 1990). However, it should be possible to address the continent's development woes by carefully utilising its enormous resources.[2] Yet socioeconomic indices across the continent overwhelmingly reflect a 'paradox of plenty', as the (mis)management of natural resources has directly promoted conflict and civil strife (Elbra 2013; Koubi et al. 2014).

Systemic corruption, argued to be a manifestation of bad leadership, is widely touted as the cause of Africa's underdevelopment or de-development (Médard 2002; Agbiboa 2010).[3] De-development can be understood as a 'process which undermines or weakens the ability of an economy to grow and expand by preventing it from accessing and utilising critical inputs needed to promote internal growth beyond a specific structural level' (Roy 1987: 56). Franks (2005: 106) asserts that 'Africa has suffered from governments that have looted the resources of the state; that could not or would not deliver services to their people; that in many cases were predatory.' Morally neutral language is used to deemphasize corruption at various levels. For instance, as in the United States, bribery becomes 'oiling the wheels' or 'service costs', stealing becomes 'pinching' and 'freeloading' (Kaptein 2012: 40). African anti-corruption activist Prof. Patrick Loch Otieno Lumumba of Kenya says, 'today we hang the good thieves and elect the big thieves in office', claiming that Africa is in the business of 'demonising saints and canonising thieves'.[4] With reference to the pillaging of public funds by our 'misleaders', Lumumba is of the opinion that we should call a spade a spade and label them as thieves rather than mitigate their acts by using a term like 'economic crime' to describe their grand larceny.

Against this backdrop, this chapter interrogates blockages to sustainable development as it pertains to a culture of corruption, while attempting to shed light on perceived cultural causes or drivers of corrupt practices in the sub-Saharan Africa context. The chapter analyses the troika of culture, corruption and development in an attempt to identify historical influences on African culture and their implications on the pervasive corruption in the sub-region. The study that forms the basis for this chapter is exploratory in nature and based on a critical review of relevant literature. Hence, data sources include primary and secondary literature drawn from scholarly and institutional databases such as the Transparency International (TI) and United Nations Human Development reports, among others. Primary search words include 'culture', 'corruption' and 'sustainable development in sub-Saharan Africa'. The overarching rationale is to analyse the relationship between the largely abstract concepts of culture (with a particular reference to ubuntu) and corruption, and their impact on sustainable development in sub-Saharan Africa. The chapter proposes an African moral worldview (ubuntu), to varying degrees common among sub-Saharan African countries, as both a necessary and an effective tool in combating corruption. The first of the four sections deals with the definition and measurement of corruption. The second and third sections highlight the cost and causes of corruption, respectively. The fourth offers analysis and recommendations, with a particular emphasis on the need for more critical engagement with ubuntu as a potential socio-moral remedy.

Defining corruption

While equally common in academic and popular discourse, the term 'corruption' is not easily defined. Many scholars have tried to do so in the abstract, or in relation to specific activities that are seen as corrupt, such as bribery, nepotism and favouritism, among others. Nye (1967: 419) defines corruption as '...behaviour which deviates from the formal duties of a public role because of private-regarding (personal, close family, private clique) pecuniary or status gains; or violates rules against the exercise of certain types of private-regarding influence'. Bribery, nepotism and misappropriation are among the prominent examples of corruption in Nye's definition. Corruption has also been said to be the misuse of entrusted power or public property for private benefit or gain (Bardhan 1997; Uzodike 1999; Mbaku 2000; TI 2015). What has been termed as 'the public-private duality' is central to these and other, similar, definitions (Ekeh 1975: 92). It means that corruption is commonly understood to take place within relationships between the public and private domains as far as the (mis)use or (ab)use for self-gain of office, power, or public resources.

Acts of corruption are not confined to the public sphere; they are equally prevalent in the private sector. 'Business owners who bribe civil servants in order to enhance their ability to gain access to foreign exchange, secure import, export, investment, and production licences, are regarded as engaging in corrupt activities' (Mbaku 2000: 13). Further, questions about whether or not private gains by public officers are reasonably deemed corruption must be clarified. Indeed, as Johnson (2004: 3) observes, situations do arise where private gain by public officers may not be considered corruption simply because: (1) the officer 'is not seeking his or her own personal gain but is seeking benefits for political supporters'; or (2) the officer 'actually enjoys personal gain but it does not significantly affect the policy outcome'. Accordingly, Johnson cautions that 'there isn't *always* an obvious, clear [and] rigid line separating what is legitimate from what is corruption…different people, and different countries can legitimately understand and define corruption differently.'

Bribery, regarded as the most common form of corruption, remains difficult to define. Nye (2002: 419) describes it as 'the use of reward to pervert the judgement of a person in a position of trust'. But, as we shall see soon enough, gift giving has been largely equated with bribery. In line with Johnson's view, what constitutes bribery must thus be understood within a context, or it could be confused with certain cultural practices. The relevance of such distinctions is that it helps challenge the (mis)conception of gift giving as constituting bribery, or the disguise of bribery in gift-giving practices across sub-Saharan Africa. Elsewhere, two other categories of corruption can be identified, namely political and bureaucratic corruption, sometimes referred to as grand and petty corruption, respectively (Chitakunye et al. 2015: 136). The former is seen as the violation of formal rules governing the allocation of public resources by public officials in response to offers of financial gain or political support (Mbaku 2000). Rather than being merely the 'diversion of public resources to non-public purpose', political corruption is employed by political coalitions to capture state apparatus towards self-benefiting ends, such as gaining a monopoly of power (Werlin 1973: 73). Bureaucratic corruption, on the other hand, is oriented towards gaining extra-legal pecuniary or non-pecuniary benefits that do not necessarily have political ramifications.

The difference between political (grand) corruption and bureaucratic (petty) corruption boils down to scale. Political corruption, as often (though not exclusively) manifested in sub-Saharan Africa, takes on the grand form of state capture[5] by leaders for self-interested reasons (TI 2015). Bureaucratic corruption is small by comparison. Notwithstanding the distinction in terms of seriousness, their insidious impacts are the same, given that one reinforces the other.

Thus, the serious corruption of politicians who sign cheques that bounce, of leaders who get millions of dollars by way of kickbacks from multinational companies, and of those who profit heavily from payments for goods that are not needed or below standard, becomes the cause of petty corruption among the ranks of police, customs officials, public servants, ministerial drivers, sweepers, medical nurses and small traders, to name but a few (Waliggo 2007).

This chapter, while clearly acknowledging the wide scope of corruption, limits its focus to political corruption, understood as 'the abuse of entrusted power by political leaders for private gain, with the objective of seizure of state power' (Ekwueme 2014: 72).

It usually involves top officers in government, including presidents, ministers, governors, members of parliament, commissioners, permanent secretaries and other key government officials. Examples of political or grand corruption include kickbacks, especially in public procurement, large-scale embezzlement of public funds, irregularity in public financing, political patronage and clientelism, among others. It also takes the various forms of unethical business deals with multinational companies, which often have long-term, large-scale implications for the wellbeing of broader society (Nye 1967, 2002; Atuobi 2007). Corruption has been described as a culture in Africa, given its prevalence in most of the countries on the continent (Hope 2000). However, corruption is 'an intractable global problem from which no nation or region can claim any exemption' (Chitakunye et al. 2015). It varies only in degrees from place to place.

Measuring corruption: Corruption Perception Index (CPI)

Corruption is a phenomenon of stealth and, as such, difficult to measure directly and objectively. However, various indirect systems of measurement have been advanced, including the TI Corruption Perceptions Index (CPI) (Kyambalesa 2006: 105; TI 2015). The CPI assesses the perception of corruption on a scale of 0 to 10. 'A 0 level denotes a country where most transactions or relations are soiled in corruption, while 10 refers to a highly transparent country' (Tanzi 1998: 577). The charts below demonstrate sub-Saharan Africa's poor CPI rating relative to other regions between 2010 and 2014. This regional picture is informed by the ranking of each country in the region. With the exception of Botswana, sub-Saharan African countries often dominate the worst end of the CPI. The trend analysis also reveals a discouraging outlook for sub-Saharan Africa. While the East European and Central Asian regions also have negative ratings for the period under measurement, it is notable that they improved from 3.0 in 2010 to 3.3 in 2014. Sub-Saharan Africa, on the other hand, slid from 3.4 to 3.3.

Figure 1.1 *CPI: Regional perception 2010–2014*

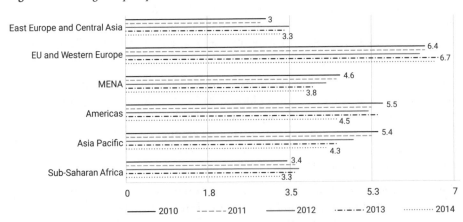

Source: Transparency International (author's compilation)

Figure 1.2 *Regional CPI trends 2010–2014*

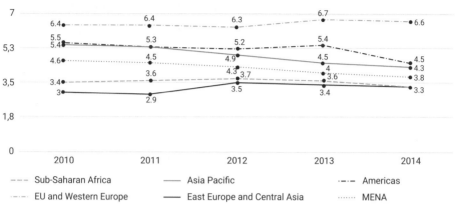

Source: Transparency International (author's compilation)

Not all scholars agree with this rating of corruption in Africa. For instance, De Maria questions the Western tendency towards measurement, as exemplified by the CPI, as a prime source of knowledge and action. He says that the 'softly declared but forcefully present business patronage in the Corruption Perception Index' emphasises the fact that the CPI is merely a tool to provide risk management data for transnational capital rather than for the supposed promotion of good governance (De Maria 2010: 146). The politicisation of the CPI is also a factor. Opposition parties have employed the corruption rhetoric to unseat governments, sometimes for their own corrupt reasons rather than to bring about accountable and good alternative governance. In this regard, CPI presents rather a 'provincialised, subjective, historically bounded and, most saliently, non-indigenous' method of scientific enquiry (Westwood and Jack 2007: 250). Indeed, as a perception-based rating, the CPI is not well aligned with experience-based indicators of corruption. Accordingly, its usefulness in understanding corruption is considered limited (Banuri & Eckel 2012: 4). The CPI must be used cautiously, since not only is it epistemologically flawed but it is also 'a trouble-making index able to be used for the purposes of political opportunism' (De Maria 2010: 149). Malawi can be cited as an example of a country where political opponents often hide their agendas behind the fight against corruption. The 2015 Nigerian general elections brought to light a similar tactic, where politicians hardly free of corruption themselves used an anti-corruption campaign to unseat the sitting administration.

Nevertheless, the CPI is used here to illustrate levels of corruption in sub-Saharan Africa. Treisman (2000: 409–410) highlights at least two reasons for reliably adopting TI data. Firstly, TI ratings and surveys are interrelated regardless of differences in time, input and methodologies. This helps mitigate against the risk of inconsistencies and guesswork. Secondly, the fact that CPI ratings predict various aspects of economic performance is noteworthy. Treisman (2000: 410) demonstrates how TI and Business International (BI) ratings converge on the economic performance of a country, especially apropos investment and growth levels, which are integral to a nation's development. Unsurprisingly, considerable correlation exists between the perceived high levels of corruption in sub-Saharan Africa and its underdevelopment, especially if compared with regions showing more transparency in the CPI (compare Figures 1.1 and 1.3).

In the section that follows, some of the costs of corruption vis-à-vis sub-Saharan Africa development are examined.

Costs of corruption

The damage caused by corruption has been extensively documented in the literature (see Nye 1967; Gould & Amaro-Reyes 1983; Khan 1996; and Chitakunye et al. 2015, among others). Particularly severe economic costs of corruption include: the diversion of talent from entrepreneurship and innovation (Murphy, Shleifer & Vishny 1991); brain drain (Osei-Hwedi & Osei-Hwedi 2000: 50); an increase in borrowing costs for governments and businesses in emerging economies (Ciocchini, Durbin & Ng 2003); slowing down business growth more than taxation (Fisman & Svensson 2007); fostering allocative inefficiencies[6] (Lien 1990); and lower levels of investment (Mauro 1998; Wei 2000).

It has been argued, however, that some positives are attached to corruption. For instance, Johnson (1975: 53) claims, and Seyf (2001: 599) goes along with his view, that 'if bribe takers belong to an entrepreneurial class and these entrepreneurs invest a significant fraction of the corruption revenue in highly productive activities with significant backward and forward linkages, the growth effects would be highly favourable'. Nonetheless, the overarching view is that the negative implications of corruption far outweigh any of its perceived or real benefits. If such benefits were substantive enough, sub-Saharan Africa arguably would not be ranking low in development indices while being high in corruption indices. Essentially, corruption is a social dilemma: beneficial to the individual and harmful to other members of society (Banuri & Eckel 2012: 2).

Some of the costs of corruption in sub-Saharan Africa have been an unimpressive economic growth and development rate (on average) across the region, hovering at just under one per cent per capita for the period 1956 to 2003; the fall in its share of world exports from three per cent in 1950 to one-and-a-half per cent in 2003; the high rate of external debt of about US$206 billion in 2000; and the decrease from a ninth of OECD per capita income levels in 1960 to an 18th in 2003 (Luiz 2006; Agbiboa 2010; David 2012). Corruption, among other factors, is directly linked with slow development in Africa.[7] Bribery and corruption can be directly linked to poverty, since the reliance on government for the provision of basic services tends to put the poor at the mercy of corrupt public officials, including police, and bureaucrats who often extort payment from them before rendering services—a violation of basic human rights in many African states. This scenario was amply illustrated recently in the on-going Dasukigate[8] investigation in Nigeria, which has revealed that an estimated $2.1 billion—earmarked for the procurement of arms and ammunition for the fight against the Boko Haram insurgency—was allegedly diverted and shared among government officials. Given the loss of life and property as a result of the insurgency, the implications of this level of corruption are far-reaching and nothing short of a tragedy.

Figure 1.3 *Regional comparison of Human Development Index 1980–2013*

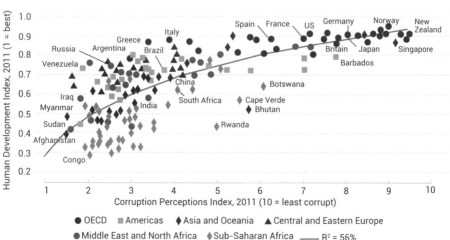

Source: United Nations Annual Human Development Index (author's compilation)[9]

Looking beyond economic factors, other dehumanising effects of corruption in both the short and long term in sub-Saharan Africa can be better illustrated by taking a human-centred approach to measuring development and using the United Nations Human Development Index (HDI), which captures both the social as well as the economic dimensions of human development (see Figure 1.4). This clearly demonstrates that, relative to other regions, sub-Saharan Africa remains at the undesirable end of the index.

Figure 1.4 *Corruption versus human development*

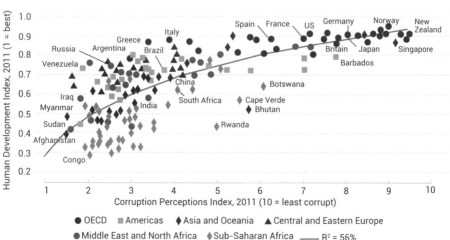

Source: Adapted from *The Economist*[10]

Figure 1.4 clearly demonstrates a strong correlation between levels of corruption (as indicated by the CPI) and development (as indicated by the HDI). Discernibly, most of the sub-Saharan African countries that have higher levels of corruption remain at the lower end of human development reports, compared with more transparent countries such as New Zealand and Norway. As the CPI improves along the horizontal axis, we observe the more transparent countries in sub-Saharan Africa such as Botswana and South Africa nudging above the 0.5 index figure in development rankings. Looking at the chart, it is as clear as daylight that corruption thwarts development in the region. It is hardly surprising that a number of prominent African writers such as Chinua Achebe and Ngugi wa Thiong'o, among others, have written about the ills of corruption, and have called for it to be stamped out. They believe the growing problems of poverty, inequality and unemployment to be pivoted on the prevalence of corruption, which in turn is a manifestation of bad leadership and institutional weakness in Africa (Fraser-Moleketi 2007: 239).

The harmful impacts of corruption are not limited to material impoverishment, understood in terms of inadequate or a lack of material wellbeing and affluence. It extends to more intangible wellness such as psychological, emotional, moral and cultural wellness. African culture is increasingly being corrupted by various influences, internally and externally (Roberts 1994; McGregor 2008). Internal factors include the distortion of African values such as solidarity, reciprocity and relatedness, with implications for the virtues of hard work, integrity and contentment integral to the ubuntu philosophy on which many cultures in sub-Saharan Africa hinge (Boateng 1983; Kamwangamalu 1999; Nussbaum 2003). It may then safely be asked: why do so many countries in the region consistently hover in the negative field on the CPI in spite of anti-corruption campaigns and efforts to nip the rot in the bud? Is corruption a cultural phenomenon? These questions become even more pertinent when corruption is juxtaposed against the humanistic principles of ubuntu. How can this paradox be resolved? An exploration of the causes of corruption may help illuminate the questions.

Causes of corruption in Africa

Various factors have been put forward as causing corruption in Africa. These range from economic to social, political to historical and cultural (Gould & Mukendi 1989; Mauro 1998; Tanzi 1998; Treisman 2000; Kyambalesa 2006; Lambsdorff 2006). Potential causes can be categorised into two groups, namely external and internal. External factors link the major causes and drivers of corruption to the influence of foreign cultures that have entered Africa over the years. From this perspective, colonialism is often blamed for having helped compromise African moral and cultural identity and integrity. Moreover, colonialism is argued to be the root cause of corruption in Africa because of its dispossession of local people and the subsequent failure to make restitution (Davidson 1994: 282). The effects of colonialism have continued to 'reverberate in profound cultural and material ways' (Westwood & Jack 2007: 247). Through education, the mark of colonialism on the African consciousness is clear. Kanu (2007) has explored the cultural and intellectual servitude, and the devaluation of traditional African culture, perpetuated by the colonialist education system and style. In exploring the dynamics in Sierra Leone, Kanu advocates for the re-appropriation of pre-colonial forms of education to rediscover the roots of African identity (cited in De Maria 2010: 148).

However, to put all the blame for corruption on foreign influence misses the mark. Internal factors that lead to various forms of socioeconomic insecurity also promote corruption. In sub-Saharan Africa, it is not unusual to hear that 'state failure to provide basic social services as a driver of corruption has led to perception of elected representatives as providers rather than facilitators of access to services through enabling policies and legislation' (Bukuluki 2013: 33). This has resulted in a culture of corruption.

The cultural dimension of corruption in sub-Saharan Africa

Hofstede (1980) defined culture as 'the collective programming of the mind which distinguishes the members of one category of people from those of another' (cited in Banuri & Eckel 2012: 5). As a response to his definition, it is interesting to ask what collective mental programme sets the people of Africa apart from other people, which may be of relevance when trying to understand the culture of corruption. Cultural explanation for the prevalence of corruption in Africa has been acknowledged (Mbaku 2000; Agbiboa 2010; David 2012). As David (2012) has noted, the 'high collectivist cultural outlook and the strong sense of obligation to family, clan, kinsfolk and cronies—which often overrides the sense of commitment to the public and individual rights and accountability' —is believed to engender corruption from a cultural perspective (see also Jabra 1976; Bukuluki 2013). Public officials who do not work to satisfy the interests of relatives, kinfolks and cronies are seen as irresponsible, if not downright stingy (Mbaku 1996). Thus, some have argued that corruption is fostered by the excessive expectations and demands placed on public officials, especially by their relatives and cronies, who expect the officers to be able to meet all their needs (Agbiboa 2010; David 2012). Others have linked corruption to the very heart of the philosophy of ubuntu. For instance, Nduku and Tenamwenye (2014: 80) observe that 'the African culture of communalism summed up in the ubuntu philosophy of "I am because you are and so you are because I am" is closely linked to political corruption in Africa.'

Analysis

Culture, as a way of life, remains integral to the very notion of sustainable development and the fight against corruption. Accordingly, anything that has an impact on culture, be it positive or negative, also impacts on development. Similarly, the complex nexus between culture and corruption is thus increasingly being acknowledged (Treisman 2000; Lambsdorff 2006; Barr & Serra 2009; Kelly 2014). As Coetzee (2012: 40) rightly observes, 'both corruption and culture are dependent on and reinforced by social interactions, for example habits. People partici-

9

pating in corruption can become dependent on a corrupt culture because they can benefit from it for their survival.'

Meanwhile, contrary to popular belief, corruption is not the cultural legacy of Africa. Various factors must be considered when discussing levels of corruption in Africa, especially the sub-Saharan region, where development has remained dismal despite the moral precepts of ubuntu. Fraser-Moleketi (2007: 241) cautions that the tendency in the corruption discourse—in both the Global North and South—to focus exclusively on the corrupted and corrupter, while neglecting complexities surrounding structural relationships embedded in the political and economic interface, is detrimental to the fight against corruption. As she sees it, this neglect tends to ignore the political economy of corruption, especially as it pertains to how multinational corporations and individuals tend to exploit vulnerable states in the name of globalisation. What happens at this interface is the erosion of value systems, whereby 'possessive individualism overrides any sense of the common good' (Fraser-Moleketi 2007: 241).

In this regard, corruption is one of the factors that distort the practice of gift giving. This is exacerbated by the encroachment internally of the external culture of materialism and individualism espoused by global capitalism. Thus, one of the founding fathers of TI, Olusegun Obasanjo, has vigorously challenged the acceptance of corruption in the name of responsibility to families and relative as 'merely an escape route by corrupt public officers ... Responsibility and challenge of leadership must encompass the courage and the ability to prevent such expectations and the foisting of a culture of temporary relief through the practice of tokenism rather than the practice of industry, hard work, self-reliance, prudence and exemplary living' (Obasanjo cited in Waliggo 2007).

Admittedly, there is hardly such a thing as one static African culture. Indeed, 'culture drifts on the open ocean of human interaction and technological development, pushed on by the winds of globalisation' (Shahadah 2014). Hundreds of years of African interaction with Asians, Americans, Europeans and Arabs have no doubt influenced African culture, even more so in this age of information and globalisation. Hundreds of years of European colonisation and exploitation of Africa and the Africans, and decades of European and American neocolonialism since political independence gradually arrived for Africa's various colonised countries allow meaningful interrogation of the dynamics of corruption in Africa from a historical perspective (Waliggo 2007). Essentially, a conflict of values has generated confusion with regard to what is right and wrong, the implication being that one culture (usually the more economically powerful one) subdues the other, or the two diffuse into a new entity (integration) (Waliggo 2007; Sylla 2014). And we can acknowledge that, while culture is dynamic, its ethics are largely static.

This has implications for the practice of gift giving, which has been, rightly or wrongly, associated with bribery and corruption in the African context. The idea of gift giving as it pertains to social solidarity—a strong tenet of African culture—is not in and of itself a corrupt practice, especially if understood within its original context before colonisation. Gift giving in Africa has cultural meaning as a gesture of goodwill, anchored on the primal place of relationship in Africa (Sigger, Polak & Pennink 2010; Sylla 2014). In practice, the gift itself is stripped of any material or monetary value, even though it is important to give the best of gifts or of one's possessions (Waliggo 2007). Moreover, value is placed instead on the receiver for the purposes of the relationship. The gesture of giving a gift stems from the cultural mindset surrounding the importance of sharing, as anchored in the communitarian cultural setup in which both the African giver and receiver exist. Accordingly, 'giving a gift to someone else is the most honourable gesture in a relationship. It is commonly accepted due to the fact that indigenous people believe in prior anticipation of new relationship even before things have taken place' (Sylla 2014: 6). In this sense, gift-giving is not corruption (bribery) and should not lead to bribery and embezzlement (Sylla 2014: 6).

A gift is different from a bribe in its intent: the former cements existing relationships, whereas the latter is often an attempt to create a new relationship for self-interested reasons (Pillay 2013). In this regard, the observation of Olusegun Obasanjo is instructive:

> In the African concept of appreciation and hospitality, the gift is usually a token. It is not demanded. The value is usually in the spirit rather than in the material worth. It is usually done in the open, and never in secret. Where it is excessive, it becomes an embarrassment and it is returned. If anything, corruption has perverted and destroyed this aspect of our culture. (cited in Larmour 2008: 225)

The perversion of traditional gift giving has changed what used to be done in appreciation for something done before the gift is even given (Egbue 2006; Atuobi 2007). Hence, gift giving, which in traditional settings had no self-interested motivation, became a ready tool for advancing people's own interest (as learnt from their colonial masters) to the detriment of others or society at large. As Fraser-Moleketi (2007: 241) observes, corruption distorts and undermines the value systems of all societies and their peoples.

A related dimension of the corruption of African cultural values is the competitive mindset that has substituted the African cooperative approach to social coexistence. As Quenum (2012: 7–8) observes, 'corruption entered the African scene as practices established by the new urban culture of competition for the control of economic resources and social influence.' In this regard, Fraser-Moleketi (2007: 247) says, 'the market fundamentalism of contemporary global capitalism and its atomising effect have created conditions under which corruption flourishes. Self-interest has taken precedence over the collective good. Our people no longer see themselves as an integral part of their communities, with the attendant responsibilities that this entails.' Hence, as the moral consciousness of the indigenous African became more influenced by the capitalist's 'winner takes all' mentality (Kaptein 2012), the culture of sharing is not only undermined but repulsed. Competition among individuals and groups dictates survival at all levels, instead of cooperation among individuals and groups. In this context, Kaptein (2012: 87) points out that, where there is only one winner, 'the use of drugs in sport, plagiarism in science, beefed up CVs, bribery over tenders, inflated profits and glossed-over losses' becomes imperative for survival.

Ironically, with the implantation of their administrative structures and culture, colonialists automatically expected Africans to behave like them regardless of traditional inclinations. While colonial administrators were cognisant of the fact that, in pre-modern Africa, everyday life was 'highly relational, life-giving, holistic, integrative and communitarian' (Quenum 2012: 7–8), they imposed public Western rules towards checkmating corrupt practices. They did this without adequate reference to the cultural worldview of the African, which underscores relationships in its communitarian setting. Yet, without necessarily alluding to moral relativism, what is corruption in a Western society may not be so in a non-Western society. Unlike in the West, where vast patronage systems are considered breeders of corruption because of the divide between the private (private/family) realm and the public (government) realm, in traditional African society, the two realms are inseparable. This, of course, has implications for the concept of corruption.

Introducing and reinforcing this dichotomy has entrenched the view that taking from the state is not really stealing in a survival-of-the-fittest scenario. Given the tendency towards tribal loyalty, especially in the highly heterogeneous societies, the public officer will eventually use their power to assist kith and kin (Guest 2004; Kelly 2014). Furthermore, as far as grand corruption is concerned, the colonialist has arguably instilled in African leaders—whom they installed to facilitate their exploitation of African wealth, especially its natural resources, while subjecting its people to economic and political enslavement—a sense of entitlement and expectation. Hence, even though the system itself did not openly teach corruption, its bearers were not exactly exemplary in using bribes to induce or force support. The resultant African political elites 'simply came to occupy the seats vacated by the colonial rulers, enjoyed a similar status of demigods and wished to hear nothing about democratic governance, strict accountability and transparency or a free press' (Fanon 1963; Waliggo 2007). Thus, the unfavourable administrative foundation laid by the colonialist, which has entrenched both the inability and unwillingness of governments to provide for the very basic needs of the people or empower them to do so for themselves, makes corrupt shortcuts an option for survival (Waliggo 2007).

Petty corruption, especially among police, is sometimes employed to support grand corruption. This is frequently driven by low wages. In a 2013 survey, the Global Corruption Barometer found that 36 countries out of an overall 107 maintained that their police were the most corrupt of all institutions. Seventeen of the 36 countries are located in sub-Saharan Africa.[11] Police corruption in Africa, as in other developing regions, have been linked largely to poverty and low wages (Treisman 2000; Andvig & Fjeldstad 2008: 27). Meanwhile, by virtue of their access to hard power, police sometimes facilitate grand corruption, especially when they unethically defend the interests of elites or political leaders. For instance, 'when wealthy and influential interests bribe the police to chase out poor homeowners to build profitable industrial plants, as they have done in a number of countries, it is police corruption in the service of the elite' (Andvig & Fjeldstad 2008: 24). Police corruption can also involve meddling with crime statistics to favour the government of the day.

Another dimension of the link between poverty and corruption, especially in sub-Saharan Africa, is the widespread consumerist and individualist culture that is at odds with the communalist and other-centred paradigm of traditional African societies. Fraser-Moleketi (2007: 247) observes that 'traditional African society was forged on the basis of communal values—this contrasts with the values of rampant free-market capitalism under globalisation, which emphasise individual wealth acquisition'. In the post-traditional social system, the 'we' approach to survival is replaced by the 'me, myself and I' approach. By implication, the growing poverty ensuing from the colonialist milking of African state resources has sometimes necessitated the latter to apply dubious means to survive. All these are fertilised by the gradual erosion of cultural values, which results from 'our formal education [having] failed to build on traditional African moral and ethical values. What was taught were Christian and Muslim moral ideas, which never penetrated into the hearts and lifestyle of the people' (Waliggo 2007).

Recommendations

A proper representation of ubuntu, taking into account modern circumstances, is not only expedient but also imperative to the attainment of broad-based development of African sub-regions. To paraphrase Mahatma Gandhi, Africa 'supplies enough to satisfy the needs of each person but not the greed of each person' (quoted in Schwartzentruber 2010: 21); hence the importance of a morally responsible approach towards the distribution of supplies. Davidson (1994: 282) advocates for an indigenous historical framing of both the problems and solutions, regardless of the contributions an external world may have made, if anti-corruption programmes were to yield desirable outcomes. Thus, in the bid to deal with corruption, we must avoid jettisoning African moral consciousness, especially as embedded in the ubuntu worldview, lest we throw the baby out with the bathwater.

Ubuntu: A realistic remedy for corruption?

Ubuntu is an African philosophy that advances the idea of 'being human through other people'. This is captured by the saying in isiZulu: *ubuntu ngumuntu ngabantu*, which translates into *I am because we are and I am human because I belong*. The concept of ubuntu, common in South Africa, is widely known in sub-Saharan Africa, as evidenced in a number of languages of the region. For instance, Mugumbate and Nyanguru (2013: 85) observe the following equivalents of ubuntu in other African countries: *bumuntu* (Tanzania), *bomoto* (Congo), *gimuntu* (Angola), *umunthu* (Malawi), *vumuntu* (Mozambique), *umuntu* (Uganda) and *botho* (Botswana). A concept of some depth, ubuntu does not yield to easy definition or theorisation. However, certain key attributes can be acknowledged that are ontologically and ethically salient. Ontologically, ubuntu accentuates the existence of a person as being intrinsically linked to other people. For instance, compared with animals, a human newborn is more likely to die if left without care, which shows its dependence on other humans for existence (Praeg 2008; West 2014). Ethically, ubuntu stresses the moral responsibility humans have towards one another, which is what makes them human. So, for instance, in its expression in Zimbabwean Shona, the word *unhu* (related to personhood) tasks an individual with acceptable human behaviour in order to qualify as an *unhu*. You are said to lack *unhu* when you do not display adequate behaviour. Thus, the saying *uri mhuka yemunhu* (you are an animal of a person) reflects an individual without *unhu* (Mugumbate & Nyanguru 2013: 86).

The implication of ubuntu for the fight against political corruption can be captured in the three maxims of ubuntuism or *hunhuism* identified by Samkange and Samkange (1980):

- The first maxim asserts that to be human is to affirm one's humanity by recognising the humanity of others and, on that basis, establishing respectful human relations with them.
- The second maxim says that, if and when one is faced with a choice between wealth and the preservation of the life of another human being, then one should opt for the preservation of life.
- The third maxim as a principle is deeply embedded in traditional African political philosophy. It dictates that the king owes his status, including all the powers associated with it, to the will of the people under him (cited in Mugumbate & Nyanguru 2013: 84).

If political leaders were to live out the assertion that their very personhood is inseparable from those of the people they lead, they would be more inclined to think in terms of common good than rampant self-interest. In this regard, Fraser-Moleketi (2007: 242) maintains that 'ubuntu is the belief in a universal bond of sharing that connects all humanity'. In other words, we are beings unto others; our humanness becomes essentially doing for others, not just for ourselves. On top of that, we recognise that personhood, in the African tradition from the perspective of ubuntu, means that our wellbeing is inextricably linked with the wellbeing of others. Any deviation from this is fundamentally a perversion of our personhood (Fraser-Moleketi 2007: 242). Equally, the third maxim unambiguously articulates the ethical responsibility of leaders towards those they lead as a priority over status and power. Arguably, it is the absence of conscious adherence to the third maxim that drives leadership in many sub-Saharan African countries today. And that is what has landed the region in its current sorry state.

Personhood, or humanness, as expressed in ubuntu, connotes a certain moral uprightness. This is captured in various ways across Africa. For instance, using a sociocultural-linguistic approach, Ademilokun (2014) employs the Yoruba[12] concept of *ewà-inú* to demonstrate how corruption is an aberration of beauty as it relates to morality among the Yoruba-speaking ethnic groups in Nigeria. Using about 30 Yoruba proverbs, Ademilokun draws out the undergirding philosophy that construes corruption as a sickness rooted in greed and lack of contentment, themselves strongly prohibited within the culture. 'This notion of proper human conduct among the Yoruba is articulated in *ewà-inú*. In Yoruba cosmology, *ewà-inú* is a notion of beauty that transcends the physical; it emphasises the individual's character and conduct' (Ademilokun 2014: 42). Against this backdrop, the African traditional worldview emphasises that a person's success is not 'essentially measured in the quantitative terms of economic wealth, but in terms of the quality of life' (Waliggo 2007). Such quality of life, derived from the success and wellbeing of others—and that includes the environment—is pertinent both to nipping corruption in the bud and fostering sustainable development.

The philosophy of ubuntu can make a profound contribution to fighting corruption, especially when applying a bottom-up approach, promoting values at the grassroots through moral re-education. Ubuntu stresses the importance of deep respect for 'the other', and this is essential if we are to overcome Western materialism (Sigger, Polak & Pennink 2010).

Conclusion

This chapter has attempted to unravel the problem of corruption, its prevalence in sub-Saharan Africa and its harmful impact on sustainable development. It furthermore stresses the dynamic nexus between corruption, culture and development within the region. In particular, it acknowledges that while corruption in Africa, as measured by the CPI, tends to create an impression that corrupt practices are part and parcel of the continent's DNA, it is, in fact, a global challenge. Importantly, this chapter highlights external influences that pervert certain aspects of African culture, and illustrates that such influences may be considered drivers of corruption. African practices such as gift giving should be understood within the traditional context, and the practice in itself is not an act of corruption if the intent is right. Finally, the chapter asserts that African cultural heritage, especially as encapsulated in ubuntu, can contribute positively in the fight against corruption by redressing the consumerist and individualist culture entrenched in modern capitalism and bad governance.

Notes

1   Sub-Saharan Africa refers geographically to the areas of the continent that lie south of the Sahara, commonly also known as Darkest Africa.

2   While largely immeasurable, development is generally used to reflect the economic, political, social, technological and cultural wellbeing of people. These are often captured by indices such as Purchasing Power Parity, Gross Domestic Product, Gross National Income and, more importantly, the Human Development Index, among other yardsticks. Africa lags in virtually all these indices (David 2012).

3   See also *Zero Tolerance to Corruption for Development: Time to Wake Up*, a speech delivered at the 3rd National Anti-Corruption Convention held on 2 December 2013 in Kampala, Uganda.

4   *Zero Tolerance to Corruption for Development: Time to Wake Up*, a speech delivered at the 3rd National Anti-Corruption Convention held on 2nd December 2013 in Kampala, Uganda.

5   The term 'state capture' is used to describe 'a situation where economic elites develop relationships with political officials through whom they exert undue influence over public policy for their own personal gain' (Atuobi 2007).

6   Allocative efficiency occurs when there is an optimal distribution of goods and services, taking into account consumers' preferences: www.economicshelp.org/blog/glossary/allocative-efficiency/.

7   See also Rose-Ackerman (1998), Justesen & Bjørnskov (2014).

8   The term 'Dasukigate' derives from 'the infamous Watergate political scandal that forced the American president, Richard Nixon, to resign from office in 1974 in order to avoid the politically worse fate of impeachment': B Jeyifoon, Dasukigate: Beyond the Outrage and Apart from the Legal Battle, What Is to Be Done? *The Nation Newspaper*, 20 December 2015. In the context of Nigeria it is linked with the diversion of monies intended for the purchase of arms and armaments for the army in its counter-insurgency war with Boko Haram to various private pockets.

9   Data available from www.hdr.undp.org/en/content/human-development-index-hdi.

10   Available at www.economist.com; see also David (2012).

11   Transparency International. Available at http://www.transparency.org/gcb2013/results.

12   Besides constituting one of the three major ethnic groups in Nigeria, the Yoruba people are also to be found in countries such as Togo, Benin, Côte d'Ivoire and in some parts of Brazil, among other places.

References

Ademilokun MA (2014) Yoruba proverbs and the anti-corruption crusade in Nigeria. *Inkanyiso: Journal of Humanities and Social Sciences* 6(1): 41–48

Agbiboa DE (2010) The corruption-underdevelopment nexus in Africa: Which way Nigeria?! *The Journal of Social, Political, and Economic Studies* 35(4): 474–509

Andvig JC and Fjeldstad O-H (2008) Crime, poverty and police corruption in developing countries. CMI (Chr. Michelsen Institute) Working Papers

Atuobi SM (2007) Corruption and state instability in West Africa: An examination of policy options. Kofi Anan International Peacekeeping Training Center Occasional Paper 21

Banuri S and Eckel CC (2012) Experiments in culture and corruption: A review. World Bank Policy Research Working Paper Impact Evaluation Series No. 56

Bardhan P (1997) Corruption and development: A review of issues. *Journal of Economic Literature* 35: 1320–1346

Barr A and Serra D (2009) The effects of externalities and framing on bribery in a petty corruption experiment. *Experimental Economics* 12(4): 488–503

Berthoud G (1990) Modernity and development. *The European Journal of Development Research* 2(1): 22–35

Boateng F (1983) African traditional education: A method of disseminating cultural values. *Journal of Black Studies* 13(3): 321–336

Bukuluki P (2013) 'When I steal, it is for the benefit of me and you': Is collectivism engendering corruption in Uganda? *International Letters of Social and Humanistic Sciences* 5: 27–44

Chitakunye P, David OJ, Derera E and Tarkhar A (2015) Transnational analysis of the impact of corruption on development in Africa: A review of literature. *Journal of Social Sciences* 42(1): 129–142

Ciocchini F, Durbin E and Ng DT (2003) Does corruption increase emerging market bond spreads? *Journal of Economics and Business* 55(5): 503–528

Coetzee JJ (2012) Systemic corruption and corrective change management strategies: A study of the co-producers of systemic corruption and its negative impact on socio-economic development, MA Thesis, Stellenbosch University

David (2012) The nexus between corruption, education and development: analysing the net effect of corruption and poor education on development in Nigeria, Honours Project, University of KwaZulu-Natal

Davidson B (1994) *The search for Africa: A history in the making.* London: James Currey

De Maria W (2010) Why is the president of Malawi angry? Towards an ethnography of Corruption. *Culture and Organization* 16(2): 145–162

Egbue N (2006) Africa: Cultural dimensions of corruption and possibilities for change. *Journal of Social Sciences* 12(2): 83–91

Ekeh PP (1975) Colonialism and the two publics in Africa: A theoretical statement. *Comparative Studies in Society and History* 17(1): 91–112

Ekwueme EO (2014) What am I doing when I am being corrupt? An epistemology of corruption. In E Nduku and J Tenamwenye (Eds) *Corruption in Africa: A threat to justice and sustainable peace.* Geneva: Globethics.net

Elbra AD (2013) The forgotten resource curse: South Africa's poor experience with mineral extraction. *Resources Policy* 38(4): 549–557

Fanon F (1963) *The wretched of the earth.* New York: Grove Press

Fisman R and Svensson J (2007) Are corruption and taxation really harmful to growth? Firm level evidence. *Journal of Development Economics* 83(1): 63–75

Franks S (2005) Our common interest: Report of the Commission for Africa. *The Political Quarterly* 76(3): 446–450

Fraser-Moleketi G (2007) Towards a common understanding of corruption in Africa. *International Journal of African Renaissance Studies* 2(2): 239–249

Gould DJ and Amaro-Reyes JA (1983) The effects of corruption on administrative performance. World Bank Staff Working Paper 580

Gould DJ and Mukendi TB (1989) Bureaucratic corruption in Africa: Causes, consequences and remedies. *International Journal of Public Administration* 12(3): 427–457

Guest R (2004) *The shackled continent: Power, corruption, and African lives.* Washington DC: Smithsonian Books

Hope KR (2000) Corruption and development in Africa. In KR Hope, BC Chikulo (Eds) *Corruption and development in Africa: Lessons from country case-studies.* London: Palgrave

Jabra J (1976) Bureaucratic corruption in the Third World: Causes and remedies. *Indian Journal of Public Administration* 22: 673–691

Johnson OE (1975) An economic analysis of corrupt government, with special application to less developed countries. *Kyklos* 28(1): 47–61

Johnson RA (2004) *The struggle against corruption: A comparative study.* New York: Palgrave Macmillan

Justesen MK and Bjørnskov C (2014) Exploiting the poor: Bureaucratic corruption and poverty in Africa. *World Development* 58: 106–115

Kamwangamalu NM (1999) Ubuntu in South Africa: A sociolinguistic perspective to a pan-African concept. *Critical Arts* 13(2): 24–41

Kaptein M (2012) *Why do good people sometimes do bad things?: 52 reflections on ethics at work.* Accessed November 2016, www.ssrn.com/en/sol3/papers.cfm?abstract_id=2117396

Kelly RM (2014) Corruption in Africa: Cultural, economic and political factors which impact corruption and potential solutions. MA Thesis, The State University of New Jersey

Khan MH (1996) The Efficiency Implications of Corruption. *Journal of International Development* 8(5): 683–696

Koubi V, Spilker G, Böhmelt T and Bernauer T (2014) Do natural resources matter for interstate and intrastate armed conflict? *Journal of Peace Research* 51(2): 227–243

Kwame Y (2006) The impact of globalization on African culture. Manuscript. Odense: University of Southern Denmark

Kyambalesa H (2006) Corruption: Causes, effects, and deterrents. *African Insights* 36(2): 102–122

Lambsdorff JG (2006) Causes and consequences of corruption: What do we know from a cross-section of countries? In S Rose-Ackerman (Ed.) *International Handbook on the Economics of Corruption.* Cheltenham: Edward Elgar

Larmour P (2008) Corruption and the concept of 'culture': Evidence from the Pacific Islands. *Crime, Law and Social Change* 49(3): 225–239

Lien D-HD (1990) Corruption and allocation efficiency. *Journal of Development Economics* 33(1): 153–164

Luiz J (2006) *Managing business in Africa: Practical management theory for an emerging market.* Oxford: Oxford University Press

Mauro P (1998) Corruption: Causes, consequences, and agenda for further research. *Finance and Development* 35: 11–14

Mbaku JM (1996) Bureaucratic corruption in Africa: The fultility of cleanups. *Cato Journal* 16(1): 99–118

Mbaku JM (2000) *Bureaucratic and political corruption in Africa: The public choice perspective.* Florida: Krieger Publishing Company

McGregor J (2008) Children and 'African Values': Zimbabwean Professionals in Britain Reconfiguring Family Life. *Environment and Planning* 40(3): 596–614.

Médard J-F (2002) Corruption in the neo-patrimonial states of sub-Saharan Africa. In AJ Heidenheimer and M Johnston (Eds) *Political corruption: Concepts and contexts.* New Brunswick: Transaction Publishers

Mugumbate J and Nyanguru A (2013) Exploring African philosophy: The value of ubuntu in social work. *African Journal of Social Work* 3(1): 82–100

Murphy K, Shleifer A and Vishny R (1991) The allocation of talent: Implications for growth. *Quarterly Journal of Economics* 106: 503–530

Nduku E and Tenamwenye J (Eds) (2014) *Corruption in Africa: A threat to justice and sustainable peace.* Geneva: Globethics.net

Nussbaum B (2003) Ubuntu: Reflections of a South African on our common humanity. *Reflections* 4(4): 21–26

Nye JS (1967) Corruption and political development: A cost-benefit analysis. *American Political Science Review* 61(02): 417–427

Nye JS (2002) Corruption and political development: A cost-benefit analysis. In AJ Heidenheimer and M Johnston (Eds) *Political Corruption Concepts and Contexts* (3rd edition). New Brunswick, NJ: Transaction Publishers

Osei-Hwedi B and Osei-Hwedi K (2000) The political, economic and cultural bases of corruption in Africa. In KR Hope and BC Chikulo (Eds) *Corruption and development in Africa: Lessons from country case-studies.* London: Palgrave

Pillay K (2013) *Decoding the culture of corruption* Accessed October 2015, www.corruptionwatch. org.za/decoding-the-culture-of-corruption/

Praeg L (2008) An answer to the question: What is ubuntu? *South African Journal of Philosophy* 27(4): 367–385

Quenum J-MH (2012) The root cause of widespread corruption in Sub-Saharan postcolonial nation-states. *Asian Horizons* 6(1): 103–108

Roberts GW (1994) Brother to Brother: African American Modes of Relating among Men. *Journal of Black Studies* 24(4): 379–390.

Rose-Ackerman S (1998) Corruption and development. Paper Presented at Annual World Bank Conference on Development Economics 1997

Roy S (1987) The Gaza Strip: A case of economic de-development. *Journal of Palestine Studies* 17(1): 56–88

Schwartzentruber P (2010) Enough for everyone's need: Reflections on a non-violent economy. Paper Presented at International Conference on a Non-violent Economy, Bhopal, India

Seyf A (2001) Corruption and development: A study of conflict. *Development in Practice* 11(5): 597–605

Shahadah A (2014) *The African culture complex: Africa should tap into its culture.* Accessed November 2015, www.africafiles.org/article.asp?ID=27377

Sigger D, Polak B and Pennink B (2010) 'Ubuntu' or 'humanness' as a management concept. CDS Research Report no 29

Sylla K (2014) Defining corruption in the cultural context of sub-Saharan Africa. In GM Mudacumura and G Morçöl (Eds) *Challenges to Democratic Governance in Developing Countries.* Heidelberg, New York, Dordrecht, London: Springer

Tanzi V (1998) Corruption around the world: Causes, consequences, scope, and cures. *International Monetary Fund Staff Papers* 45(4): 559–594

TI (Transparency International) (2015) What is corruption? Accessed November 2015, www.transparency.org/what-is-corruption/?gclid=CjwKEAiAp_WyBRD37bGB_ ZO9qAYSJAA72IkgwpIL4z5ijNr9PzIB6K2yJ1dks4zOiBF_jzyeUa4zABoCknvw_wcB#define

Treisman D (2000) The causes of corruption: A cross-national study. *Journal of Public Economics* 76(3): 399–457

Uzodike UO (1999) Development in the new world order: Repositioning Africa for the twenty-first century. In JM Mbaku (Ed.) *Preparing Africa for the Twenty-First Century: Strategies for peaceful coexistence and sustainable development.* Aldershot: Ashgate Publishing Ltd

Waliggo JM (2007) *Corruption and bribery: An African Problem?* Accessed November 2015, www.africafiles.org/article.asp?ID=14619

Wei S-J (2000) How taxing is corruption on international investors? *Review of Economics and Statistics* 82(1): 1–11

Werlin HH (1973) The consequences of corruption: The Ghanaian experience. *Political Science Quarterly* 88(1): 71–85

West A (2014) Ubuntu and business ethics: Problems, perspectives and prospects. *Journal of Business Ethics* 121(1): 47–61

Westwood RI and Jack G (2007) Manifesto for post-colonial international business and management studies: A provocation. *Critical Perspectives on International Business* 3(3): 246–265

2 | Integrating indigenous knowledge into rural development in Botswana: A case study

Malatsi Seleka

Arguments for integrating cultural aspects into developmental processes have grown tremendously over the past two decades. The development community now calls for culturally sensitive approaches to prosperity since it is culture that provides the fundamental essence of identity, preference, obligations and responsibilities that are important to rural development (Kelly 2005: 6). The integration of various forms of cultural knowledge into rural development planning plays a fundamental role in formulating sustainable development interventions. Today, more than ever before, indigenous knowledge (IK)[1] that derives from culture offers power to achieve desired developmental objectives, to manage scarce resources for development, and to effect improvements in the lives of rural populations (Gabriel 1991).

An awareness of the different purposes and functions of IK in sustainable rural development has seen it adopted as a key component of rural development planning and management strategy (Sillitoe et al. 2004). IK is entrenched in the cultural environment of all people, irrespective of spatial and temporal factors. People are historically and traditionally bound and thus have their own, particular knowledge systems that enable them to survive and develop (Malla & Loubser 2003: 277). IK can be divided into various fields, including knowledge about agriculture, nutrition, healthcare practices, environmental management, poverty alleviation, community development and education. Rural development attempts to address developmental setbacks, and integrating IK into rural development planning can aid the process.

Various approaches to integrating IK into rural development planning have been adopted by development practitioners in Africa and elsewhere. In Botswana, participatory approaches to rural development planning have been utilised. The *kgotla*[2] traditional institution has been established as a medium for consultation and collaborative communication between local communities and development planners. It is a process that aims to document and promote culture as well as IK for integration into rural development planning (Mokwena & Fakir 2009: 11–12). However, rural livelihoods have remained stagnant despite the participatory approach; rural development projects have not lived up to expectations. A common belief is that the ineffectiveness and inefficiency of rural development initiatives have been the result of limited integration of 'indigenous wisdom' into rural development planning and the introduction instead of predesigned development initiatives that ignore IK systems.

This chapter discusses the nature and extent of IK integration into rural development planning in Botswana, using the village of Mmankgodi as a case study. The author set out to answer the following research questions:

- *In what ways is IK integrated into rural development planning?*
- *To what extent do communities contribute local knowledge to rural development planning?*
- *What are the barriers that stop IK from being integrated into rural development planning?*

Background

Historically, rural communities in Botswana relied on cultural structures and traditional knowledge to sustain their livelihoods. Cultural practices established satisfactory standards of economic prosperity based on norms and values. Over the years, it was common practice to maintain cultural systems that imparted knowledge and skills that made communities respond to undesirable living conditions (Maripe 2012: 5–6). Communities survived on subsistence agriculture and devised self-help initiatives guided by their IK and social services provided by the chiefs. However, reliance on culture and IK for development by rural communities changed when Botswana gained independence in 1966, and the subsequent discovery and mining of diamonds in the late 1960s. Diamonds provided a significant share of government revenue, a good proportion of which was used for socioeconomic development initiatives (Harvey & Lewis 1990). The advent of diamond mining placed Botswana on a sustained self-generating development path, hence government was able to commit to rural development. The first step to improving rural livelihoods was the introduction of the Accelerated Rural Development Programme (ARDP) in 1973. The programme's primary objective was to push services towards far-flung rural areas, where most of the poorest people lived (Harvey & Lewis 1990).

In its efforts to improve rural livelihoods, the ARDP did not take into account the importance of integrating culture and local knowledge into its processes. Instead, it took up a top-down approach to rural development planning. While the ARDP led to improvements in public services, which increased employment in rural areas, it did little to strengthen the rural economy and enhance rural livelihoods. This was attributed to the centralised process of development, which facilitated a top-down approach. Communities became the passive recipients of this new development style (Dipholo 2002: 68–69). As rural development remained a government priority, rural development programmes such as the ARDP were constantly reviewed to measure their impact. This led to the realisation that, to develop rural areas, communities should be more than passive recipients of development—they should also participate in the planning and management of the process. Participatory mechanisms then became central to community development strategy, ultimately informing the National Rural Development Policy (NRDP). Development administrators acknowledged that, for rural development to be effective and sustainable, they should integrate IK into the planning process to achieve interventions compatible with local conditions and customs. Rural communities' livelihoods around the country do, after all, depend on natural resources, and culture and IK are widely used in managing them in a sustainable way, be it for poverty alleviation, drought management, or other interventions. With the realisation that you cannot divorce rural communities from their culture, rural development administrators in Botswana adopted participatory approaches to enhance their planning strategies (Cassidy et al. 2011: 77).

A participatory approach can be described as a dynamic process whereby recipients of a development intervention intended to improve their wellbeing determine and shape its nature (World Bank 1994: 77–78). This approach has given communities a platform to share their IK and perceptions on rural development resource use and management. Local institutions like the *kgotla* have been utilised to collect IK from communities during rural development planning processes. The importance of assimilating IK into rural development in Botswana remains paramount, as national development principles are drawn from culture, which forms the basis for IK. In present-day Botswana, rural development processes are culturally sensitive and take IK into account (Maripe 2012: 2).

Like any other country, Botswana has a wealth of IK that has been recognised by academics, policymakers and development practitioners. Government has made significant efforts to develop the country's IK systems, including setting up a research department to lead research on IK. The unit is housed under the Ministry of Infrastructure, Science and Technology (Nfila & Jain 2011: 11). In addition, the University of Botswana in 2008 established the Centre for Scientific Research, Indigenous Knowledge and Innovation (CesrIKi), which has tremendously raised awareness of the importance of integrating IK in socioeconomic processes (Neba et al. 2012: 8–12). In the policy space, the National Policy on Research Science, Technology and Innovation is currently the only policy adopted in Botswana that comprehensively articulates the importance of IK in development and recognises it as a vital component of improving rural livelihoods. It calls for the documentation, preservation, integration and promotion of IK across all economic sectors (Ministry of Communications, Science and Technology 2005: 21–24). In addition, the National Policy on Natural Resource Conservation and Development, as well as the National Policy on Culture, narrowly enunciate the importance of IK in rural development.

Defining IK

While the term 'IK' does not have a universally accepted definition, it typically refers to local knowledge that is location and culture specific (Ngwasiri 1995: 1). All definitions of IK have a similar emphasis, namely on knowledge derived from experiences and observation from current and past generations (Materer et al. 2002: 2–3). Grenier (1998: 6) defines IK as the knowledge and skills used by communities to survive in their environment. This definition is also consistent with that of Ponge (2013: 7–8), who says IK is a set of shared knowledge regarding everyday life practices in a particular society. He further points out that this knowledge varies from one community to the next, and that it informs people's decision-making. Melchias (2001), cited in Eyong (2014: 121), defines it as characterising and explaining historical practices and activities within particular societies that have been modified to help the communities cope with environmental dynamics. This definition corresponds with that of Odora-Hoppers (2002: 5–7), who describes IK as knowledge that is fixed in the social history of individuals or communities; this knowledge includes people's historical development as well as their social and economic disposition, and the logical and innovative nature of their personality as a group. As Odora-Hoppers's definition is broad and covers all aspects of IK, it has been adopted as a framework for this chapter.

In its broadest sense, IK is considered social knowledge that contains all the economic, political, social, and other worldly aspects of traditional routines. The salient features of IK are that it is firmly linked to subsistence practices, and it is also context, location and culture specific, usually transmitted orally and informally. It is often categorised into knowledge about agriculture, natural resources management, poverty alleviation, healthcare, community development and education (Tanyanyiwa & Chikwanha 2011: 132–134). Within the scope of this chapter, the discussion is limited to IK's role in community development.

The IK/culture nexus

The concept of IK is synonymous with culture. Odora-Hoppers (2002: 5–7) says that, to define IK, culture should form a fundamental basis of the definition. Culture, naturally, has its own array of definitions, and also does not have a universally fixed understanding. Hofstede (1980: 97) defines culture as a common living system that distinguishes one community from another. Odora-Hoppers (2005: 3–4), on the other hand, sees it as the entirety of community behaviour that informs beliefs, arts and other human products generated through human work and thought. This corresponds to the definition by Spencer-Oatey (2008: 1–3), who describes culture as a composite of norms and values as well as behavioural traditions shared by a particular group of people. Matsumoto (1996: 2–3) also defines culture as shared group attitudes, behaviour, values and beliefs among a particular community that are passed on from one generation to another. While these definitions vary to some extent, they all articulate the collectiveness and sharing of certain traits that define culture. The key characteristics of culture are that it is learnt, collective, based on symbols, integrated and dynamic (Spencer-Oatey 2008: 1–3).

The relationship between culture and IK is indisputable. Culture is entrenched in social processes that produce knowledge considered to be indigenous (Pottier 2003). IK also results from people co-existing with the environment, which occurs within a cultural context (Weedon 2004: 3–6). Sen (1999: 190–192) states that the cultural landscape affects human activities, which has a bearing on knowledge production. Culture assigns social meanings to human behaviours, which further influences knowledge acquisition. Moreover, within a cultural sphere, individuals interact and form knowledge webs, creating the backward and forward flow of information among them. This flow of information is imperative to acquiring IK (Abraham &

Platteau 2004: 211–213). Mutebi (2004: 289–292) shares this opinion, saying that culture is a building pillar of society. It facilitates interactions between individuals, groups and the environment through which IK is being produced and shared.

It is impossible to divorce IK from culture, since the latter is fundamental to the former. Where culture exists, the acquisition of unique knowledge specific to a group of people will follow.

The case for integrating IK into rural development planning

Rural development can be understood in a number of ways, depending on how one defines the term 'development' itself. Generally, development is considered a change process that is multidimensional and interdependent (Krishnamurthy 2000: 1–5), and it goes beyond economic factors. Therefore, development should be viewed as a process that reconstructs overall social and economic conditions and structures (Todaro 1985: 13). The term 'rural', while understood differently depending on the location, typically refers to a geographic area situated outside cities and towns. It often refers to a less densely populated part of a particular place (Sears & Reid 1995: 2). The concept of rural development has come to signify a whole set of policies, programmes and strategies broadly covering the field of rural reconstruction (Krishnamurthy 2000: 3), which aims to improve and sustain living conditions of disadvantaged populations in rural areas (Lele 1975).

Integrating IK into the rural development planning process is now generally assumed to be a good, if not vital, practice. Social researchers associated with the formulation of development assistance policies now acknowledge the contribution of local communities to development projects (Lalonde 1991). Conventions such as the International Labour Organization (ILO) Convention 169 (1989) and the Rio Declaration (1992) also supported the integration of IK in rural development. And the 2002 World Summit on Sustainable Development held in Johannesburg, South Africa, reaffirmed the vital role of integrating IK into planning sustainable development interventions (IFAD 2003).

Hoskins (1990: 14–15) argues that development initiatives introduced over the past decade have failed to improve rural livelihoods, because IK was not integrated into the planning and implementation of projects. Local communities have deep knowledge of their environment, which guides their priorities and practices when it comes to development, and these should be respected and considered when designing new projects and strategies. The World Bank (1998: 3–4) shares this view, stating that IK characterises a significant element of universal information on development matters. Making use of IK enhances the quality of development projects, because it is more likely to introduce relevant and appropriate interventions that can improve lives of rural populations.

The integration of IK in development planning should lead to efficient, effective and sustainable rural development. Okafor (1982: 130–143) mentions that local people are likely to be more familiar with specific circumstances of the development environment than technically competent development planners, and can therefore make a positive contribution to the process. On the strength of their knowledge of local conditions and taking into account projects' constraints and benefits, beneficiaries can play an active role in determining the scope and nature of projects (Van Heck 2003: 10–16). The integration of IK into rural development planning means involving local communities in developmental processes and enabling them to shape decisions that affect their lives. Having more independence and control over their lives, people will be empowered (Oakley 1991: 2–4) to become more self-reliant and able to sustain their own processes of development. This can bring about holistic transformation of the local communities and better material wellbeing of the people. Self-transformation of communities as an outcome is one of the biggest benefits of integrating IK into rural development planning (Makumbe 1996).

Mmankgodi, Botswana: A case study

The study that formed the basis for this chapter used the social constructivism theory by Vygotsky (1978) as a tool of inquiry at the village of Mmankgodi in Botswana to highlight some relevant and complex issues regarding culture, indigenous knowledge and rural development. This theory emphasises the importance of culture and context in understanding what happens in society, and how it relates to activities taking place socially (Kukla 2000). The theory further stresses the importance of the knowledge, beliefs and skills that individuals bring to development (Bouwen & Taillieu 2004: 138–142). Societies do not exist separately from their communal setting and culture (Risse 2009). The latter shapes who we are, how we think, what we know and what our preferences are. Social constructivism sets a clear guideline for the importance of culture in human development. Thus, it is relevant to the study which looked at the structural and societal aspects of IK integration into rural development.

Furthermore, the study made use of Hamdi and Goethert's (1997) Community Action Planning (CAP) framework, which strives to empower communities to design, implement and manage development projects in their environments (Sanoff 2000: 275–276). It is a framework that allows communities to play a role at all stages of the development project cycle that take place in their social space. Communities know best the nature of their own problems and have preferences when it comes to tackling them, so their participation in the projects is an obvious requirement (Luthi 2012: 20–23). It is also important that sound structures, skills, knowledge and technical know-how are in place, and that the right institutions are involved if effective integration is to be achieved (Denters & Klok 2010: 588–589). Community development should be viewed as a long-term process, and projects should be designed with flexible time schedules to allow people to take full advantage to participate. The CAP model provides a clear direction for effective community participation (Rakody & Schlyter 1981), looking at it from a long-term perspective, which further speaks to the sustainability of projects.

Research methodology

The research in Mmankgodi village was designed as a qualitative study.[3] Besides primary data sourced by way of in-depth interviews and focus group discussions, it used secondary data from already published documents such as journals, policy documents and books.

Thirty-two respondents participated in the study, eight of whom were personally interviewed and 24 of whom participated in focus group discussions. The eight interviewees were picked from among community development administrators at the Social and Community Development Department (S&CD), the Village Development Committee (VDC), the Village Extension Team (VET) and tribal administration, which is made up of the chieftaincy and support officers employed by the government. Those interviewed were purposively selected on the grounds of their knowledge in the field. Four focus group discussions were held, attended by six members each. Participants were selected using snowball sampling.

Study area

The study was conducted in Mmankgodi village in the Kweneng District of Botswana (Fig. 2.1). Mmankgodi village lies 35km west of Gaborone, Botswana's capital. The reason for selecting Mmankgodi is that it is rural, yet not too far from Gaborone, which makes it easily accessible. Mmankgodi has a large farming community with a population of approximately 4 997 according to the 2011 Botswana population census.

Figure 2.1 *Map of Botswana showing the location of Mmankgodi village*

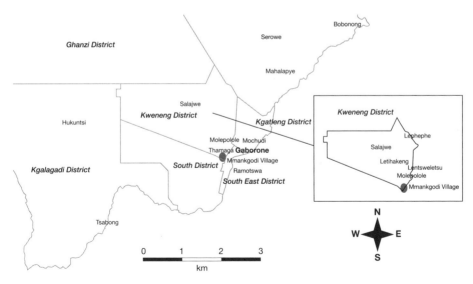

Demographics of the respondents

The age distribution of all participants varied widely. The key informants ranged in age from 25 to 75 years; two of them were over the retirement age of 65, with the remaining interviewees falling under the economically active age groups. Focus group discussion members' ages ranged from 15 to 75 years. With the 45 to 55 years age group being the largest (seven respondents), the 15 to 25, 25 to 35, 35 to 45 and 55 to 65 age groups all counted four participants each. Only 1 person in the age group 65 to 75 took part in focus group discussions.

Out of 32 participants in the study, 15 women and 9 men participated in the focus group discussions, while three women and five men were interviewed as key informants.

Education levels of participants also ranged widely, from primary education to secondary and tertiary education. Of the 8 interviewees, 4 had tertiary education, 1 had secondary education and 3 did not disclose their educational levels. Among the participants of the focus group discussions, 13 had primary, 8 secondary and 3 tertiary education. While the education levels of participants varied, they all demonstrated awareness of IK, culture and development initiatives in Mmankgodi.

Data analysis

Thematic analysis was employed as a method to analyse the collected data. It entailed finding, scrutinising and reporting patterns within the data, and categorising and defining the data set in detail (Braun & Clarke, 2006). The information was organised thematically with descriptions tied to each specific research question, as per the objectives of the study.

Findings

In what ways is IK integrated into rural development planning?

Any knowledge integration process should be supported by strategies flexible enough to accommodate divergent perceptions (Berkes 2009: 1693–1702). This study revealed that rural development administrators in Mmankgodi responsible for integrating IK into development plans do not have written guidelines, and nor do they have any expertise in effective knowledge exchange. Community development workers at the S&CD office said that, in the absence of a documented strategy on integrating IK, they relied on community-level institutions such as the VDC to involve communities in rural development planning and management. It also emerged that community development workers took advantage of community gatherings, usually held as *kgotla* meetings to engage the community and involve it in documenting relevant IK for rural development. Community members confirmed that their engagement with development matters happens through *kgotla* meetings.

The S&CD officers said they knew how important it was to create an atmosphere conducive to knowledge sharing, and that was the reason for using the *kgotla* as a forum for gathering community input on the development process. In fact, the *kgotla* seems to be the only way S&CD officers could engage the community that gathers in large numbers for those meetings. Furthermore, community members who were usually most knowledgeable about IK were village elders who invariably preferred the traditional *kgotla* meeting to other forms of exchanging information.

No documented structure exists to enable IK integration into the rural development planning process. The CAP framework proposes the effective integration of IK into the development process by way of a cohesive structure supported by trained and skilled facilitators. However, the S&CD officers have not been trained in this regard; instead, they rely on the *kgotla* meeting chaired by the kgosi, or chief, and other senior villagers. As community development workers, the S&CD officers are the primary link to the community. The fact that they have not received training in IK integration methodology and practice renders the whole process ineffective.

To what extent do communities contribute local knowledge to rural development planning?

Communities should be given more opportunities to contribute IK in the development process (Van Heck 2003: 10–16). Since the general point of rural development is to improve community living conditions, its mandate is to empower local populations, and this should be done by giving people significant opportunity to contribute during the planning process. When communities are satisfied that their contributions are applied, rural development projects have a higher chance of survival and sustainability. Being given an equal opportunity to contribute to the process, the communities are more likely to take ownership of projects being implemented. Furthermore, it is clear that communication between the community and development workers is poor. Community members who participated in the study claimed that they had never received communication on developmental issues before discussions were held during *kgotla* meetings. This, they say, places them at a disadvantage, because they do not have the opportunity to think through issues to make informed decisions during the meetings. The fact that whatever topic is discussed is new to their ears leads to low interest in participating meaningfully, so they resist sharing the knowledge they do have.

Accordingly, community members felt that the opportunity for them to contribute IK for rural development planning was limited. The general consensus was that the *kgotla* forum did not offer them enough of a platform to contribute meaningfully. One participant claimed that community members were given barely five minutes to talk during *kgotla* meetings, which was not enough to make a valid point and possibly convince development workers about a given subject. More time was needed so that more matters could be discussed. Youth and women, in particular, felt they had limited opportunities to contribute within the space of the *kgotla*, an institution dominated by elderly males. Women tend to be sidelined and rarely have a chance to contribute. However, S&CD officers disagreed with the claims, saying that all members of the community were given an equal opportunity to contribute their knowledge. Upon further investigation, the VDC committee members backed the statements of the community members with regard to having limited opportunities to contribute during *kgotla*.

What are the barriers that stop IK from being integrated into rural development planning?

Integrating IK into rural development planning is often limited by a multitude of barriers, and it is important to understand and anticipate these (Oakley 1991: 3).

The Mmankgodi village faces a host of hindrances. The women, youth and elderly participants of the focus group discussions identified the participatory structure as a barrier to effective knowledge sharing. They said the *kgotla*, used to facilitate knowledge sharing, disadvantages some community members. Since it has been established as a male-dominated institution, women's voices are often disregarded during proceedings, even when it comes to voicing their opinions on developments that would affect them directly, for example in agricultural projects. Moreover, most of the youth in the village does not attend development meetings held at the *kgotla*, as the platform is not conducive for the community to state their concerns openly and share suggestions.

The S&CD officers admitted that a number of factors hinder the process. Lack of resources, for instance, forces them to rely on a single method of collecting and storing IK for development planning integration. They rely extensively on *kgotla* meetings because of budget constraints, while if adequate resources were available, they would facilitate IK collection and documentation at ward level. It also emerged that the S&CD offices have rendered the VDC less important. This, participants felt, has crippled their chances of articulating IK for documentation in rural development planning and management. They acknowledged the VDC as their village-level parliament, where they are free to express their views, but they were concerned about the lack of recognition the S&CD gives the VDC.

Lastly, misconceptions held by development administrators about the rural population hinder integration. Community participants said development administrators often imposed their own preconceived ideas of particular development situations and undermined contributions from the community in the belief that community members were not educated enough or trained in development practice. This has led to suggestions that community contributions to development projects in the area are of no use. A common belief among participants was that their suggestions were thrown away or shelved, which made them lose interest in integrative development planning; they felt their voices did not matter.

Conclusion

The integration of IK into rural development planning is a fundamental component of sustainable rural development. This view is widely shared by development practitioners across the globe. This chapter investigated the nature and extent of IK integration into rural development planning in the Mmankgodi village in Botswana.

It shows that integrating IK into the development process in Mmankgodi is limited by various factors. This can be attributed to the centralised nature of rural development processes in the country. And while the *kgotla* serves as a structure to facilitate IK integration, no documented guidelines and strategy for this task are in place. The situation is exacerbated by the usually disjointed procedures and setups that are meant to foster IK collection and documentation. A number of barriers affect the overall process of collecting, documenting and integrating IK into the rural development process.

Claims made in state publications of culture and IK integration in development processes in Botswana do not seem to reflect reality, since such integration does not exist in practice. Therefore, no conclusion can be reached other than that the integration of IK in the rural development planning process in Botswana is significantly limited.

Recommendations

Several gaps and opportunities exist in culture and IK integration into rural development planning in Mmankgodi and, by extension, Botswana.

1. Set up an effective participatory network. IK integration in project planning and management seems to be disjointed, resulting in poor accountability for community participation and contribution. This calls for the establishment of a sound and inclusive participatory network that gives every member of the community equal opportunity to contribute their IK.
2. Formulate and implement an integration strategy that is focused on the specific objective of bringing about the efficient and effective exchange of IK. The strategy should also contain guidelines to ensure the smooth exchange of information for rural development planning.
3. Provide IK facilitation training. Development workers at village level are the first contact of the community in the development process; it is important for them to be skilled in handling communication and participatory practices to ensure quality IK collection and documentation. Development workers in Mmankgodi should receive training in facilitation skills and be made aware of the importance of integrating IK in rural development planning.
4. Formulate and implement improved communication strategies. Poor communication between development workers and the community adversely affects IK sharing. There is a need for community-based information centres for the display, storage and dissemination of project information. The community should be sensitised on the values, objectives and timelines of projects so that they can contribute meaningfully.

Notes

1 Different scholars have used the terms 'indigenous people' and 'indigenous knowledge' differently, as cited in this chapter. The first refers to people living traditionally who, to some extent, have maintained their own social, economic, cultural and political institutions since colonisation and the establishment of new states. The second speaks to the wisdom or information that derives from their experiences, guided by a traditional lifestyle. The United Nations refers to indigenous knowledge as 'indigenous, local and traditional knowledge'. Some indigenous people have partly adopted modern lifestyles that they have blended with their traditional preferences. In Botswana, the Basarwa (San) are regarded as indigenous people due to their traditional lifestyle. There are also other ethnic groups that have maintained the traditional fabric of their ways of life; they live indigenously and use their indigenous knowledge to survive in their local environment. This chapter takes into account spatial factors and originality (originating from a particular locality) as well as traditional lifestyle when referring to 'indigenous knowledge' and 'indigenous people'. The concept of 'locality' or 'being local' (as in terms 'local knowledge' and 'local people') is often viewed as a component of indigeneity itself.

2 A *kgotla* acts as a local-level platform for consultative developmental and policy discussions between government and communities (Sharma 2010). It is a public community meeting or traditional law court functioning in Botswana. Headed by the village chief, a *kgotla* makes decisions by consensus.

3 Qualitative research methodology is intended to divulge a target audience's behaviour and the insights that drive it in regard to precise topics or issues. It uses in-depth studies of smaller groups of people to guide and support the formulation of a hypothesis. The results of qualitative research are descriptive rather than predictive (Neuman 2012).

References

Abraham A and Platteau JP (2004) Participatory development: Where culture creeps in. In V Rao and M Walton (Eds). *Culture and Public Action* (212–233). Stanford: Stanford University Press

Berkes F (2009) Evolution of co-management: Role of knowledge generation, bridging organizations and social learning. *Journal of Environmental Management* 90: 1692–1702

Bouwen R and Taillieu T (2004) Multi-party collaboration as social learning for interdependence: Developing relational knowing for sustainable natural resource management. *Journal of Communty and Applied Social Psychology* 14(3): 137–153

Boven K and Morohashi J (2002) *Best practices using indigenous knowledge*. Paris: United Nations Educational Scientific and Cultural Organization

Braun C and Clarke V (2006) Using thematic analysis in psychology. *Qualitative Research in Psychology* 3(2): 77–101

Cassidy L, Wilk J, Kgathi DL, Bendsen H, Ngwenya BN and Mosepele K (2011) Indigenous knowledge livelihoods and government policy in the Okavango Delta, Botswana. In DL Kgathi, BN Ngwenya and MBK Darkoh (Eds). *Rural Livelihoods, Risk and Political Economy of Access to Natural Resources in the Okavango Delta, Botswana.* UK: Nova Science Publishers, 76–96

Denters B and Klok PJ (2010) Rebuilding Rombeek: Patterns of citizen participation in urban governance. *Urban African Affairs* 583–587

Dipholo K (2002) Trends in participatory development. *Journal of Social Development in Africa* 59–79

Eyong C T (2014) *Indigenous knowledge and sustainable development in Africa: Case study on Central Africa.* Bonn: University of Bonn

Gabriel T (1991) *The human factor in rural development* Lancashire: Belhaven Press

Government of Botswana (2005) *Botswana national research, science and technology plan.* Gaborone: Government Printers

Grenier I (1998) *Working with indigenous knowledge.* Ottawa: International Development Research Centre

Hamdi N and Goethert R (1997) *Action planning for cities: A guide to community practice.* London: John Wiley & Sons Publishers

Harvey C and Lewis SR (1990) *Policy choice and development performance in Botswana.* Houndsmill: Macmillan

Hofstede G (1980) *Culture's consequences: International differences in work-related values.* London: Sage Publishers

Hoskins M (1990) Trees for the People. *CIKARD News* 2(1): 14–15

IFAD (International Fund for Agricultural Development) (2003) *Indigenous peoples and sustainable development.* Rome: International Fund for Agricultural Development

Kelly G (2005) *Report on threats to the practice and transmission of traditional knowledge. Regional report: Asia and Australia.* Canberra, ACT: AIATSIS

Krishnamurthy J (2000) *Rural development: Challenges and opportunities.* New Dehli: Nice Printing Press

Kukla A (2000) *Social constructivism and philosophy of science.* New York: Routledge

Lalonde A (1991) *African indigenous knowledge and its relevance to environment and development activities.* Winnipeg: Indiana University Press

Lele U (1975) *The designing of rural development.* London: Johns Hopkins University Press

Luthi C (2012) *Community-based environmental sanitation planning approaches for the South: The household-centred approach.* Berlin: University of Berlin

Makumbe JM (1996) *Participatory development: The case of Zimbabwe.* Harare: University of Zimbabwe

Malla MW and Loubser CP (2003) Emancipatory indigenous systems: Implications for environmental education in South Africa. *South African Journal of Education* 23(4): 276–282

Maripe K (2012) *Safeguarding cultural heritage as a strategy for development in the 21st century.* Gaborone: University of Botswana

Materer S Valdivia C and Gilles J (2002) *Indigenous knowledge systems: Characteristics and importance to climatic uncertainty.* Columbia: University of Missouri-Columbia

Matsumoto D (1996) *Culture and psychology.* California: Pacific Grove

Melchias G (2001) *Biodiversity and conservation.* Enfield: Science Publishers

Ministry of Communications, Science and Technology (2005) *Botswana national research science and technology plan.* Gaborone: Government Printers

Mokwena L and Fakir E (2009) *Democratic Decision Making and Development at the Local Level: Lessons from rural Botswana.* Johannesburg: Centre for Policy Studies

Mutebi F (2004) Reassessing popular participation in Uganda. *Public Administration and Development* 29: 289–304

Neba A, Andrae-Marobela K, Totolo O, Mazonde IN, Rutherford B, Graham K, et al. (2012) *Higher education institutions-industry stakeholder relationships: A case study of the University of Botswana's Centre for Scientific Research, Indigenous Knowledge and Innovations (CesrIKi's) partnership with indigenous knowledge systems (IKS).* Gaborone: University of Botswana

Neuman LW (2012) *Basics of social science research: Qualitative and quantitative approaches.* Wincosin: Pearson Publishers

Nfila RB and Jain P (2011) *Managing indigenous systems in Botswana using information and communication technologies.* Bulawayo: University of Botswana

Ngwasiri DN (1995) *Knowledge is of two kinds.* Wageningen: CTA Bulletin

Oakley P (1991) *Projects with the people: The practice of participation in rural development.* Geneva: International Labour Office

Odora-Hoppers C (2002) *Indigenous knowledge and the integration of knowledge systems.* Claremont: New Africa Books

Odora-Hoppers CA (2005) *Culture, indigenous knowledge and development: The role of the university.* Johannesburg: Centre for Education Policy Development

Okafor FC (1982) Community involvement in rural development: A field study in Bendal. *Community Development Journal* 17(2): 134–140

Ponge A (2013) *Integrating indigenous knowledge for food security: Perspectives from the Millenium Village Project St Bar-Sauri in Nyanza Province in Kenya.* London: University of London

Pottier J (2003) *Negotiating local knowledge: An introduction.* London: Pluto Press

Rakody C and Schlyter A (1981) *Upgrading in Lusaka: Participation and physical changes.* Stockholm: The National Swedish Institute for Building Research

Risse T (2009) *Social constructivism and European relations.* Oxford: Oxford University Press

Rubin A and Babbie E (1997) *Research methods in social work.* Washington: Brooks Publishing Co.

Sanoff H (2000) *Community participation methods in design and planning.* London: John Wiley and Sons

Sears DW and Reid JN (1995) *Rural development strategies.* Illinois: Nelson Hall Publishers

Sen A (1999) *Development as freedom.* Oxford: Oxford University press

Sharma KC (2010) Role of local government in Botswana for effective service delivery: Challenges, prospects and lessons. *Commonwealth Journal of Local Governance* 7: 1–8

Sillitoe P, Bicker A and Pottier J (2004) Participating in development: approaches to indigenous knowledge. *Anthropology Matters* 6: 1–8

Spencer-Oatey H (2008) *Culturally Speaking: Culture, Communication and Politeness Theory* (2nd edition). London: Continuum

Tanyanyiwa IV and Chikwanha M (2011) The role of indigenous knowledge systems in the management of forest resources in the Mugabe area, Masvingo, Zimbabwe. *Journal of Sustainable Development in Africa* 13(3): 132–149

Todaro M (1985) *Economic development in the Third World.* London: Orient Longman

UNESCO (United Nations Educational, Scientific and Cultural Organization) (2013) *Mapping research and innovation in the Republic of Botswana.* Paris: UNESCO

Van Heck B (2003) *Participatory development: Guidelines on beneficiary participation in agricultural and rural development.* Rome: FAO

Vygotsky LS (1978) *Mind in society.* Cambridge: Harvard University Press

Weedon C (2004) *Identity and culture: Narratives of difference and belonging.* Milton Keynes: Open University

World Bank (1994) *World development report.* Oxford: Oxford University Press

World Bank (1998) *Indigenous knowledge for development: A framework for action.* Washington DC: World Bank

3 How Africans trade their riches for roads and bridges: Three stories

Dunia Prince Zongwe

In the past decade, African nations have entered into several contractual arrangements in terms of which they have traded natural resources for major infrastructure works. While these projects have had a substantial impact on the economies of the host countries, little is known about the design and occurrence of these unconventional deals. Thus, questions arise about the special characteristics and various descriptions of these large investment contracts, as well as their real and likely outcomes. To make sure this way of transacting is to their advantage, countries on the continent involved in such arrangements need to interrogate these contracts thoroughly.

After an in-depth review of the deals, three models of contracting have been identified. The three stories told in this chapter illustrate them using examples of contracts from Angola, the Democratic Republic of the Congo (DRC) and Ghana. Such contractual models try to shield these important investments from local politics and the political culture in countries facing daunting accountability and capacity challenges. The contractual models discussed here are sometimes referred to as resources-for-infrastructure (R4I) contracts; the question is, what makes them attractive to governments of host countries?

To understand how the different models have been applied in the three countries under scrutiny, this chapter explains the basic concept and workings of the R4I contract, followed by a discussion of each of the three examples of R4I contracting, ending with a summary of the lessons that can be learnt from the practice.

What is a resources-for-infrastructure investment contract?

R4I contracts are highly complex contractual arrangements. Simply put, an R4I contract would creatively combine, say, a mining or oil venture and an infrastructure project (1) to extract minerals or hydrocarbons, and (2) to pay for major infrastructure projects with revenues generated from those extractive activities. Under this arrangement, the host state gets the infrastructure and the foreign investor gets the extracted resources (Zongwe 2015: 39).

Contracts

R4I arrangements are contractual in nature. The answer to the question as to which acts or facts constitute a contract varies within legal systems and from one legal system to another. In Africa's rural areas, where most Africans still live (although migration to cities from rural areas is rapidly increasing), the way people envision formal agreements conflicts, to some degree, with the Western understanding of contracts, which, for historical reasons, nearly all states in Africa have incorporated into their laws.

This chapter views contracts from an economic perspective. It refers to a contract as the terms of an economic exchange in which parties to the exchange specify certain consequences for their property rights. Put differently, in order to generalise across legal systems, the chapter defines a contract as an agreement by at least two parties who furthermore indicate how their property rights will be changed or affected by their agreement.

Investment contracts

The R4I model is a way of transacting foreign direct investment (FDI). Put another way, the R4I deals are *investment* contracts. Investment is the committal of money for profit, and FDI is the category of cross-border investment that reflects the objective of an entity in one economy to obtain a lasting interest in an enterprise resident in another economy (IMF 1993: 86). The hallmark of FDI—as opposed to portfolio investment (e.g. purchases of securities)—is the transfer of physical property (e.g. plant or equipment) that is bought or built (Sornarajah 2010: 8).

That R4I arrangements are investment contracts cannot be overemphasised, given the fact that several experts have erroneously equated R4I contracts to trade agreements.[1] Edinger & Jansson (2008: 8) describe R4I contracts as barter trade agreements. In the DRC, the Governor of the Central Bank concluded that the R4I contract struck by the DRC and China is a barter agreement (Tshitenge Lubabu 2009).

It is critical to locate FDI within the broad field of international economic law to make sure that R4I contracts are properly labelled as investment contracts rather than trade agreements or other economic arrangements, as did Bräutigam, for example (2009: 46).[2] An investment contract is distinct and distinguishable from a trade agreement because the nature of the business activities underlying these two contract types differs, even if mining investments often translate into increased exports of primary commodities. Whereas a trade transaction characteristically consists of a *once-off* exchange of goods and money, an FDI deal initiates a *long-term* relationship, a 'lasting interest' (IMF 1993: 86) between the foreign investor and the host state, which may span more than 30 years (Dolzer & Schreuer 2008: 3). The long-term nature of the economic exchanges that investment contracts regulate involves, almost invariably, significant risks of losses for foreign investors and host states. Incidentally, both FDI law and R4I contracts are techniques for the allocation and mitigation of these risks.

Defining resources for infrastructure

R4I deals are, as mentioned above, contractual in nature and best categorised as investments. However, defining R4I deals as investment contracts does not say much about the basic concept and content of those deals. So, how can the concept be framed, and the ordinary and special characteristics of R4I contracts be described?[3]

An R4I contract is an elaborate and complex network of agreements between a host state and another state investing in the host state (1) to develop and extract natural resources (minerals and/or hydrocarbons), (2) to use the revenues generated or expected from the extraction of resources to pay for (3) major infrastructure projects in the host state. Thus, the essential clauses of an R4I contract are the resource development agreement, the loan agreement and the agreement on infrastructure development. In the ordinary course of events, the essential agreements are provided for in a framework agreement, which is a vital contract document from a conceptual and structural perspective.

Resource development agreement
The parties agree that the foreign investor will prospect for natural resources and carry out feasibility studies. Most importantly, they agree to extract and export those resources to the investor's home country or to third parties. As will be illustrated later by the three stories on R4I deals, the resource development agreement may take the form of a production sharing agreement or an off-take agreement.

Loan agreement
In exchange for the promise to grant rights to specified natural resources, the investing foreign state gives a loan to the host state to construct infrastructure that will be built by contractors from the same foreign state. As the loan is often on concessional terms, it is sometimes seen as aid (Alves 2013: 7–8). The loan is paid out directly to the contractor and the developer, and never reaches state coffers.

Infrastructure development agreement
The parties agree that the foreign investor will construct and/or rehabilitate infrastructure. The host state selects the infrastructure to be developed. The scale of R4I contracts varies widely. At the top end of the scale, R4I contracts can be used for national reconstruction, as has been done in Angola and the DRC. Generally, R4I contracts are best suited for massive, large-scale infrastructure projects. Nonetheless, at the bottom end of the scale they serve for small infrastructure projects.

The political culture of resource extraction
How are R4I contractual arrangements able to navigate the political cultures in the adverse circumstances typical of resource-rich countries in the developing world? 'Political culture' refers to the pattern of beliefs, assumptions, attitudes and practices that underlie and give meaning to political processes such as granting mining licenses to foreign investors. A report by the Multilateral Investment Guarantee Agency (2011) attests to the singularity of risk in the extraction of natural resources in developing countries, especially conflict-torn and fragile states such as Angola or the DRC.

Africa is a place in the Global South that foreign investors generally perceive as risky—riskier, at any rate, than its sister continents. Unfortunately, these negative perceptions are often as inaccurate as they are widespread. They tend to overlook countries with decent track records such as Mauritius, Cabo Verde, Botswana, South Africa, Namibia and the Seychelles.[4]

A fundamental concern of modern foreign investment law is that host states will behave opportunistically after the investment contract is signed and the foreign investor has sunk capital into an investment project. Once money has gone into a project, the bargaining positions of the parties change. This is a problem known as 'political risk' (Yackee 2008: 807).

Regime change or changes to host states' existing political and economic policies are the main political risks to foreign investment (Sornarajah 2010: 69–70). Those changes are the greatest threat to the effective implementation of R4I contracts in Africa. Many factors may precipitate the materialisation of political risks. These risk factors include ideological hostility, nationalism, ethnicity, changes in industry patterns, uncertain legal frameworks, the absence of a bilateral investment treaty (BIT), onerous contracts, regulation of the economy, environmental and human rights concerns, and contracts agreed to by previous regimes (Sornarajah 2010: 77; Comeaux & Kinsella 1997: 18). In a nutshell, the principal risk faced by foreign investors relates to the political culture of the host country.

The context in which most countries in Africa evolve are marked by accountability, capacity and security issues. According to Transparency International (TI), almost half of the most corrupt countries[5] globally in 2015 were in Africa.[6] Of the 18 countries in that category of countries, eight were African.[7] Ranked from the most corrupt, these countries were Somalia, Sudan, South Sudan, Angola, Libya, Guinea Bissau, Eritrea and Zimbabwe.[8] Moreover, the Fund for Peace ranks countries in terms of institutional capacity. It had, as of October 2016, a list of at least 38 failed states. Of these 38, 26 were located in Africa.[9] In descending order of state failure, these African countries were Somalia, South Sudan, Central African Republic (CAR), Sudan, Chad, the DRC, Nigeria, Burundi, Zimbabwe, Guinea Bissau, Eritrea, Niger, Kenya, Côte d'Ivoire, Cameroon, Uganda, Ethiopia, Libya, Liberia, Mauritania, Mali, Congo-Brazzaville, Rwanda, Sierra Leone, Angola and Egypt.[10]

The reason, ultimately, why R4I contracts may be useful to those nations lies in governance issues. If a host country is faced with governance challenges, the need for greater transparency, or an institutional failure to build infrastructure, it makes sense for that country to resort to R4I contracts.[11] It is in that sense that R4I contracts can be viewed as a mechanism to bind host governments into performing a governance function—that is, public investments in social and economic infrastructure.

Unsurprisingly, as the World Bank report on the ease of doing business demonstrates, it is hard to do business in countries on the continent plagued by conflict, corruption or institutional dysfunction.[12] Effectively, the World Bank shows that countries with the least conducive regulatory environment for business are Eritrea, Libya and South Sudan.[13]

Political risks

There are four major types of political or non-commercial risk: expropriation, war and political violence, breach of contract, and currency restrictions (Baker 1995: 13; Ossman 1996: 369). That is, the adverse political culture and economic context, known as 'resource curse', manifests itself in individual foreign investments in the form of regulatory changes, breach of contract, transfer and convertibility restrictions, failure to honour sovereign guarantees, and civil disturbance (MIGA 2011: 23).

Expropriation is 'the most severe form of interference with property' (Dolzer & Schreuer 2008: 89), even though it is *prima facie* lawful (Sornarajah 2010: 406). States have the right to expropriate or the 'right of eminent domain', an entitlement stemming from the states' territorial sovereignty (Dolzer & Schreuer 2008: 89). International law recognises the right of states to change their economic and other policies. This right is an inherent aspect of state sovereignty. The political culture and security situation of host countries are relevant to the assessment of investment risks because insecurity and instability in the host country increase the odds of asset losses for investors.

Host government interference with state–investor contracts is another political risk. The state may, for one reason or another, decide unilaterally to vary the terms of the contracts it has signed with foreign investors. If intangible assets, including contract rights, are protected property rights, then they may be expropriated, which in turn may lead to a duty to compensate (Reinisch 2008: 417). These breaches may occur where a government wishes to review and rescind contracts that an illegitimate previous government entered into, where it is economically efficient[14] or necessary to preserve economic equilibrium (Dolzer & Schreuer 2008: 77),[15] where the contracts are onerous, or where they have been concluded in violation of applicable laws or as a result of corruption.

A third type of political risk is restrictions imposed on transfers, or the conversion or exchange of currency. Local currency regulations may partially or entirely restrict the transfer, conversion, repatriation, or exchange of funds. For example, the host state may license banks and brokers to handle foreign exchange, thereby limiting the availability of foreign exchange for commercial transactions—a move that has engendered a great deal of corruption in some least-developed countries (Baker 1995: 13). However, the risk of currency restrictions is lower in the case of natural resources and commodities, whose output is sold in the export market, thereby yielding hard currency directly (Comeaux & Kinsella 1997: 15).

The R4I model and local political cultures

Investment-specific devices protect foreign investors from political risks by internationalising investment contracts. These devices are stabilisation, choice-of-law clauses, arbitration, damages, waiver of sovereign immunity, waiver of the local remedies exhaustion requirement, currency conversion, repatriation, interest rates, *force majeure* clauses, state interest in the project, and state-as-party clauses.

Internationalisation (achieved chiefly through stabilisation, choice-of-law and arbitration clauses) requires investor–state contracts to go through a process that propels them to a higher legal orbit. A few of these devices are discussed below.

Takings clauses

Takings clauses protect foreign investors by restraining the right of host states to interfere with property or property rights. They achieve that purpose by requiring that lawful takings serve the public interest, are non-discriminatory, and compensate investors aggrieved by the takings. Like most international investment contracts, R4I contracts contain takings clauses by which African parties undertake never, and in no circumstances whatsoever appropriate, to nationalise, nor expropriate, directly or indirectly, the joint venture as well as its property.

Stabilisation clauses

Stabilisation clauses aim to prevent future changes in the legislation of the host state from varying the terms of an investment contract to the detriment of an investing foreign party. The key element of a stabilisation clause is the stripping of the host government's right unilaterally to alter a foreign investor's rights by changing its municipal law (Comeaux & Kinsella 1997: 139). Foreign investors stand to lose in any agreement with the host state if the state legislates in a way that varies any contractual right or right to property located within its territory (Sornarajah 2010: 281). It is therefore in the investor's interests to immunise foreign investment from a range of legislative amendments in a given area, for example taxation, environmental controls and other regulations, as well as to prevent the destruction of the contract itself before it expires (Sornarajah 2010: 281). International investment law comes off as particularly well suited to protect investors' rights, even in circumstances where key constituencies in the host country lobby for legislative amendments or a cancellation of an investment contract.

However, stabilisation clauses cannot deliver on their promises, because constitutional theory prescribes that a sovereign state cannot bind its actions by contract and that it can always change its legislation. Nonetheless, they do raise the legitimate expectations of the parties, which are factored into the assessment of damages when dispute settlement fora award compensation.

Choice-of-law clauses

Another technique to protect foreign investment is to incorporate a choice-of-law clause in the investment contract. Choice-of-law clauses exclude the application of the domestic laws of the host state and subject the contract to some external standards like the 'general principles of law' (Sornarajah 2010: 281). The default contract provision is that the law of the host state is the governing law, because, in the majority of cases, it is the place of performance under the contract. However, some jurisdictions put limitations on choice-of-law clauses.

Because of the well-established principle of party autonomy in contract law, parties to an investment contract may choose the legal system that will apply to the contract. A party to the contract can therefore choose a legal system other than that of the host state to apply to the contract. Parties usually select a neutral, commercially sophisticated, well-developed body of law such as English law or New York law (Comeaux & Kinsella 1997: 135).[16] By choosing a foreign legal system, a foreign investor can prevent a host state that wishes to evade contractual obligations from taking unfair advantage or counting on the parochialism of domestic courts in the event of a dispute over the terms of the contract.

The weakness of choice-of-law clauses is that they do not have the desired effect of subjecting investment contracts to a system higher than that of the legal system of the host state (Sornarajah 2010: 284–285). A foreign legal system chosen by either or both parties will have only a co-equal, and not a superior, authority (Sornarajah 2010: 284–285). Admittedly, in every legal system, the freedom to choose a foreign law as the law that applies to the contract cannot rule out mandatory provisions of national laws.

Arbitration

Arbitration is another contractual device that protects foreign investment. An arbitration clause refers for adjudication to a neutral forum—often an international mechanism like the International Center for the Settlement of Investment Disputes (ICSID)—all disputes between the host state and the foreign investor. An arbitration clause is preferable to an equivalent provision in a BIT because the arbitration clause can be tailored to the needs of the parties and can, unlike BITs, be used in conjunction with stabilisation and choice-of-law clauses (Comeaux & Kinsella 1997: 134). Typically, a foreign investor will not trust the ability of a developing country and its courts to adjudicate on investor–state dispute impartially and independently. Reference of disputes to the domestic courts of a country other than the host country raises issues of sovereign immunity (Sornarajah 2010: 286).

The state-to-state business model

R4I contracts hold an arsenal of contractual devices to shield foreign investors from political and other types of risk they may face in host countries. One of the key observations is that, of all the protective devices designed to insulate foreign investors from the political culture of host states, the state-to-state model seems to be the silver bullet. This should not come as a surprise, because cultivating strong relations with host states is one winning strategy for the mitigation of political risk.

The state-to-state business model that characterises China's FDI and R4I contracts in Africa has played a vital role in the success of Sino-African joint ventures. Beijing's support for Chinese state-owned corporations has been decisive in directing FDI in Africa as opposed to other regions (Alden et al. 2008: 7). The dramatic upsurge of China's FDI in the mining sectors of Africa is as a result of the support of the Chinese central government (Alden et al. 2008: 7) and the solid financial support provided by Chinese state-backed banks (Alden et al. 2008: 16).

The state-to-state business model typical of China's FDI in Africa has lessons for conventional wisdom and debates on the effectiveness of investment contract clauses in attracting FDI.[17] It suggests that it serves the promotion and protection of Chinese FDI in Africa more effectively than BITs, though China has also signed BITs with many countries in Africa. That said, while there are differences between the state-to-state model used by Chinese investors and the traditional international project finance structures, both rely and depend on state involvement, usually through the grant of a concession (Rehbock phone interview, 3 May 2010).[18]

The Angola story

Among the many countries with first-hand experience of R4I dealing, the choice of the Angolan story is deliberate. The R4I contract between Angola and China is the first major example—the archetype—of R4I contracts and, ultimately, a potent template for how post-conflict countries can effectively embark upon national reconstruction (Davies 2010: 14). This is the reason why the 'Angola model' and 'Angola mode' have become nicknames for R4I contracts in general.

The 2004 deal

'When the war ended in 2002, the Angolan government approached traditional donors, including the International Monetary Fund and the Paris Club, for loans to fund its post-conflict reconstruction, but they were not forthcoming. China offered Angola a colossal US$2 billion line of credit to finance infrastructure projects as part of a historic deal that is now commonly known as the "Angola model" or the "Angola mode"' (Zongwe 2010). That deal helped repair, modernise and expand Angola's infrastructure destroyed by the country's civil war.

In 2004, Angola and China sealed an intergovernmental framework agreement (the Angola–China R4I deal) for the post-conflict reconstruction of Angola. The Angola model is structured to (1) channel China's massive loans to develop infrastructures and (2) pay back the loans with exports of oil to China by Angola. That manner of financing infrastructure development constitutes the signature of the Angola model. Following that model, the Angolan Cabinet approved a host of infrastructure contracts that it signed with Chinese corporations in the context of the country's national reconstruction programme.[19]

Loan repayment

The loan agreement involved two state-owned corporations, namely Angola's oil parastatal, Sonangol, and China's oil company, China Petroleum & Chemical Corporation (Sinopec). 'The loan agreement provided for the terms and conditions for the lending of money to Angola through the Sonangol-Sinopec joint venture pursuant to an intergovernmental framework agreement between Angola and China' (Zongwe 2010). In terms of the loan agreement, China Exim Bank was the lender and the Sonangol–SSI joint venture the debtor. Just like the credit decision of a rational lender is based primarily on estimated cash flow (Malloy 2004: 90), so China Exim Bank's decision to grant a loan to the Sonangol–SSI joint venture took into account the venture's cash flow. The total amount of the debt in terms of the R4I contract was US$4.5 billion. At US$70 per barrel—the average crude spot price by January 2010 (IEA 2010: 40)—the total reimbursement would have required the export to China of around 642 857 140 barrels. The Angola–China contract mandated a daily payment of 10 000 barrels (Vines et al. 2009: 47). That is equal to about 176 days or six months of exports, all other things remaining constant.

The financing of the infrastructure projects was highly leveraged in the sense that the bulk of the finance came from debt as opposed to equity. High leverage enabled China Exim Bank to risk a smaller portion of its equity investment in the joint venture and to reduce the cost of capital by substituting lower-cost tax-deductible interest for higher-cost taxable returns on equity (Baragona 2004: 141). The reimbursement proper dispenses with monetary intermediation. The Angolan government simply sets off the US$4.5 billion infrastructure loan against an equivalent amount in taxes, dividends and royalties that Chinese investors would have been required to pay in terms of an ordinary investment contract.

The Angola–China contract provides for a concessional interest rate, London Interbank Offered Rate (LIBOR) plus one-and-a-half per cent, with a grace period of up to three years (Vines et al. 2009: 47) for the first loan of US$2 billion, repayable over 17 years; and the rate for the second loan of US$2 billion decreased at one-and-a-quarter per cent (Bräutigam 2009: 176). The interest on these loans is close to market rates, implying that Chinese investors were risk tolerant or estimated their investments in Angola to be low-risk. The decrease in interest rate for the second loan is probably a sign of the growing confidence of Chinese firms in the relative safety of their investments in Angola. In any event, these loan agreements contained better terms than contracts with Angola's traditional partners, which demanded higher interest rates and guarantees of oil, with no grace periods (Campos & Vines 2008: 18).

Infrastructure projects for national reconstruction

On 3 April 2006, the Angolan Cabinet approved four infrastructure contracts for the supply, installation and commissioning of a nationwide fibre-optic telecommunication network within the framework of the credit line extended by China Exim Bank for a total value in Kwanzas equivalent to US$276 307 189.[20] The four approved contracts or projects refer to four corresponding basic telecommunication networks,[21] namely the first project covered the Luanda–Malanje–Kuito axis;[22] the second spread over the Lueala–Negage–Uíge, Chibia–Cahama–Ondjiva, and Benguela–Tchindjenje–Longonjo axes;[23] the third expanded the metropolitan network of the capital city of Luanda;[24] and the fourth covered the axis Cuito–Huambo–Lubango.[25] Telecommunication lines also reached adjacent localities in the provinces of Bengo, Benguela, Bié, Cuanza-Norte, Cuanza-Sul, Cunene, Huambo, Huíla, Luanda, Malanje, Moxico, Uíge and Zaire.

As shown below, the Angolan government published a list of these contracts by Cabinet resolution.[26]

Table 3.1 *Angolan infrastructure contracts with Chinese corporations*

Infrastructure projects/contracts	
Rehabilitation of the city of Luanda	Rehabilitation of the city of Luanda and five municipalities, namely Kilamba Kiaxi, Rangel, Ingombota, Cazenga and Sambizanga
Rehabilitation of infrastructure in Cazenga-Cariango	Construction of the principal channels and branches of the drainage system as well as the construction of infrastructures in the municipalities
Construction of a drainage system and rehabilitation of infrastructure in Precol and Suroca	Construction of the principal system for rehabilitation of infrastructure in Suroca and Precol
Construction of central and auxiliary drainage systems and rehabilitation on Senado de Câmara, Rio Seco and Maianga	Construction of the main extension system and infrastructure works on Senado de Câmara, Rio Seco and Maianga
Distribution project for water supply	Renovation of 300 kilometres of water supply, 300 fountains, 2 800 valves, 30 000 meters, 13 pumps and 5 control stations
Construction of 215 500 houses in 24 cities and 18 provinces	Construction of 215 500 housing units with one total construction area of 31 436 709 m^2
Rehabilitation of the road between Luanda, Sumbe and Lobito	Rehabilitation of a total of 497 kilometres of road, including reconstruction of roads, bridges and ditches
Rehabilitation of the roads between Malanje and Saurimo, and Luena and Dundo	Rehabilitation of roads with a total length of 1 107 km, including reconstruction of roads, bridges and ditches
Rehabilitation of the railway of Luanda	Rehabilitation of railways with a total length of 444 km, including reconstruction of roads, bridges, ditches and other installations
General rehabilitation of the railway of Benguela	Rehabilitation of railways with a total length of 1 547.2 km, including reconstruction of roads, bridges, ditches and other installations
General rehabilitation of the railway of Moçamedes	Rehabilitation of railways with a total length of 1 003.1 km, including reconstruction of roads, bridges, ditches and other installations
New International Airport of Luanda	EPC, preparation, supply and construction contract for a new airport, including car park, cargo areas and other constructions
Studies and technical projects	**Description**
Projects for the building of housing	Project for the construction of 215 000 housing units with a total construction area of 31 436 709 m^2
Rehabilitation of infrastructure	Project for the rehabilitation of five public infrastructures

Table 3.1 *Continued*

Studies and technical projects	Description
General and urban planning of the new city of Luanda	General planning of one new city, including management and investment proposals and urban planning
General and urban planning of the administrative centre of Luanda	General planning of an administrative centre, including ministerial office buildings, a supreme court building, parliament, presidential house, etc.
Landscape project for Luanda	Landscape project for the administrative centre of Luanda

Source: Zongwe (2010)

Drawing information from the Angolan Ministry of Finance, the Chatham House report *Thirst for African Oil* (Vines 2009: 63) lists infrastructure projects by phase and by sector.

Table 3.2 *Projects financed by China Exim Bank (phase 1)*

Sector	Number of contracts	Total value (in US$ million)
Health	9	206.1
Education	8	217.2
Energy and water	8	243.8
Agriculture	3	149.8
Transport	1	13.8
Social communication	1	66.9
Public works	1	211.7
Total	**31**	**1 109.3**

Table 3.3 *Projects financed by China Exim Bank (phase 2)*

Sector	Number of contracts	Total value (in US$ million)
Health	1	43.8
Education	3	229.6
Energy and water	3	144.9
Agriculture	1	54.0
Fisheries	3	266.8
Post	4	276.3
Public works	2	89.5
Total	**17**	**1 104.9**

The extensions

The Angolan example proves that a joint venture acting as a vehicle of finance for large-scale infrastructure works in a given R4I contract could be retained to serve the same purpose in subsequent R4I contracts. Thus, in May 2007, China Exim Bank granted an additional US$500 million to finance 'complementary actions' in Angola—these are projects from the first phase that had not been budgeted for (Vines 2009: 47). These projects included water and energy networks, water treatment plants and new telecommunications lines (Vines 2009: 47).

Table 3.4 *Complementary actions*

Sector	Total value (in US$ million)
Health	159.4
Education	145.6
Energy and water	76.5
Education and health	1.7
Fisheries	40.0
Telecommunications	56.3
Public works	65.5
Total	**545.0**

Source: Vines et al. 2009: 63

Institutionalising the model

The Angolan story is further proof that the R4I model could be completely institutionalised instead of being used for specific purposes only. In March 2011, the Angolan president instituted by decree the *Fundo Petrolifero de Angola,* the Oil for Infrastructure Fund (O'Neill 2012). Although the fund was later replaced by a sovereign wealth fund, the *Fundo Soberano de Angola*, the Angolan experience nevertheless offers that possibility.

The Congo story

Like Ghana, the Democratic Republic of the Congo (DRC) sealed two R4I deals, one with China, the other with South Korea. However, unlike Ghana, neither of these long-term deals has been completed yet. The first R4I contract was signed in 2008 and the second in 2011.

The Sicomines deal

The earlier R4I contract, the Sicomines deal, has as its objective the exchange of copper and cobalt to China for a programme of nationwide infrastructure construction in the DRC. Though valued at US$9 billion, the DRC—under pressure from the International Monetary Fund (IMF)—renegotiated the deal and reduced its value from US$9 billion to US$6 billion, suspending the remaining US$3 billion of the initial value of the deal.

The mining project

The DRC framework agreement states that the Chinese and Congolese parties will formalise their cooperation by constituting a mining joint venture to which the Congolese will cede, through national mining company *Générale des Carrières et des Mines* (Gécamines), the mining rights and titles involved in the cooperation.[27]

The framework agreement contains a number of guarantees whereby the DRC warrants, inter alia, that mining titles and rights awarded to the joint venture, Sicomines, will be free of all defects,[28] and that mineral deposits whose rights have been ceded to Sicomines contain mining reserves envisaged by the parties to the agreement.[29]

Important guarantees in the agreement come in the form of guarantees against political risk. The DRC guarantees that, one year after the approval of the agreement by the Chinese government, it will commit to obtaining from the Congolese parliament the enactment of legislation securing the financial regime (i.e. tax, customs and excise, and foreign exchange) applicable to the DRC–China joint project because of its specificity.[30] The DRC also makes the commitment that it will in no circumstances appropriate, nationalise and expropriate, directly or indirectly, the mining joint venture or the latter's property.[31] It further promises to respect the BIT between China and the DRC signed on 18 December 1997.[32] Finally, the DRC guarantees the security of China's mining and infrastructure investments and the reimbursement of the infrastructure to be built in accordance with the framework agreement.[33]

The Sicomines joint venture

The resource side of R4I contracts entails the establishment of a joint venture between a national mining or oil corporation and a Chinese state-owned corporation. The joint venture between the DRC (through Gécamines) and China (through a consortium of Chinese state-owned corporations) has been incorporated in terms of Congolese corporate laws.[34] The joint venture is known as *La Sino-Congolaise des Mines* (Sicomines). The Congolese state participates in Sicomines through Gécamines, while the Chinese state participates in the joint venture through a consortium of state-owned corporations consisting of China Railway and Engineering Corporation (CREC) and SinoHydro.

Sicomines will have to generate profits for the reimbursement not only of the mining investments, but also the infrastructure investments made by China.[35] To guarantee that the Chinese parties recover their investments in the mining and infrastructure projects, the parties agreed that the Chinese will have a 68 per cent interest in the joint venture and that Gécamines will own the remaining 32 per cent.[36] Some R4I contracts promote state-to-state partnerships through joint ventures like *La Compagnie Minière de Bélinga* (COMIBEL) in Gabon and *La Sino-Congolaise des Mines* (Sicomines) in the DRC. These partnerships are preferable to mining concessions because, in addition to the exploitation of natural resources, they develop national mining/oil corporations. They thus fall within

China's win–win philosophy, which favours joint ventures with host countries in Africa. This despite the fact that the law in the DRC requires that mining investors form joint ventures with Congolese nationals. They also revive the developmental role of host states, with joint ventures acting as vehicles for the finance of infrastructure projects. The revival runs counter to the mining/oil reforms initiated by international financial institutions (IFIs) in many an African country. These reforms consisted in weakening the state as a development agent by urging countries in Africa to privatise mining/oil sectors or remove state monopolies in those sectors (Campbell 2009: 3).

Repayment through the joint venture

China's decision to advance loans and build infrastructure was based on the Sicomines joint venture, which constitutes security for the mining rights and titles granted to the consortium of Chinese corporations.[37] The capital structure in Sicomines is 32 per cent for the DRC and 68 per cent for the consortium of Chinese state-owned corporations engaged in the DRC–China R4I contract. A great many analysts have criticised the capital structure of these ventures. While critics are right in their concerns, they are asking the wrong questions. They are asking whether the capital structure is unconscionable or unfairly disadvantageous, instead of whether the profit-sharing formula reflects the respective contributions of the parties and creates the right incentives for the parties to apply their best efforts at *a given time during the lifetime of the contract*.

In this model, the capital structure is justified by the need to guarantee that the Chinese Consortium recoups the capital it has sunk into the mining/oil and infrastructure projects. It is difficult to be too precise as to the appropriate share for foreign investors. Nonetheless, it is evident that a formula that does not allocate a high share of the revenues to the foreign investors for cost recovery *in the early stages* of resource exploitation will remove the incentives for the investors to commit substantial finance to projects, especially when political risk and transaction costs are high in the host country, as is the case in the DRC.

The parties have agreed that, to facilitate the reimbursement of infrastructure investments, the DRC undertakes to exonerate the mining and infrastructure projects of the R4I contract from all customs and excise requirements, mining royalties, and taxes (direct or indirect) within the country or at import or export.[38] All taxes paid by Sicomines during the reimbursement period will be accounted for as infrastructure expenses.[39] During the reimbursement phase of China's mining investments, the capital structure of Sicomines in the DRC is 30 per cent of debt in the form of a shareholders' loan bearing no interest to Sicomines, and the remaining 70 per cent is equity.[40] The DRC Framework Agreement stipulates that reimbursement of China's equity investments in the Sicomines joint venture will be at an annual interest rate of 6.1 per cent.[41] This derogation is most probably a signal that the risk of default by the DRC in reimbursing China's investments is above average.

The DRC Framework Agreement arranges the reimbursement of the mining and infrastructure investments in three periods.[42] The first period will reimburse the mining investments, and the second the first half of infrastructure investments. The third and final period will be commercial, a time during which the DRC will directly share in the profits and will no longer have to apply them to the reimbursement of the mining and infrastructure investments. If Sicomines has not reimbursed the loans, with interest, 25 years after its inception, the DRC government undertakes to reimburse Chinese investors by other means.[43]

National reconstruction

Just as the Sino-Angolan R4I contract provided for several infrastructure projects aimed at Angola's national reconstruction, so the R4I contract between the DRC and China covers construction, rehabilitation and modernisation projects nationwide. And, as was the case with the Sino-Angolan R4I contract, the implementation of the infrastructure projects envisaged by the Sino-Congolese R4I contract is divided into phases. The first phase, still in progress, is valued at US$350 million, while the second, which began in March 2010, is valued at 400 million US dollars.[44] Below is a list of the projects to be implemented within the framework of the R4I contract between the DRC and China.[45]

Table 3.5 *List of projects to be implemented within the framework of the Sicomines deal*

Number	Projects	Length (in km)	Description
1	**Railway**		
	Tenke–Kolwezi–Dilolo		Rehabilitation and modernisation
	Sakania–Lubumbashi–Kamina–Mwene Ditu–Kananga–Ilebo	1 833	Modernisation
	Kinshasa–Matadi	365	
2	**Railway**		
	Ilebo–Kinshasa	1 015	Construction
3	**Roads**		
	3.1 Tarred roads		
	Kasindi–Beni–Komanda–Niania	520	Construction
	Komanda–Bunia	71	
	Lubumbashi–Kasomeno–Kasenga	207	
	Kasomeno–Pweto	336	
	Likasi–Kolwezi	180	
	Bukavu–Kamanyola	55	
	Moba slip road	462	
	3.2 Bridge over the Lualaba River	0.110	Construction

Number	Projects	Length (in km)	Description
3	**3.3 Tarred roads (bitumen)**		
	Pweto–Kalemie–Fizi	730	Construction
	Fizi–Uvira-Kavinvira	142	
	Bukavu–Goma–Beni	590	
	Niania–Bafwasende–Kisangani	363	
	3.4 Tarred roads (asphalt)		
	Matadi–Boma	135	Rehabilitation
	Uvira–Kamanyola	85	
	Moanda–Banana	9	
	Mbuji Mayi–Mwene Ditu	135	
	3.5 Untarred roads		
	Kananga–Mbuji Mayi–Kasongo–Kindu–	887	Rehabilitation
	Kolwezi–Kasaji–Dilolo	426	
	Dilolo–Sandoa–Kapanga–Kananga	709	
	Kasaji–Sandoa	139	
	Boma–Moanda–Yema	125	
	Niania–Isiro	232	
	–	220	
4	**Public roads**		
	City of Kinshasa	250	Rehabilitation
	Other cities: Lubumbashi, Bukavu, Kisangani, Kananga, Mbuji Mayi, Goma, Matadi, Bandundu, Mbandaka, Kindu	300	
5	**Airports**		
	Goma airport		
	Bukavu airport		
6	**Hospitals and medical equipment**		
	10 hospitals, each with 150 beds, one in each province		Construction
	21 hospitals, each with 150 beds, one in each province		
	Hospital in the centre of Kinshasa		Rehabilitation and completion
7	**Energy (electricity)**		
	Kakobola Hydroelectric Dam (Bandundu)		Construction
	Katende Hydroelectric Dam (Kasai Occidental)		
	Electric distribution network in Kinshasa		Rehabilitation
	Electric distribution network in Lubumbashi		

Number	Projects	Length (in km)	Description
8	**Training centres for public works**		Construction and rehabilitation
9	**Housing**		
	2 000 houses in Kinshasa		Construction
	3 000 houses in provinces		
10	**Health centres**		
	145 health centres equipped with 50 beds, one in each territory		Construction and equipment
11	**Two modern universities**		Construction

As can clearly be seen, the R4I contract between the DRC and China is wide-ranging. It covers such basic socioeconomic infrastructure as railways, roads (tarred and untarred), public roads, bridges, airports, hospitals and medical equipment, electricity and power generation, training centres for public works, housing, health centres and universities.

The Musoshi deal

R4I contracts may accommodate small-scale projects. The Musoshi deal between the DRC and a consortium of South Korean corporations is one such example. In terms of that agreement, signed in July 2011, the South Korean investors will build a water supply system in Kinshasa, the DRC's capital city, in return for copper.

The Ghana story

Ghana has experience with two R4I deals. In 2007, Ghana and China entered into a R4I contract whereby China was to build a hydroelectric dam at Bui in Ghana in return for the export of cocoa products to China. The Bui dam was completed in 2013. Then, in 2010, Ghana entered into another R4I deal with China in terms of which China was to conduct various large-scale infrastructure projects in Ghana in exchange for oil.

The Bui hydroelectric dam

At the time of its signature in 2007, the R4I contract to build the Bui dam in north-western Ghana was the single largest Chinese-funded project in the country.[46] Like the 2004 Sino-Angolan deal and the 2008 Sino-Congolese deal, the R4I contract for the Bui dam attracted the largest finance since independence.[47] What is more, the Bui hydroelectric power project is by far the largest foreign investment in Ghana since the construction of the Akosombo hydroelectric power project in the early 1960s (Baah et al. 2009: 98–99).

The Bui dam project illustrates the prohibitively high costs of financing infrastructure as a result of credit risk, payment insecurity and low creditworthiness of most resource-rich countries in Africa. Since gaining independence in 1957, successive

Ghanaian governments have tried unsuccessfully to find foreign investor funding to build the Bui dam.[48] In other words, the cost of searching for a suitable foreign investor to fund the Bui dam project has proven to be prohibitively high for Ghana. The traditional route of a mining or oil deal on the one hand and a separate infrastructure project on the other was not viable.

It was only by signing the R4I contract in 2007, half a century after independence, that Ghana no longer needed to incur search costs for the Bui dam project. The R4I model merges mining or oil deals with infrastructure projects in one contract. Without R4I contracts, host governments have to seek out contractors to build infrastructure projects at much greater costs. Simply put, R4I contracts make transactions possible that would not otherwise have materialised because of high transaction costs.

Loan repaid with cocoa

Payment by means of a buyer's credit, coupled with a concessional loan, is the financial structure of the 2007 Ghana–China R4I contract. The buyer's credit of US$298.5 million and the concessional loan of US$263.5 million covers 90 per cent of the construction costs of US$622 million of the Bui dam in the Bui National Park in the centre-west of Ghana.

The Sino-Ghanaian R4I contract does not provide for a joint venture between a Ghanaian national mining or oil corporation and a Chinese state-owned corporation. Instead, the parties have agreed that the Ghana Marketing Board, a state-owned institution, will export cocoa products to China to pay for the construction of the Bui Dam (Otoo phone interview, 19 April 2010). The Ghana Marketing Board does not produce cocoa directly; it contracts with middle companies, which in turn negotiate the price of cocoa with cocoa farmers (Otoo phone interview, 19 April 2010).

The Bui infrastructural complex

The Bui dam project involves the construction of an entire complex. The complex will consist of a main dam in the Bui gorge and two smaller saddle dams in the neighbouring Banda Hills, a power house and a switchyard, transmission lines from Bui to Kumasi and Kenyasi, access roads in and around the dam site, irrigation systems and the nucleus of a metropolis called Bui City.[49]

The Bui Dam was completed in February 2013 at the cost of US$622 million.[50] The contract that Ghana and China had signed is of the resource-for-infrastructure kind, whereby China (through the state-owned corporation, SinoHydro) built the Bui dam in exchange for Ghana's exports of cocoa products to China. The dam has a maximum generation capacity of 400 megawatts and a net average annual energy production of 1 000 gigawatt hours per year, a generation capacity that is crucial in meeting the country's future energy needs.[51] The Bui dam has been immensely significant for Ghana's economy. It helped propel economic growth, which further led to Ghana achieving a middle-income country status (Baah et al. 2009: 99).

The 2010 deal

In September 2010, Ghana signed a framework agreement valued at US$10.4 billion with the state-owned Export-Import Bank of China (Eximbank). This R4I contract, the largest in dollar value in Ghana, is of the Sino-Angolan type, because it involves infrastructure development on a national scale and in various sectors. It covers the development of a road and railway system from Kumasi to Paga, Ghana's eastern corridor roads network, as well as other sectors of the economy.[52] The contract entails two constituent projects—one to promote the exploitation of mineral deposits, and the other a road and railway project to open up the upper-western, upper-eastern, eastern, middle, and northern regions of Ghana for development.[53]

The deal provides for an intricate network of contractual relationships. This is a highly complex arrangement because of the number of parties involved and the contractual obligations that link them.

The Master Facility Agreement

This contract differs from the Angolan and Congolese models in that the most important agreement under the framework agreement is its loan agreement, the Master Facility Agreement (MFA). The Ghanaian Ministry of Finance and Economic Planning has published a summary of the MFA, which states that the MFA is the 'umbrella loan agreement for the loan'.[54] The state-owned China Development Bank (CDB) granted—through the MFA—a US$3 billion loan to Ghana for the construction and/or development of a gas project, and a surveillance and monitoring system enhanced by information and communications technology (ICT) in exchange for the supply of oil to the Chinese firm, UNIPEC Asia.[55]

The MFA is based on four principal finance documents, namely the Five Party Agreement, the Accounts Agreement, the Charge over Accounts Agreement, and the Subsidiary Agreement.

Offtake agreement

The resource component of the 2010 deal takes the form of an offtake agreement similar to the one in the 2007 Bui dam deal. So, Ghana's R4I contracts prominently feature offtake agreements as far as resource exploitation goes. This differs from the Angolan and Congolese deals, which involve joint ventures between state-owned resource firms from the host state and the foreign investor.

The parties to the offtake agreement are Ghana's national oil firm, the Ghana National Petroleum Corporation (GNPC), and UNIPEC Asia. The agreement provides for the sale of crude oil by GNPC to UNIPEC Asia to repay the loan.

Infrastructure development

This deal dwarfs the Bui dam project in sheer scale, the extent of infrastructural works to be executed and the amount of money involved. Specifically, it covers 12 projects, including a railway line, a port, fishing harbours and landing sites, a free zone, an irrigation project, a petroleum terminal, a toll road, an incubation facility for small and medium enterprises, and an information and communications technology (ICT) system to manage road traffic and monitor oil-extractive activities. Of all these projects, the development of gas infrastructure and the construction of a multimodal transportation system are among the most ambitious projects of this Sino-Ghanaian deal.

Conclusion

Several lessons can be learnt from these three stories about exchanging natural resources for national infrastructure. Wells (2014: 85) says R4I contractual models, inherently, are neither good nor bad for host countries, and they should be evaluated like any other business arrangement. Similarly, the good and bad lessons to be learnt from R4I contracting should not lead to inflexible prejudices about the nature of those contracts.

First, R4I contracts have the ability to attract substantial finance for infrastructure development. Thanks to the R4I model, Angola, the DRC and Ghana have all managed to attract the largest investment since gaining independence. Second, the natural resources that could be traded for infrastructure can consist of minerals, hydrocarbons, or agricultural products, as has been the case in Ghana. The latter example (swapping agricultural products for infrastructural works) demonstrates that R4I contracts are not only usable by countries richly endowed with minerals and hydrocarbons; they can also be used effectively by countries that simply export agricultural products.

Moreover, R4I contracts are effective in sheltering foreign investors from local political culture. A good example is the contractual provision that channels the financing of infrastructure directly to the contractor, bypassing the bureaucracy of the host state. This decreases the risk of infrastructure money being embezzled. Perhaps the greatest lesson is that the model is well suited to a country's reconstruction needs after a war or a serious and deep economic crisis. Finally, R4I deals can be used for projects at various scales. They can be used for nationwide projects or reconstruction work, or massive, large-scale infrastructure works, and for small-scale projects.

The three stories show that the resources-for-infrastructure contractual model gives pride of place to the state as an agent of development. It marks the return of the developmental state in development practice. This is a remarkable departure from the neo liberal slant pervasive in classic foreign direct investment law. It accounts in no small measure for the happy outcomes of Sino-African joint ventures.

The Angola model is the essence of China's win–win game plan for the country. It fulfils the interests both the Angolan and the Chinese parties, and therein lies its charm. After 27 years of war, Angola's infrastructure was shattered and the government badly needed finance that could match the magnitude of the destruction. Luanda searched the Western capitals and leading capital markets in vain, and eventually found the finance in Beijing. The two governments signed a deal that gave Luanda a large loan to fund Chinese construction of Angolan infrastructure, in return for Angola's oil exports to China. This is a unique and innovative investment contract that suits Angola's circumstances.

The R4I model is rich in lessons for other resource-rich countries in Africa struggling to attract infrastructure investments. Countries endowed with minerals and hydrocarbons, with daunting capacity limitations and resurging from conflict, might see in this model a pragmatic path for a fast-tracked post-conflict reconstruction programme. Countries like Zimbabwe, Sudan, Chad, the DRC, Guinea, Côte d'Ivoire, Niger, Cameroon and Congo-Brazzaville could all benefit from this model. It could serve to diversify their economies, create employment for citizens, and construct backbone economic or social infrastructure such as hospitals, health centres, training centres, schools and universities.

Lessons can be learnt from the way in which the R4I model structures investments to bring down to efficient levels risk and transaction costs, yielding concrete results despite institutionalised corruption in host countries. The offset clause embedded in the reimbursement mechanism bypasses state bureaucracy, thereby warding off the risk of embezzlement.

The greatest lesson of all comes from the Angola story, which tells of how a country that had experienced conflict since its independence moved from trading oil for weapons to trading oil for development.

Acknowledgement

This chapter derives some of its content from the doctoral dissertation 'Ore for Infrastructure: A Contractual Model for the Optimization of China's Investments in the Mining Sectors of Africa' by Dunia Prince Zongwe (Cornell University 2011).

Notes

1   Examples of such views can be found in Collier (2008) and Keenan (2009).

2   R4I contracts are described incorrectly as 'long-term trade' agreements.

3   This section is partly reproduced from Zongwe (2015).

4   See Mo Ibrahim Foundation, IIAG data portal. Accessed June 2016, www.mo.ibrahim. foundation/iiag/data-portal/.

5   'Most corrupt countries' refers to the lowest tenth on the list of transparency/corruption of Transparency International.

6   Transparency International, Corruption Perceptions Index 2015. Accessed October 2016, www.transparency.org/cpi2015.

7   Transparency International, Corruption Perceptions Index 2015. Accessed October 2016, www.transparency.org/cpi2015.

8   Transparency International, Corruption Perceptions Index 2015. Accessed October 2016, www.transparency.org/cpi2015.

9   The Fund for Peace, Fragile States Index 2016. Accessed October 2016, www.fsi.fundforpeace.org/.

10 The Fund for Peace, Fragile States Index 2016. Accessed October 2016, www.fsi.fundforpeace.org/

11 Vivien Foster, Lead Economist, Sustainable Development Department, Africa Region, World Bank, 6 January 2010).

12 World Bank, Doing business 2010. Accessed June 2016, www.doingbusiness.org/EconomyRankings/?regionid=7

13 World Bank, Doing business 2010. Accessed June 2016, www.doingbusiness.org/EconomyRankings/?regionid=7.

14 *Gioacchino v. American Family Mutual Insurance Company*, 64 P.3d 230 (Colo. 2003).

15 Dolzer & Schreuer (2008) state that a renegotiation can serve to preserve 'economic equilibrium'.

16 Another option is to choose the law of the host state stabilised on the date of the agreement, but only as pertaining to certain issues on which the investment contract is silent or incomplete: See *Maritime International Nominees Establishment v. Government of the Republic of Guinea* (ICSID Case No. ARB/84/4), ad hoc Committee Decision of Dec. 22, 1989, 5 ICSID Rev. For. Inv. L.J. 95, 111–112 (1990).

17 On the capacity of bilateral investment treaties to attract foreign direct investment, see Sauvant & Sachs (2009).

18 She explained that project finance had always implied some kind of state involvement.

19 Resolução No. 61/06, de 12 de Julho de 2006, Diário da República de 4.9.2006. art. 1 (Angl.).

20 Resolução No. 27/06, de 3 de Abril de 2006, Diário da República de 26.11.2006. art. 1 (Angl.) [hereinafter Angolan Telecommunication Resolution].

21 Angolan Telecommunication Resolution art. 2.

22 Angolan Telecommunication Resolution art. 2(a).

23 Angolan Telecommunication Resolution art. 2(b).

24 Angolan Telecommunication Resolution art. 2(c).

25 Angolan Telecommunication Resolution art. 2(d).

26 Resolução No. 61/06, de 12 de Julho de 2006, Diário da República de 4.9.2006. art. 1 (Angl.). Annex.

27 DRC Framework Agreement art. 3.1.

28 DRC Framework Agreement art. 13.1.

29 DRC Framework Agreement art. 13.2.

30 DRC Framework Agreement art. 15.1.

31 DRC Framework Agreement art. 15.2.

32 DRC Framework Agreement art. 15.3.

33 DRC Framework Agreement art. 15.6.

34 DRC Framework Agreement art. 3.2.

35 DRC Framework Agreement art. 3.3.

36 DRC Framework Agreement art. 3.4.

37 DRC Framework Agreement art. 9.3.

38   DRC framework agreement art. 14.2.

39   DRC framework agreement art. 14.2.4.

40   DRC Framework Agreement art. 12.

41   DRC Framework Agreement art. 12.

42   DRC Framework Agreement art. 12.

43   DRC Framework Agreement art. 13.3.4.

44   Programme sino–congolais: Quid de l'évaluation de la 1ère phase. Radio Okapi, 30 March 2010. Accessed January 2016, http://www.radiookapi.net/actualite/2010/03/30/programme-sino-congolais-quid-de-l%25e2%2580%2599evaluation-de-la-1ere-phase.

45   DRC Framework Agreement Annex C.

46   The 2010 Ghana–China R4I contract is currently Ghana's largest investment in financial terms.

47   The total amount of infrastructure finance in a single R4I contract can be very large relative to the size of the host economy: US$4.5 billion in Angola in 2004–2007 and US$ 9 billion in the DRC in 2008 (before the amendment of the DRC–China R4I contract in August 2009).

48   Bui Power Authority, *Project Background.* Accessed November 2017, http://www.buipower.com/node/139.

49   Bui Power Authority, Project Background. Accessed November 2017, http://www.buipower.com/node/139.

50   Bui Power Authority, Project Background. Accessed November 2017, http://www.buipower.com/node/139.

51   Bui Power Authority, Project Background. Accessed November 2017, http://www.buipower.com/node/139.

52   Ghana, Ministry of Finance and Economic Planning, US$3 Billion Term Loan Facility Agreement Between China Development Bank (CDB) and Government of Ghana (GOG)—Summary. Accessed November 2017, https://www.coursehero.com/file/20492203/CDB-Loan-Summary-050112/.

53   Ghana, Ministry of Finance and Economic Planning, US$3 Billion Term Loan Facility Agreement Between China Development Bank (CDB) and Government of Ghana (GOG)—Summary. Accessed November 2017, https://www.coursehero.com/file/20492203/CDB-Loan-Summary-050112/.

54   Ministry of Finance and Economic Planning of Ghana, US$3 Billion Term Loan Facility Agreement Between China Development Bank (CDB) and Government of Ghana (GOG)—Summary.

55   Ministry of Finance and Economic Planning of Ghana, US$3 Billion Term Loan Facility Agreement Between China Development Bank (CDB) and Government of Ghana (GOG)—Summary.

References

Alden C, Large D and Soares de Oliveira R (Eds) (2008) *China returns to Africa: A rising power and a continent embrace.* New York: Columbia University Press

Alves AC (2013) *China's economic statecraft and African mineral resources: Changing modes of engagement.* Southern African Institute of International Affairs Occasional Paper No. 131. Accessed June 2016, www.saiia.org.za/occasional-papers/17-china-s-economic-statecraft-and-african-mineral-resources-changing-modes-of-engagement/file

Baah AY, Otoo KN & Ampratwurm EF (2009) Chinese Investments in Ghana. In Baah AY & Jauch H (Eds) *Chinese Investments in Africa: A labour perspective.* Accessed June 2016, www.cebri.org/midia/documentos/315.pdf

Baker JC (1995) *Foreign direct investment in less developed countries: The role of ICSID and MIGA.* Westport, CT: Greenwood Publishing Company

Baragona KC (2004) Project finance. *Transnational Lawyer* 18: 139–158

Bräutigam D (2009) *The dragon's gift: The real story of China in Africa.* Oxford: Oxford University Press

Collier P (2008) Laws and codes for the resource curse. *Yale Human Rights and Development Law Journal* 11(1): Article 2

Comeaux PE and Kinsella NS (1997) *Protecting foreign investment under international law: Legal aspects of political risk.* New York: Oceana Publications Inc.

Campbell B (Ed.) (2009) *Mining in Africa: Regulation and Development.* London: Pluto Press

Campos I and Vines A (2008) Angola and China: A pragmatic partnership. Center for Strategic and International Studies Working Paper, Washington

Davies M (2010) How China is influencing Africa's development. OECD Development Centre Background Paper. Paris: OECD

Dolzer R and Schreuer C (2008) *Principles of international investment law.* Oxford: Oxford University Press

Edinger H and Jansson J (2008) China's Angola model comes to the DRC. *The China Monitor* 34: 4–6

IEA (International Energy Agency) (2010) *Key world energy statistics.* Paris: IEA

IMF (International Monetary Fund) (1993) *Balance of payments manual.* Washington DC: IMF

Keenan PJ (2009) Curse or cure? China, Africa, and the effects of unconditioned wealth. *Berkeley Journal of International Law* 27: 84–126

Malloy MP (2004) International project finance: Risk analysis and regulatory concerns. *Transnational Lawyer* 18: 89–106

MIGA (Multilateral Investment Guarantee Agency) (2011) *2010 World investment and political risk.* Washington DC: The World Bank

O'Neill D (2012) Angola fund launch leaves questions unanswered. *Euromoney.* Accessed June 2016, www.euromoney.com/Article/3112458/Angola-fund-launch-leaves-questions-unanswered.html

Ossman G (1996) Legal and institutional aspects of the MIGA. *Journal of International Banking Law* 11: 359–392

Reinisch A (2008) Expropriation. In P Muchlinski, F Ortino & C Schreuer (Eds) *The Oxford handbook of international investment law.* Oxford: Oxford University Press

Sauvant KP & Sachs LE (Eds) (2009) *The effect of treaties on foreign direct investment: Bilateral investment treaties, double taxation treaties, and investment flows.* Oxford: Oxford University Press

Sornarajah M (2010) *The international law on foreign investment* (3rd edition). Cambridge: Cambridge University Press

Tshitenge Lubabu MK (2009) Jean-Claude Masangu Mulongo: 'Nous avons réalisé des choses qui paraissaient impossibles'. *Jeune Afrique.* Accessed June 2016, www.jeuneafrique.com/200386/archives-thematique/jean-claude-masangu-mulongo-nous-avons-r-alis-des-choses-qui-paraissaient-impossibles/

Vines A, Wong L, Weimer M & Campos I (2009) *Thirst for African oil: Asian national oil companies in Nigeria and Angola.* London: Chatham House

Wells LT (2014) Comments by Louis T. Wells. In H Halland, J Beardsworth, B Land & J Schmidt (Eds) *Resource financed infrastructure: A discussion on a new form of infrastructure financing.* Washington DC: The World Bank

Yackee JW (2008) Bilateral investment treaties, credible commitment, and the rule of (international) law: Do BITs promote foreign direct investment? *Law & Society Review* 42: 805–832

Zongwe DP (2010) On the road to post-conflict reconstruction by contract: The Angola model. *Social Science Research Network Electronic Journal.* Accessed October 2016, www.researchgate.net/publication/228286407_On_the_Road_to_Post_Conflict_Reconstruction_by_Contract_The_Angola_Model

Zongwe DP (2015) Seeing the whole elephant: A comprehensive framework for analyzing resources-for-infrastructure contracts as intended by the parties. *Southern African Journal of Policy and Development* 1: 38–48

Interviews

Kwabena Nyarko Otoo, Director of Labour Research & Policy Institute in Ghana, 19 April 2010

Elke Rehbock, Associate, Greenberg Traurig, 3 May 2010

PART 2

AN AFRICA OF GOOD GOVERNANCE,
DEMOCRACY, RESPECT FOR HUMAN RIGHTS,
JUSTICE AND THE RULE OF LAW

4 | The *Tinkhundla* monarchical democracy: An African system of good governance?

Hlengiwe Dlamini

The *Tinkhundla* monarchical democracy, instituted in 1978, is a unique political system that distinguishes Swaziland in the Southern African region. In siSwati, the indigenous language spoken in Swaziland, an *inkhundla* (plural: *tinkhundla*) is an administrative subdivision smaller than a district but larger than a chiefdom (*unphakatsi*). *Tinkhundla* serve as electoral constituencies. Swaziland is divided into 55 *tinkhundla*. The Constitution of the Kingdom of Swaziland (2005) defines the government of Swaziland as democratic, participatory and *Tinkhundla*-based, one that emphasises the devolution of state power from central government to *tinkhundla* areas. Individual merit serves as the basis for election or appointment to public office.[1]

The main precept of the *Tinkhundla* system is that it is non-partisan. The 2005 constitution does not allow the existence of political parties in Swaziland, although Section 25 of the document allows for the freedom of assembly and association. The importance of the *Tinkhundla* lies in the fact that they serve as electoral constituencies and each *inkhundla* unit elects one representative to the Swazi House of Assembly, the lower chamber of a bicameral parliament, or *libandla*. The *Tinkhundla* non-partisan political system is therefore an indigenous Swazi political system. It endured and survived the third democratic wave[2] (Huntington 1993; Eisenstadt 2000: 3–17; Abrahamsen 2000; Berg-Schlosser 2004) that blew over Africa in the 1990s. The resilience of the system raises questions about its authenticity, relevance, acceptability and adaptability to the current day and age.

In political science literature, scholars have been critical of the *Tinkhundla* system of governance, arguing that it has given rise to an absolute monarchy and a no-party state, where executive authority lies exclusively in the hands of a king as the head of state, governing with his advisory council and traditional advisers (Jackson & Rosberg 1982; Mzizi 2004: 94–110; Bohler-Muller & Lukhele-Olorunju 2011; Motsamai 2011: 42–50; Woods 2014). Critics of the system point to the fact that it is devoid of political parties and competition, and is therefore an antiquated system that falls short of the democratic ideals set for the Southern African Development Community (SADC), of which Swaziland is a signatory.[3]

This chapter examines the origin and nature of Swaziland's *Tinkhundla* system of governance to be in a position to make a pronouncement on its suitability or otherwise as a model of governance for a 21st-century African country. One cannot assess the *Tinkhundla* political system by exclusively using the benchmarks of Western liberal democracy. An African insider perspective is needed to interrogate the historical authenticity of *Tinkhundlaism*, instead of blithely disparaging it. Nyamnjoh (2009: 67) makes a strong case for a careful consideration of African modes of knowledge, saying that

> [while academic perceptions are] shaped and reshaped over time and given the importance of cultural diversity in a fast-globalising world, conscious efforts [should be made] to encourage the production and consumption—in Africa and the rest of the world—of cultural products created by Africans...who are crying out for the space and means to tell the stories of African creativity with dignity.

I argue that the *Tinkhundla* political system evolved from a combination of Swazi monarchical culture and tradition, and Western political tradition. The coexistence of heavy doses of Western political liberalism and Swazi monarchical culture led to the collapse of the constitutional monarchy, which was replaced with the *Tinkhundla* system of governance in 1978. For the *Tinkhundla* system to survive liberal democratic challenges in the 1990s, it had to demonstrate malleability without necessarily complying with multipartyism.

The evolution of *Tinkhundla*

1968 Westminster model

Swaziland inherited a Westminster-style constitution when it gained independence in 1968. It was based on a mixture of ideas from the Western political and Swazi monarchical tradition, in which the king ruled as executive head of state. During the constitutional debates in the 1960s, which culminated in the drafting of the independence constitution, the Swazi National Council (SNC)[4] and the pro-royalist party—the Imbokodvo National Movement (INM)[5]—argued for a constitutional order in which the Swazi king was the chief executive with unrestrained powers. The British colonial authorities held a contrary view and proposed a constitutional monarchy akin to that of the United Kingdom, in which the monarch would serve as ceremonial head, while 'modern politics' would be the business of the Western-educated elite, who would emanate from multiparty elections.[6] In the end, the British struck a compromise with the Swazi traditionalists in the Swazi National Council and the Imbokodvo Movement by agreeing to allow King Sobhuza II of Swaziland to be head of state with executive powers that would be checked by the legislature and judiciary. The legacy of the British political modernisation project for Swaziland was therefore in the liberal democratic tradition.

Liberal democracy, otherwise known as Western democracy, is characterised by fair, free and competitive elections between multiple distinct political parties. In practical terms, liberal democracies hinge on a constitution to delimit the powers of government and enshrine the social contract. The purpose of a constitution is often seen as limiting the authority of government through the separation of powers, an independent judiciary, and a system of checks and balances between the various arms of government (Vile 2012). De Smith (1964: 106) says that

The idea of constitutionalism involves the proposition that the exercise of governmental power shall be bounded by rules, rules prescribing the procedure to which legislative and executive acts are to be performed and delimiting their permissible content. Constitutionalism becomes a living reality to the extent that these rules and the arbitrariness of discretion are in fact observed by the wielders of political power, and to the extent that within the forbidden zones upon which authority may not trespass there is significant room for the enjoyment of individual liberty.

Constitutionalism, in essence, concerns itself with two fundamental pillars: limiting government power and protecting the fundamental rights, freedoms and civil liberties of the individual (Vile 2012). Freedom of association allows the unrestrained formation of political parties and trade unions. The media is expected to be free and unfettered. Liberal democracy is therefore considered as the hallmark of good governance (Holden 1993). And this is what the British bequeathed to the Swazis.

The British provided for a constitutional monarchy in the 1968 constitution, with checks and balances that rendered the Swazi king accountable to the legislature and judiciary.[7] The *Ngwenyama*[8] was vested with the power to appoint the prime minister, nominate six senators (half the senate) and six members of parliament. The king was made an executive authority and acted on behalf of the cabinet, which he appointed after consultation with the prime minister. The king participated in the modern governance of the country, but traditional aspects of Swazi kingship—including the nomination of members of the Swazi National Council and succession to the royal throne in the event of the king's death—were left to the extra-constitutional domain. The king operated in a dual capacity—as the monarch of a modern government whose powers were defined by the constitution, and as the monarch of the traditional sphere of government, which was regulated exclusively according to culture and tradition.

The 1968 Westminster-model constitution required the *Ngwenyama* to act on many issues in accordance with the advice of his cabinet and not unilaterally. Section 12 of the document stated categorically that 'the constitution [was] the supreme law of Swaziland and if any law...[was] not consistent with this constitution, that law [would] to the extent of the inconsistency, be void'. Any alteration of this entrenched provision would require a vote at a joint sitting of the House of Assembly and the Senate, and winning a majority of no fewer than three-quarters of all members' votes cast. The decision would then be submitted to the people for approval in a referendum that had to be supported by no fewer than two-thirds of all valid votes cast. It was only after this process that the bill would be submitted to the *Ngwenyama* for his assent. In essence, the 1968 Westminster constitutional model contained the main tenets of liberal democracy, including a written constitution, a multiparty system, a bill of rights, separation of powers, and the independence of the judiciary.

Establishing the *Tinkhundla* system

The aftermath of Swaziland's independence saw an uneasy coexistence between the principle of the separation of powers enshrined in the constitution and the powers of the king conferred by Swazi culture and tradition. This would eventually culminate in the collapse of the inherited Westminster constitution. Swazi culture and tradition dictated that the monarch was supreme and he expected to be revered unchallenged. King Sobhuza II disagreed with the idea of the separation of powers and multiparty democracy, considering them both un-African and unsuitable for the people of Swaziland. Consequently, he began to declare his intention publicly to revisit the independence constitution.[9] The revision of the inherited Westminster independence constitutions by former British colonies was a common trend in post-colonial Africa. Most African countries previously ruled by Britain gradually modified, amended, revised, or changed their constitutions, and erected single-party structures (Welch 1991: 85, Smith 2005: 421–451). In 1970, for instance, Lesotho abandoned its colonially inherited constitution on grounds that it did not tally with traditional African democracy (Khaketla 1972). Similar justifications were made all over the continent to defend the imposition of single-party states; multipartyism was perceived as divisive and un-African, whereas the single-party state was very close to traditional African consensus politics (Huntington & Moore 1970; Jackson & Rosberg 1982; Ake 1991; Barya 1993; Ayittey 1994). This prevailing justification of one-party rule in Africa corresponded with King Sobhuza II's political philosophy. The ruler consistently rejected Western liberal democracy in favour of the traditional African mode of politics that had no room for multipartyism.[10]

A pretext for discarding the 1968 constitution was provided by a conflict between the Swazi judiciary and the legislature over the first multiparty elections that took place in independent Swaziland in May 1972. The elections set in motion a series of events that culminated in the overthrow of the independence constitution. The royal party—Imbokodvo National Movement—won the elections overwhelmingly with 21 seats, while the opposition Ngwane National Liberatory Congress (NNLC) managed to capture the remaining three seats. This was the first time in Swaziland's modern political history that the opposition joined the House of Assembly.

The presence of the opposition displeased King Sobhuza II, who could be now openly challenged. Motloso (1998) says the number of seats held by the opposition was not significant, but it did confirm the fears of the Swazi traditionalists that the independence constitution made it possible to challenge royal prerogatives. The Swazi government interpreted the opposition 'victory' as a constitutional crisis. It intended to solve the problem by doing away with the constitution; to do this, it needed a pretext.

Government claimed that one of the opposition candidates, Bhekindlela Thomas Ngwenya, was not a Swazi national but a South African citizen. Although Ngwenya had been allowed by Swazi electoral law to stand for election as an opposition candidate, he was deported back to South Africa after the elections. Yet he decided to come back to Swaziland and fight for his rights through the Swaziland High Court, which eventually ruled Ngwenya a Swazi citizen by birth. King Sobhuza II saw the case of Ngwenya as a proof that the judiciary was able to challenge the authority of the Swazi government, which led him to abolishing the constitution on 12 April 1973. The king proclaimed

> I, Sobhuza II, king of Swaziland, hereby declare that, in collaboration with my cabinet and supported by the whole nation, I have assumed supreme power in the Kingdom of Swaziland and that all legislative, executive and judicial power is vested in myself and shall, for the time being, be exercised in collaboration with my cabinet ministers.[11]

King Sobhuza II imposed one-man rule by decree and this gave him unfettered authority. But his method of governance by decree did not go down well with the international community, especially the Commonwealth, which was critical about the king's high-handed governance style in a modern nation and without a parliament. Against the backdrop of international pressure on the Swazi monarchy to establish a state of law, King Sobhuza II established the Royal Constitutional Commission to 'inquire into the fundamental principles of Swazi history and culture as well as the modern principles of constitutional and international law',[12] which would guide government to write a new constitution for Swaziland. He urged the Swazi people to cooperate with the commission, which was given the task of studying a future constitution that would be suitable and would 'safeguard national interests and guarantee freedom, justice, peace, order, good government and the happiness and welfare of the entire nation'. The Royal Constitutional Commission presented its report to the king in July 1975; it was never publicised.[13] Review commissions were appointed to work on a new constitution that would take into consideration the views of the Swazi monarchy (Matsebula 1988).

The last Royal Constitutional Review Commission produced a final report in 1978. This report was adopted and paved the way for the *Tinkhundla* political system, which came into effect in 1978. It was developed in terms of the Establishment of Parliament Order (1978) and the Regional Councils Order (1978)[14]. The architects of the system portrayed it as a homegrown system that incorporated elements of Swazi traditional governance with the king at the centre, and elements of Western governance reflected in the bicameral legislature.[15] By repealing the independence constitution and introducing the *Tinkhundla* system, Swazi leaders wanted to expand the role and influence of existing traditional structures of government as a counterbalance to monarchical rule. To achieve this, they simply aligned traditional institutions with modern structures of government to ensure that government was organised around the monarch. Faithful to Swazi culture and tradition, the *Tinkhundla* system espoused a no-party or partyless system of government reminiscent of traditional African politics based on consensus rather than political parties competing for dominance.[16]

Instead of establishing a single political party to which everybody belonged, the *Tinkhundla* system elevated King Sobhuza II to a father figure to the nation, one who has the responsibility of directing political activities in the kingdom in a conflict-free, harmonious way. Thus, the *Tinkhundla* system vested sovereignty in the king and not the people of Swaziland. It catapulted the king to the position of a 'benevolent despot', as dictated by Swazi culture and tradition[17]. It entrenched the absolutism of the Swazi monarchy, which, to a large extent, can be compared to the absolutism that existed in 17th century France, during which Louis XIV proudly declared, *'L'Etat, c'est moi!'* (I am the state!). Just as he believed it was his divine right to rule, referring to it as *'la grâce de Dieu'* (by God's grace) (Rowen 1961), the Swazi king saw himself as the incarnation of the Swazi state and a beneficiary of ancestral spiritual powers under the *Tinkhundla* system (Kuper 1978; Bischoff 1988; Wanda 1990; Baloro 1994; Mkhatshwa 2004; Mamba 2006; Mkhaliphi 2015). The choices of holders of political office were left in the hands of the king and his close aides, and not the people of Swaziland. *Tinkhundla* democracy is therefore royal-guided democracy.

The idea of political parties, whether single or multiple, seemed too westernised for King Sobhuza II, who therefore endeavoured to invent something he considered typically African. Accordingly, he maintained the 1973 ban on all political parties and made it unlawful for anyone to organise and canvass for political support under the banner of a political party. Although the Order-in-Council decree (1978) made Swaziland a partyless state by banning all political parties, including the royal Imbokodvo National Movement, the Swazi king incarnated and radiated the spirit of a characteristic one-party state in Africa, since he was the sole authority to sanction candidates for political office.[18]

The similarities between the African one-party state model and the *Tinkhundla* no-party state model were glaring to the extent that the two models were almost indistinguishable. The governments of the one-party states in Africa, just like the government of Swaziland, were made up of individuals drawn mainly from the ruling party that had wrested power at independence. In both the one-party and the *Tinkhundla* models, a clearly identifiable culture prevailed of the systematic neutralisation of the opposition through a series of strategies, including coercion, cooptation, accommodation and exclusion. The president of a one-party state was usually the chairman of the national party and tighly controlled its operations. The Swazi king was the source of all authority, like the leader of the single party, and was responsible for appointing officials to all office. Using his overbearing influence in the *Tinkhundla* system, the Swazi king was at liberty to exclude the Western-educated radicals and reformers from gaining a foothold in the political arena.

Tinkhundla *and its hybrid dimensions*
Tinkhundla incorporated the bicameral legislature that existed under the 1968 independence constitution. The system underwent amendments in 1993 and 2005, which made provision for up to 69 members in the Swazi House of Assembly. The king appoints ten members, including at least 5 women; 55 are elected by universal adult suffrage from a list provided by the *tinkhundla* units and 4 women are elected

by the National Assembly and the Senate (1 from each of the 4 administrative regions of Swaziland). The Senate has up to 30 members. Ten members, including at least 5 women, are appointed by the House of Assembly and 20 by the king, including at least 8 women. The king appoints the prime minister, and can revoke any law passed by parliament (Levin 1991; Dlamini 2005; Bohler-Muller & Lukhele-Olorunju 2011; Norris, Frank & Martinez i Coma 2014).

The no-party state established by *Tinkhundla* means political parties cannot be represented in elections. Consequently, candidates running for elective positions must do so on individual merit that has to be weighted by the electorate. There are 55 constituencies, each composed of several chiefdoms (Dlamini 2005; Vandome, Vines & Weimer 2013). The nomination of candidates takes place at chiefdom level by a show of hands and under the eyes of the local chief, who can exert considerable influence over the choice of nominees (Dlamini 2005; Vandome, Vines & Weimer 2013). Nominated candidates run for primary elections at the chiefdom level, but they cannot campaign. Campaigning is permitted only in the last round, when winners from individual chiefdoms compete against one another at the constituency level (Dlamini 2005; Vandome, Vines & Weimer 2013). Nominated candidates are then reduced to three per *inkhundla* (Dlamini 2005; Vandome, Vines & Weimer 2013; Hausken & Ncube 2013; Norris, Frank & Martinez i Coma 2014). Essentially, the *Tinkhundla* monarchical system of governance negates multipartyism on the one hand and the institutionalisation of a no-party state on the other. But in the late 1980s, Africa came under a tornado of political liberalisation in the shape of multiparty competition, the antithesis of *Tinkhundlaism*. How was the *Tinkhundla* system of a no-party state to survive these presssures?

The winds of change of the 1980s and 1990s

Internal and external pressures brought political changes to the African continent, starting in the late 1980s. The collapse of communism in the Union of Soviet Socialist Republics (USSR), representing a model for one-party states, the destruction of the Berlin wall in 1989, and the weakening of Russia's hegemony in the Eastern bloc countries had a ripple effect throughout Africa (Bratton 1998; Joseph 1998; Olsen 1998; Eisenstadt 2000). Demands for democratisation and the introduction of multi-party systems increased as multilateral financial institutions such as the World Bank and the International Monetary Fund (IMF), as well the major Western countries, especially the USA and the UK, insisted on these as preconditions for financial aid to African countries.

The clamour for multipartyism was widespread on the continent, although the dynamics varied from region to region, and from country to country. Against the backdrop of democratic change, the 15 Southern African Development Community (SADC) member states committed to promoting common democratic political and other shared values and systems, to be transmitted through democratic, legitimate and effective institutions (Saurombe 2012: 1–34). At the same time, African civil societies were resuscitated in an internationalised zeitgeist favourable to political liberalisation. African citizens began openly to voice their discontent with repressive governments and regimes, which had done little or nothing to improve the living conditions of their countryfolk through the years (Bratton 1998; Joseph 1998; Olsen 1998; Eisenstadt 2000).

In the spirit of the wave of democracy that rolled through the continent, Swazi civil society became reinvigorated from 1990. It went on the offensive, leaving the Swazi government on the back foot in its response to calls for democratic change. As a result, the country began to experience an unprecedented upsurge of labour and political action, led predominantly by trade unions such as the Swaziland Federation of Trade Unions (SFTU) and the Swaziland Federation of Labour (SFL), and political groupings such as the People's United Democratic Movement (PUDEMO) and Ngwane National Liberatory Congress (NNLC). Several faith organisations were also active at the time. The two largest political organisations, PUDEMO and NNLC, led the charge of democratic change in Swaziland (Kabemba 2004; Söderbaum 2007: 319–337). These civil society movements operated freely, notwithstanding the ban on multipartyism.

Pressure for constitutional reforms mounted and the Swazi king, Mswati III, resorted to appointing a succession of committees and commissions to study the issue of constitutional reform. The first of these commissions, which came to be known as Vusela I, travelled throughout Swaziland to hear the views of the people about the type of constitution they wanted. And what they wanted was the introduction of multiparty democracy and a constitutional monarchy similar to the one in Lesotho.[19]

In response, the king appointed the *Tinkhundla* Review Commission (TRC) in 1992. The commission was charged with reviewing the *Tinkhundla* system to make it more acceptable to the citizens. The TRC was asked to make appropriate recommendations to promote the democratic process without reverting to multipartyism. The TRC was accountable only to the king and its reports were confidential. Members of the public were allowed to make submissions to the commission in person only—no other representation was acknowledged. Because the TRC was appointed by the king alone, people viewed it with mixed feelings. Organised pro-democracy civil society groups denounced the commission as undemocratic and questioned the terms of its appointment.

As a result of the planned revision, the TRC recommended, inter alia, the adoption of a new constitution. It reported the division among Swazi citizens, with some people demanding a multiparty political system and others rejecting it as a solution. The TRC considered both options and indicated that a multiparty democracy was not the only system of democracy possible. However, it did conclude that the Swazi people's views on a multiparty system or the unbanning of political parties was a consideration for the future.

Further engagement by King Mswati III on constitutional reform culminated in the 2005 Constitution of the Kingdom of Swaziland. The reformed *Tinkhundla* system of democracy and governance was incorporated into the document.

The reformation of Tinkhundla

The 2005 constitution adapted the *Tinkhundla* system to contemporary Swazi needs—it is an administrative instrument for service delivery on the one hand, and a political philosophy and system of governance on the other. The aim was to ensure Swazi people could participate directly in the country's governance. The new constitution clearly articulates the point that *Tinkhundla* is the central pillar that defines Swaziland's political system and constitutional dispensation. Section 79 of the constitution reads that

> The system of government for Swaziland is a democratic, participatory, *tinkhundla*-based system that emphasises devolution of state power from central government to *tinkhundla* areas, and individual merit as a basis for election or appointment to public office.[20]

The document contains elaborate provisions encouraging and supporting the decentralised system of governance (especially chapters V and VII). The decentralised structure is made up as follows:
1. The administrative regions of Hhohho, Manzini, Shiselweni and Lubombo.
2. Urban government (the urban government shall, within boundaries, form an *inkhundla*).
3. Chiefdom level—an *inkhundla* is constituted by numbers of chiefdoms as defined by the Boundaries Committee.

It was partly in the spirit of decentralisation that the 55 *tinkhundla* were established in the country. The central government intended to shift significant functions and responsibilities to lower levels of administration such as the village councils (*bucopho*). But in reality, government transferred only limited power, resources and responsibilities to the *tinkhundla*. Consequently, matters in the domain of education, health, commerce and infrastructure continued to be handled from the capital Mbabane and not in the lower administrative echelons.

The *Tinkhundla* political system has demonstrated the ability to remodel itself following scathing criticism during the 1990s. Based on the TRC review of *Tinkhundla*, the system of voting was changed to enable people greater say in the election process. Originally, *Tinkhundla* did not provide for a secret ballot and the election process itself was indirect, since voters were allowed to vote only for an electoral college, which then selected members of parliament. The TRC recommended the inclusion of a secret ballot and direct representation. As Prince Majawonke Dlamini pointed out (Dlamini interview, 27 October 2016), the electorate was to be allowed to choose their representatives in a general election at which multiple candidates, pre-selected at community level, presented themselves. Giving people the opportunity to choose their own candidates was considered 'democracy' by the Swazi monarch. Consequently, King Mswati III rebranded the *Tinkhundla* system of governance as a 'monarchical democracy', in which the king supposedly rules together with his people (Veenendaal 2016: 183–198).

In recent years, the Swazi system of governance has been deemed even more flexible and adaptive, since it allowed people of different political affiliations to stand for elections.[21] Accordingly, opposition candidates were welcomed in the 2013 legislative elections. Yet, while everyone is constitutionally free to stand for election, one can do so only as an individual and not as a member of a political party. Moreover, candidates are pre-selected through a nomination process that takes place at the chiefdom level. The local chief can exert considerable influence over the choice of nominees, even though community members are also allowed to voice their preferences. Winners from individual chiefdoms later compete against one another at the *tinkhundla* constituency level, where the electorate is invited to select a candidate of their choice. For the 2013 elections, nearly 415 000 Swazis registered to vote—an increase from 350 000 in 2008. More than 80 per cent of former members of parliament running for re-election lost their seats in 2013 (Laterza 2013), possibly an indication of the Swazi electorate becoming empowered and politically conscious of the type of representation they want. A few well-known pro-democracy activists were elected to the House of Assembly that year. For instance, Jan Sithole, historic leader of the trade unions who had been at the forefront of the anti-monarchy struggles in the 1990s was one of them (Laterza 2013).

Reaction to reforms

The *Tinkhundla* political system has undergone some reforms in introducing the secret ballot and giving people a choice among multiple candidates for parliament. However, that does not appear to go far enough in the minds of critics. *Tinkhundla* has been widely criticised for being outdated and having no place in the 21st century (Rana 2004; Fombad 2007; Bohler-Muller & Lukhele-Olorunju 2011; Motsamai 2011, 2012). Scholars criticise the system specifically for its rejection of multipartyism. Motsamai (2012: 2) describes *tinkhundla* elections as being 'organised', since they maintain the political status quo in Swaziland. *Tinkhundla* elections are therefore seen as non-events, because people believe they simply recycle the same old pro-royal favourites (Motsamai 2012: 2).

Opposition to the *Tinkhundla* system comes from both international and domestic quarters. Swazi civil society has been at the forefront of a campaign to introduce multipartyism after it was banned with the imposition of the state of emergency and disbanding of political parties in 1973. Political contestation from pro-democracy organisations advocating for multipartyism accompanied the run-up to both the 2008 and 2013 legislative elections. Internationally, *tinkhundla* elections have been branded undemocratic. Election observers of the Commonwealth Expert Team questioned the credibility of the 2003 elections, saying they resulted in a toothless parliament because, in the absence of an opposition, all parliamentarians were selected by the monarchy. The 2008 Report of the Commonwealth Expert Team (Vandome, Vines & Weimer 2013) highlighted the need for political plurality and a revision of sections of the 2005 constitution that impede a functioning civil society. The report further stated that political parties neither registered nor participated in the elections (Vandome, Vines & Weimer 2013). In 2013, the African Union Elections Observer Mission to Swaziland also emphasised the apparent contradiction in the constitution in terms of the electoral system (Norris, Frank & Martinez i Coma 2014). It says Section 14(1b) 'guarantees fundamental human rights including the rights to freedom of association and assembly'. The same guarantees are assured by Articles 10 and 11 of the 2002 African Charter on Human and Peoples' Rights, to which Swaziland is a signatory. But, despite the existence of these documents, Swaziland citizens still do not fully enjoy their right to assemble and associate freely (Norris, Frank & Martinez i Coma 2014). The mission also pointed out that candidates in the elections were allowed to contest the results only as individuals and not under the banner of a political party. Based on its observations and consultations with various stakeholders inside and outside Swaziland, the mission urged the Kingdom of Swaziland to review Section 79 of the constitution, which speaks of the system of government for Swaziland as being 'democratic, participatory, *Tinkhundla*-based', so that it conforms with Section 14(1b) as well as Section 25, which addresses the protection of freedom of assembly and association. It also urged the country to align itself with the international principles of free and fair elections and participation in the electoral process, and particularly with the Durban Declaration on the Principles Governing Democratic Elections in Africa (1998) (Norris, Frank & Martinez i Coma 2014).

Conclusion

The *Tinkhundla* political system was an indigenous Swazi system of governance that borrowed elements from British bicameralism and Swazi culture and tradition. The system provided for an all-powerful executive, the *Ngwenyama*, with unfettered powers to ensure peace and stability. The system was born in 1978 during a constitutional void that followed the repeal of the 1968 independence constitution by King Sobhuza II, who set out to rule by decree and reign as a benevolent despot without any challenge to his power. This one-man rule attracted international criticism that resulted in the king instituting the *Tinkhundla* system to establish the legislative arm of government.

The system came under fire in the 1990s following democratic reawakening on the African continent. In response to harsh criticism, King Mswati III introduced reforms to the *Tinkhundla* system that involved decentralisation and the devolution of powers to lower echelons of administrative units. Nonetheless, resource constraints were a serious challenge to decentralisation.

The voting system was improved and Swazis were given the opportunity to elect members of the legislature on a non-partisan basis. Individual members of different political affiliations, including former opponents of the *Tinkhundla* system, were allowed to run for parliamentary seats. The capacity of the *Tinkhundla* system to evolve and assume certain aspects of the Western democratic way to better address fundamental human rights may be the key to its future survival in an ever-changing world. Therefore, the system needs to be further interrogated and fine-tuned to respond to the development needs of Swaziland.

Notes

1 The Constitution of the Kingdom of Swaziland, Act 25, Chapter VII, Article 80.

2 The expression 'the third democratic wave' was used by Huntington (1993), who described the sweep of the third-wave moment of democratic impulse throughout Africa. This wave was characterised by mass movements against authoritarian rule and the demand for liberalisation and expansion of political spaces.

3 According to the policy framework of the SADC region, 'democracy' and 'popular participation' are considered to be part of the imperatives of economic development and human security.

4 The Swazi National Council was a traditional council of notables selected by the Swazi king. It served as the custodian of Swazi culture and tradition. Its exclusively male membership was extremely conservative and suspicious of Western liberal political ideas.

5 King Sobhuza II was reluctant to form a political party before the first elections of 1964 because he felt he was above party politics. But he was convinced by the settler population to form a political party and contest elections if he expected to be relevant in Swazi politics. The Swazi National Council formed a political party, which they preferred to call the Imbokodvo National Movement.

6 For details on the protracted constitutional discussions between the British and the pro-royal camp made up of the Swazi National Council and the Imbokodvo National Movement, see Dlamini (2016).

7 The Constitution of the Kingdom of Swaziland, 1968.

8 The title *Ngwenyama*, reserved for the Swazi monarch, means 'the lion and the number one citizen of the Kingdom of Swaziland'.

9 King Sobhuza II condemned the independence constitution in several public speeches (Kuper 1978: 318–335) and this was a harbinger for the overthrow of the document.

10 Traditional African politics was based on consensus as a central principle of political organisation. This system avoided the problems of multipartyism inherited from the West (Wiredu 1995: 54–64; Jackson & Rosberg 1982; Potholm 1979).

11 Swaziland Government Gazette Extraordinary, Vol. XII, 17 April 1973.

12 *The Times of Swaziland*, 21 September 1973.

13 Public Library of the US Diplomacy. Constitutional Commission Makes its Report, 13 June 1975. Accessed October 2016, www.wikileaks.org/plusd/cables/1975MBABAN00987_b.html.

14 In Swaziland, local government in rural areas was created through two instruments, namely the Regional Councils Order, 1978, and the Establishment of Parliament Order, 1978 (amended in 1992).

15 Report of the *Tinkhundla* Review Commission: Government Gazette Extraordinary, No 855 of 1992; for a more comprehensive study on the *Tinkhundla* system of government, see: Baloro (1994); Bischoff (1988); Mamba (2006); Mkhaliphi (2015); Mkhatshwa (2004); Wanda (1990).

16 President Julius Nyerere of Tanzania argued that traditional Africa was a classless society and this structure did not necessitate Western multiparty democracy. Rather, the one-party consensual system was more appropriate and closer to African culture and tradition

(Grundy 1964: 379–393). The *Tinkhundla* system is very similar to the traditional Nepalese *panchayat* (councils) system of government, which King Mahendra of Nepal established after staging an auto-*coup d'état* in 1960. The king described the partyless system as a meaningful democratic form of government closer to Nepalese culture and tradition (Burghart 1994: 1–13).

17 The Swazis literally worshiped King Sobhuza II and saw him as a ruler who was always right and had to be praised.

18 In one-party states in Africa, the leader of the party is responsible for selecting candidates for municipal and legislative elections and for animating the political life of the nation. Although there was no political party in Swaziland, King Sobhuza II was the sole authority to sanction the candidature of those who aspired to sit in parliament.

19 Lesotho is a constitutional monarchy. The monarch is the head of state and the prime minister is the head of government who appoints a cabinet: Constitution of Lesotho, Order 16 of 1993.

20 The Constitution of the Kingdom of Swaziland Act 2005.

21 Magagula M, Progressives are not our enemies, *Times of Swaziland*, 23 June 2013.

References

Abrahamsen R (2000) *Disciplining democracy: Development discourse and good governance in Africa*. London: Zed Books

Adebajo A (2010) *The curse of Berlin: Africa after the cold war*. London: Hurst

Ake C (1991) Rethinking African Democracy. *Journal of Democracy* 2(1): 32–44

Ayittey GB (1994) Africa betrayed. *Orbis* 38(1): 119–123

Baloro J (1994) The development of Swaziland's Constitution: Monarchical response to modern challenges. *Journal of African Law* 38(1): 19–34

Barya JJB (1993) The new political conditionalities of aid: An independent view from Africa. *IDS Bulletin* 24(1): 16–23

Beaulieu E and Hyde SD (2009) In the shadow of democracy promotion: Strategic manipulation, international observers, and election boycotts. *Comparative Political Studies* 42(3): 392–415

Berg-Schlosser D (2004) Indicators of democracy and good governance as measures of the quality of democracy in Africa: A critical appraisal. *Acta Politica* 39(3): 248–278

Bischoff P (1988) Why Swaziland is Different. *Journal of Modern African Studies* 26(3): 457–471

Boahen AA (Ed) (1985) *General History of Africa. Vol II: Africa under colonial domination 1880–1935*. Paris: UNESCO

Bohler-Muller N & Lukhele-Olorunju P (2011) Swaziland: The last gasps of an absolute monarch? AISA Policy Brief 54. Accessed October 2016, www.ai.org.za/wp-content/uploads/downloads/2011/11/No-54.-Swaziland-The-Last-Gasps-of-an-Absolute-Monarch.pdf

Bollen K (1993) Liberal democracy: Validity and method factors in cross-national measures. *American Journal of Political Science* 37(4): 1207–1230

Bonner P (1982) *Kings, commoners and concessionaires: The evolution and dissolution of the nineteenth-century Swazi state*. Cambridge: Cambridge University Press

Bratton M (1998) Second elections in Africa. *Journal of Democracy* 9(3): 51–66

Burghart R (1994) The political culture of panchayat democracy. In M Hutt (Ed) *Nepal in the nineties: Versions of the past, visions of the future*, 1–13. London: School of Oriental & African Studies, University of London

Crush J (1980) The colonial division of space: The significance of the Swaziland land partition. *The International Journal of African Historical Studies* 13(1): 71–86

De Smith SA (1964) *The new commonwealth and its constitutions*. London: Stevens

Dlamini LG (2005) *Socio-economic and political constraints on constitutional reform in Swaziland.* Doctoral dissertation, University of the Western Cape. Accessed October 2016, www.etd. uwc.ac.za/xmlui/bitstream/handle/11394/2134/Dlamini_MPA_2005.pdf?sequence=1

Dlamini HP (2016) Constitutional developments in the Kingdom of Swaziland 1960–2005. Doctoral dissertation, University of Pretoria

Eisenstadt T (2000) Eddies in the third wave: Protracted transitions and theories of democratization. *Democratization* 7(3): 3–24

Fatton R (1990) Liberal democracy in Africa. *Political Science Quarterly* 105(3): 455–473

Fombad CM (2007) Swaziland Constitution of 2005: Can absolutism be reconciled with modern constitutionalism? *South African Journal on Human Rights* 23(1): 93–115

Grundy KW (1964) The 'class struggle' in Africa: An examination of conflicting theories. *The Journal of Modern African Studies* 2(3): 379–393

Hausken K and Ncube M (2013) Production and conflict in risky elections. African Development Bank Group Working Paper No 173

Holden B (1993) *Understanding liberal democracy*. London: Harvester Wheatsheaf

Huntington SP & Moore CH (1970) *Authoritarian politics in modern society: The dynamics of established one-party systems*. New York: Basic Books

Huntington SP (1993) *The third wave: Democratization in the late twentieth century*. Norman: University of Oklahoma Press

Jackson RH and Rosberg CG (1982) *Personal rule in Black Africa: Prince, autocrat, prophet, tyrant*. Berkeley: University of California Press

Joseph RA (1998) Africa, 1990–1997: From abertura to closure. *Journal of Democracy* 9(2): 3–17

Kabemba CK (2004) *Swaziland's struggle with political liberalisation* (No 3). Electoral Institute of Southern Africa

Khaketla BM (1972) *Lesotho, 1970: An African coup under the microscope* (No 5). Berkeley and Los Angeles: University of California Press

Kirk-Greene AHM (1980) The thin white line: The size of the British colonial service in Africa. *African Affairs* 79(314): 25–44

Kuper H (1964) The colonial situation in Southern Africa. *The Journal of Modern African Studies* 2(2): 149–150

Kuper H (1978) *Sobhuza II, Ngwenyama and King of Swaziland: The story of an hereditary ruler and his country*. New York: Africana Publication

Laterza V (2013) Elections in Swaziland: Liberal democracy and its discontents. Swazis want reform, but do they want a multi-party system? Accessed November 2017, https://www.academia.edu/4755539/Swaziland_liberal_democracy_and_its_discontents

Levin R (1991) Swaziland's *Tinkhundla* and the myth of Swazi tradition. *Journal of Contemporary African Studies* 10(2): 1–23

Mamba MA (2006) *Tinkhundla*: A study of a system. MA thesis, University of Swaziland

Matlosa K (1998) Democracy and conflict in post-apartheid Southern Africa: Dilemmas of social change in small states. *International Affairs* 74(2): 319–337

Matsebula JSM (1988) *A History of Swaziland.* Johannesburg: Longman

Mkhaliphi T (2015) The extent to which the *Tinkhundla*-based system of government articulates the decentralization principles: A practitioner's analysis. Paper presented at a research seminar, University of Swaziland

Mkhatshwa AM (2004) An assesment of the *Tinkhundla* system of government 1973–2003. BA Project, University of Swaziland

Mohiddin A (1968) Ujamaa: A commentary on President Nyerere's vision of Tanzanian society. *African Affairs* 67(267): 130–143

Motsamai D (2011) Can Southern Africa's last absolute monarchy democratise? *Africa Security Review* 20(2): 42–50

Motsamai D (2012) Swaziland's Non-Party Political System and the 2013 *Tinkhundla* Elections. Breaking the SADC impasse? *Institute for Security Studies Situation Report.* Accessed November 2017, https://www.files.ethz.ch/isn/151815/Swaziland_Sit_Rep_14Aug12.pdf

Mzizi B (2004) The dominance of the Swazi monarchy and the moral dynamics of democratization of the Swazi state. *Journal of African Elections* 3(1): 94–110

Ngwome GF and Ngwa NF (2004) *Multipartyism and democracy in Africa: A Development Tool or a Liability? Challenges.* Saarbrücken: Lap Lambert Academic Publishing

Norris P, Frank RW and Martinez i Coma F (2014) *The year in elections 2013: The world's flawed and failed contests. The Electoral Integrity Project.* Accessed October 2016, www.dash.harvard.edu/handle/1/11744445

Nyamnjoh FB (2009) Open access and open knowledge production processes: Lessons from CODESRIA (Institutional review). *African Journal of Information and Communication: Scholarly Communication and Opening Access to Knowledge* 10: 67–72

Oliver R and Atmore A (2004) *Africa since 1800.* Cambridge: Cambridge University Press

Olsen GR (1998) Europe and the promotion of democracy in post-Cold War Africa: How serious is Europe and for what reason? *African Affairs* 97(388): 343–367

Pain JH (1978) The reception of English and Roman-Dutch law in Africa with reference to Botswana, Lesotho and Swaziland. *The Comparative and International Law Journal of Southern Africa* 11(2): 137–167

Potholm CP (1979) *The theory and practice of African politics.* New Jersey: Prentice Hall

Rana M (2004) Unfit for a king. *Harvard International Review* 26(1). Accessed October 2016, www.hir.harvard.edu/interventionismunfit-for-a-king/

Rowen HH (1961). 'L'etat c'est a moi': Louis XIV and the state. *French Historical Studies* 2(1): 83–98

Russel B (2013) *History of Western philosophy*. London: Routledge

Saurombe A (2012) The role of SADC institutions in implementing SADC treaty provisions dealing with regional integration. *PER: Potchefstroomse Elektroniese Regsblad* 15(2): 1–34

Scheuerman WE (2006) Survey article: Emergency powers and the rule of law after 9/11. *Journal of Political Philosophy* 14(1): 61–84

Simelane HS (2002) The state, landlords, and the squatter problem in post-colonial Swaziland. *Canadian Journal of African Studies* 36(2): 329–354

Smith B (2005) Life of the party: The origins of regime breakdown and persistence under single-party rule. *World Politics* 57(3): 421–451

Söderbaum F (2007) Regionalisation and civil society: The case of Southern Africa. *New Political Economy* 12(3): 319–337

Stevens RP (1963) Swaziland political development. *The Journal of Modern African Studies* 1(3): 327–350

Tande D (2009) *Scribbles from the den: Essays on politics and collective memory in Cameroon*. Bamenda: African Books Collective

Uduigwomen AF (2002) *Schools of law and military decrees*. Thrissur: Ebenezer Printing Press & Computer Services

Vandome C, Vines A & Weimer M (2013) *Swaziland: Southern Africa's forgotten crisis*. London: Chatham House

Veenendaal W (2016) Monarchy and democracy in small states: An ambiguous symbiosis. In S Wolf (Ed.) *State size matters*. Wiesbaden: Springer Fachmedien

Vile MJC (2012) *Constitutionalism and the separation of powers*. Indianapolis: Liberty Fund

Wanda BP (1990) The shaping of modern constitution in Swaziland: A review of some social and historical factors. *Lesotho Law Journal* 6(1): 137–178

Welch CE (1991) The single party phenomenon in Africa. *TransAfrica Forum* 8(3): 85

Wiredu K (1995) Democracy and consensus in African traditional politics: A plea for a non-party polity. *The Centennial Review* 39(1): 53–64

Woods D (2014) Monarchical rule in Swaziland: Power is absolute but patronage is (for) relative(s). *Journal of Asian and African Studies*, DOI: 10.1177/0021909615596451

Interviews

Prince Majawonke Dlamini, Senior Regional Officer, Ministry of *Tinkhundla* Administration, Manzini, 27 October 2016

5 | Rights-recognition theory: An African perspective

Sabelo Wiseman Ndwandwe

Given Africa's history, human rights are among the most urgent concerns on the African continent. African people have suffered a great deal of deprivation in terms of their rights. Debate continues among African moral and political philosophy scholars about the extent to which international human rights are an unwelcome Western imposition on the continent (Cobbah 1987: 309). Central to this debate is the question of applicability—that is, whether international human rights instruments, given the individualist and rationalist Western emphasis, are suitable for the Afro-communitarian[1] ethic. Questions raised by intellectuals who engage in this debate draw attention to tensions between African cultural values and international human rights norms, which are typically dominated by a Western, individualist ethos. The search for an articulation of human rights that will appeal to authentic aspects of African traditions is what guides this debate. This has led a number of scholars to try to form an Afro-communitarian theory of human nature that might underwrite international human rights without sacrificing any of the core principles of African communitarianism.

This chapter examines the tendency in these debates to consider personhood—or the state of being an individual—as a core foundation for human rights. The arguments focus typically on the ontological differences between the African and Western formulations of the concept of personhood. Such an emphasis, however, conceals power asymmetries between the West and Africa that not only affect the political and economic relationships between these actors, but also have a direct bearing on the ability of the stronger counterpart to enforce their human rights standards. The chapter avoids complicating the question of human rights with that of personhood by advancing and developing an account of African rights based on rights recognition. It furthermore tries to find practical similarities between African and Western conventions that may inform public policy and be relevant to current African realities without losing sight of past conditions.

The first section considers African theories of rights that articulate a theory of human nature as grounds for rights, showing that they are controversial and have provoked an internal conflict within African political philosophy. I begin with a critical discussion of Gyekye's attempt to construct a theory of human nature based on *equality between community and individuality* as grounds for rights. I discuss some criticism of the theory and show how controversial it has proven to be in attempting to derive an Afro-communitarian theory of rights based on attributes of individuals. I then assess Metz's theory of human nature based on the *capacity for communal relationships* as grounds for an African theory of rights. I also examine a debate between Oyowe and Metz about the latter's views on the rights that remain authentic to sub-Saharan customs. In section two, I discuss a thesis of rights recognition outlined by Boucher and argue that an alternative approach to human rights may be found in an African moral theory that is not based on the rights of an individual, but rather on customary practice among living communities. In the final section, I develop an African theory of rights recognition that, in my opinion, better accommodates the African understanding of social and customary underpinnings of rights.

African theories of rights using the ontology of personhood

It is commonly understood that, in African societies, an individual's status as a person depends on their fulfilling certain roles within relationship circles (Wiredu 2008). This norm is different from the Western way of thinking, which holds that human rights are based on each person's capacity to exercise rational autonomy. It is commonly assumed that African and Western scholars' ideas about human nature are in conflict, the former being more communalistic and the latter more individ-ualistic. This difference in understanding of what makes us human and the rights that come with it has led some African scholars[2] to attempt to articulate ontological theories of personhood that would explain what Africans consider intrinsic rights of a human being. On its own, this idea remains contentious and has provoked inter-nal conflict within African moral and political philosophy circles. Below, I examine some theories of rights formed using the human nature tenet and discuss controver-sies that have arisen as a result of this approach.

Gyekye's moderate communitarianism

Gyekye's moderate communitarianism is a perspective on human nature which considers equality between community and individuality as the grounds for human rights. Gyekye (1992a) draws attention to the metaphysical and moral status of a person in a community, arguing that Afro-communitarian ethics typically follow the apparent connection between the two. This notion is probably the most debat-ed topic in contemporary African moral and political philosophy.[3] Central to the debate is the question of whether a person can be considered self-sufficient and their identity independent of anything external and, as such, having precedence over com-munity, or whether the person is by nature communal, having natural and essential relationships with other people. A moral question, to some extent linked to this, is the status of individual rights. In other words, are rights so important that they may not be overridden by a conflicting interpretation of communal life or the common good, which is the bedrock of African communities? Moreover, should cultural rel-ativism apply to rights?

Both Gyekye (1992a) and Wiredu (1990) have tried to explore answers to these questions from the perspective of personhood in African ethics. For Gyekye (1992a), the rights of individuals, their duties to others and their sense of common good all derive from the concept of personhood. Wiredu (2008) agrees, stating that traditional African society is moderately communitarian, and implying strong familial bonds and a broad scope of obligations and reciprocities. However, he notes, 'to adjust the interests of the individual to those of the community is not to subordinate one to the other' (Wiredu 2008: 334). Gyekye (1992a) agrees with Africa's early socialist leaders that African society places more emphasis on the group than on individuals, on solidarity than on personal interests, and on the communion of persons than on autonomy. This political position was grounded in the ideology of socialism, so it is unclear how this social conception of the individual's status can be logically linked to metaphysics. Gyekye (1992a) takes a different direction from that of the philosopher kings,[4] arguing that they have been mistaken in thinking that African communitarianism would easily fit modern socialism. He says, 'African communitarianism does not invariably conceive of the person as *wholly* socially constituted' (Gyekye 1992a: 101).

Menkiti (1984) understands personhood in the African context as being something conferred by the community He thus maintains the ontological primacy of the community over the individual. The implication is that, in the African worldview, it is the community that defines a person. And it is this 'radical, excessive and unrestricted' view that Gyekye (1992a: 103) believes is 'unsupportable', because it fails to allow sufficient room for the exercise of individual rights. While agreeing with Menkiti (1984) that a person is by nature a social being, Gyekye (1992a) goes on to say that the person is by nature also other things. 'A person possesses other attributes and failure to recognise them may result in pushing the significance and implications of a person's communal nature beyond limits' (Gyekye 1992a: 106). Personhood is not a function of one's membership of a community only. He says a more satisfactory grounding of human rights in contemporary African thought must fully take into account the human being's individuality, since these rights belong essentially to the individual (Gyekye 1997: 59). Dignity and autonomy are two inalienable attributes of people who are capable of valuation and choice. These attributes allow for the free exercise of individual rights, which in turn enhances the cultural development and success of the community (Gyekye 1992a: 110–111). Both Gyekye (1992a) and Wiredu (1990) agree that Afro-communitarian ethics promote an understanding of human dignity that underwrites individual rights and surpasses communal values.

Oyowe (2014)[5] finds this reading of human nature both conceptually and practically flawed. He says a theory of human rights conceived from this view is not appealing (Oyowe 2014: 337), because the idea of assigning equal moral status to the individual and the community is potentially 'counterproductive'. He argues that attempts to meet social objectives usually entail undermining the rights of one of the sides (Oyowe 2014: 337–338). The undeniable conflict in practice between individual rights and communal good is another reason we shouldn't be persuaded by Gyekye's argument for human nature as the basis of a theory of human rights (Oyowe 2014: 338). Matolino (2009) agrees with this position, saying that moderate communitarianism does not take the notion of individual rights seriously, a view which Gyekye rejects. Matolino (2009: 169) further claims that, if human rights are only contingent on an appropriate social context and matched with attendant responsibilities, the distinction between moderate and radical communitarianism, as argued by Gyekye, dissipates.[6] Moreover, if individual rights come to crash morally with communal values, the community has the authority and responsibility to preserve its integrity and stability by various means; such means are likely to include restrictions to individual rights. If this were to happen, 'Gyekye does not tell what rights can be abridged and what rights are incorrigible' (Matolino 2009: 169).

Metz (2012b) agrees with Matolino (2009) that Gyekye is ambiguous about which moral rights he believes are firmly fixed and which ones the state may justly enforce. Famakinwa (2010: 73) adds the argument that Gyekye's recognition of rights is not for the sake of the individual, but for the community. He says the individual, even in Gyekye's viewpoint, has value only by being a member of the community. So, this means that both radical and moderate communitarianism favour the community over the individual. Famakinwa (2010: 73) thus asserts that 'the gap between radical and moderate communitarianism is not as wide as Gyekye believes.'[7]

Metzian ubuntu moral theory

Metz (2012a) urges us to turn our attention away from Gyekye's conception of human nature and focus instead on his Metzian theory of human nature, which he considers a better basis for human rights. He articulates a theory of dignity that he considers to be true to sub-Saharan African values, yet in opposition to Western thinking about human rights as a function of dignity (Metz 2012a: 21). Despite arguing along the lines of moderate communitarians like Gyekye and Wiredu, Metz (2012a: 63) takes a position that implies 'friendliness as the master value'. All these scholars agree that human dignity underwrites equal basic rights and the obligation not to interfere coercively with others. For Metz (2010; 2012a; 2012b), a human being has dignity insofar as they have the *capacity for communal relationships*. By this, he means a combination of identity and solidarity—in other words, to identify with others is to share a way of life with them, and to exhibit solidarity is to care about their quality of life. The combination of sharing a way of life and caring for others' quality of life is equivalent to 'friendship' or 'love' in a broad English sense (Metz 2012b: 69). He adds that 'the Afro-communitarian conception of dignity entails that we have dignity in virtue of our capacity for "loving" relationships' (Metz 2012a: 27). To sum up, Metz argues that the Afro-communitarian conception of human dignity and the *capacity for communal relationships* provide the most acceptable basis for a theory of human rights, and this foundation is true to sub-Saharan African values. Just like Gyekye (1997) and Wiredu (1990), he subscribes to a moderate communitarian viewpoint, which holds that interest in and contributing to the common good do not necessarily subvert individual rights. Following Gyekye (1997), Metz (2012b: 63) indicates that the 'common good' includes each and every interest of an individual; it does not imply a wellbeing that would sacrifice the interests of an individual for the benefit of a particular group or for the greater good.

Oyowe (2014)[8] disagrees. He does not accept human dignity as being a solid enough basis for an African theory of human rights, arguing that it is unreliable. Oyowe (2013: 104) believes Metz's theory of rights fails to deliver on what he claims to be key features in Afro-communitarian ethics as it relates to human rights. 'Metz's ubuntu moral theory battles with three challenges: 1. It evokes the question of where the fundamental value lies in this theory. 2. In seeking to integrate two potentially conflicting and non-instrumental values, his theory undermines its communitarian status. 3. He erroneously construes rights as duties' (Oyowe 2013: 124).[9] It is also significant to note that Metz's account attempts to combine two insights—the impression that rights are conferred in the individual on the one hand, while on the other hand, it maintains commitment to the communal view of personhood as the characteristic shared in sub-Saharan African cultures. Oyowe (2014: 340) then points out that it is in combining these insights that Metz's Afro-communitarian theory of human rights runs into major difficulties. It is not clear that finding dignity in the individual's capacity for community, not the community itself, can adequately capture what is distinctive about sub-Saharan African sense of community. In his words, 'Metz's conception of dignity which resides in the individual's *unexercised* capacity for community casts doubt on the theory's claim to be communitarian' (Oyowe 2013: 108). This view of human nature represents individuals as existing outside networks of relationships that constitute community; it is contrary to views held by theorists in sub-Saharan Africa that place individuals within relationships (Oyowe 2014: 341).

Debate between Metz and Oyowe

Oyowe (2014: 342) points out that the Metzian understanding of human dignity is close to the Western one, which Metz (2012: 20) claims to reject. Part of what is valuable about friendship or communal relationships is that people come together and stay together 'of their own accord' (Metz 2013: 109–110). It therefore appears that the Kantian capacity for individual choice plays an essential role in the Metzian conceptualisation of human dignity. Oyowe (2014: 342) points this out, saying the capacity for community upon which Metz grounds human dignity is actually heavily dependent on Kant's capacity for autonomy, and therefore the latter is doing more work in Metz's own account. If this were correct, then Metz would have sacrificed core African values to make his case for a theory on which to base human rights.

This discussion shows that having friendly relationships, as a *master value* in the Metzian reading of human dignity, is not the only worthwhile attribute; individual freedom is another. The capacity to engage in communal relationships seems secondary if individuals hold intrinsically the capacity to make deliberative choices, one of which is to form relationships with their communities. Thus, it adds no value to maintain that what makes human beings special is their capacity to act in ways that promote community (Oyowe 2014: 342). Moreover, the claim that the dignity of a human being is linked to their capacity to make choices (particularly in promoting community) narrows down unjustifiably the range of options available to human agency (Oyowe 2014: 343). This shows that Metz splits one fundamental aim into two (equally valid aims), which renders his thesis unsuitable as a basis for a theory of human rights. Oyowe (2013: 124) then concludes that the ubuntu ethic is not an entirely suitable grounding for public morality in the modern-day industrialised and globalised societies of Africa. While I disagree with Oyowe's claim, I also find it problematic to agree with Metz on his conceptualisation of ubuntu as grounds for a theory of human rights.

The purpose of this argument is not to restate the debate between the two scholars, but rather to show how basing human rights on a particular reading of dignity runs into unnecessary controversy. I try to resolve this with an alternative suggestion, which contends that cultural problems typically identified by African philosophers do not stem from any particular concept of personhood and the conflict of ideas between Western and African ontologies. Human rights[10] have translated poorly in Africa, precisely because their universality is premised on the natural attributes of the human being, which leaves out historical factors that played a significant role in human evolution. As the British idealist,[11] Green (1917), explains, natural rights theorists fail to account for how rights develop within (and make no sense outside of) a political community in which people recognise them in one another. Boucher (2011: 756) adds to this argument, saying that 'they are deluded in thinking that the higher essence of a person is somehow separable from political society and its norms'. Human rights do not follow from natural or essential facts about persons, but instead from their actual social recognition. They do not depend upon any comprehensive doctrine or philosophical theory of human nature, but are firmly embedded in and depend upon moral communities. In a nutshell, they are a statement of what that society wants to become.

Rights-recognition thesis

Recognition theory arises in the context of customary international law. Customs are taken to be expressive of the will of people, and they are justified through being introduced to the common good (Suarez quoted in Boucher (2011)). Boucher (2011: 755) explains what Green means by the term *recognition* by drawing two sens-es of his thesis: '1. recognition makes rights, and 2. recognition is a way of knowing or acknowledging those rights'. The fundamental claim is that customary practice creates rights, and then it becomes the responsibility of intellectuals in the form of jurisprudence, lawyers, philosophers and policymakers to set up a system to identify and codify them. Rights-recognition scholars submit that customary international law and the rights-recognition thesis offer better accounts of what it means to have universal rights and obligations, and articulate more effectively the duties of states to uphold these rights and obligations.[12] Martin (1993) emphasises the importance of embodying these rights institutionally, and the role of states, not just individuals, in enforcing them. Human rights require more than moral justification—they must also be socially recognised. Without such recognition they become mere claims, even if morally valid, and cannot qualify as being human rights. The question now is, how do we explain the concept of human rights from a *recognition* thesis perspective? Further, how will this lead to the African recognition theory of human rights I seek to develop? In addressing these questions, I will 1. give a brief critique of natural rights—rights based on a theory of dignity, as discussed earlier; and 2. provide the basis for an approach that I believe better accommodates the African understanding of rights within the socio-cultural context.

A critique of personhood as a basis for human rights

Rights-recognition theorists consider unsustainable theories of human rights that are based on normative principles dissociated from the social context within which these rights developed. They have not rejected fundamental rights, grounding them instead in a theory that incorporates social recognition into their definition, and validating them through an emphasis on the contribution to the common good (Boucher 2009).[13] The international lawyer Fiss (quoted in Boucher 2011: 762), explains that 'human rights are not derived from a common understanding of human nature, nor are they deduced philosophically from first principles—they are the articulation of aspirations immanent in a culture—a statement of what that society wants to become, which provides a standard by which to judge it'. Following this thinking, a rights-recognition thesis marks a fundamental shift away from the assumption that human rights are inherent to human beings by virtue of the latter's own humanity, or that they have some 'divine or natural origin' (Boucher 2009: 289).

A contemporary reading of human rights—having shifted from a traditional idea of natural rights to more contemporary conceptualisations as in the recognition thesis—originated from British Idealism, which in turn borrowed from the Hegelian tradition. However, communitarian and moral constructivist theorists have come to dominate this tradition, among them philosophers like Michael Walzer, David Miller, Rex Martin, Gerry Gaus, John Charvet, Jeremy Waldron and Richard Rorty. The central premise in the works of these scholars was about the rights of citizenship (as part of a community) being a prerequisite for human rights, while human rights are not a prerequisite for the rights of citizenship. In this reading of rights, human rights arise within a community and make no sense outside that context. A community setting is therefore a prerequisite for human rights, and not the other way around. Within this interdependence, there is a sense of overlapping communities that shape each other reciprocally; standards of behaviour employed in one group extend into the other as part of human progress and globalisation (Boucher 2009: 287). I return to this point as I develop an African recognition theory of human rights, and champion the consensus-seeking nature of traditional African political thought as fertile ground for a recognition thesis.

Human rights

Following Green's insight that rights are *powers* that are *recognised* as upholding a *common good* (quoted in Boucher 2011), I propose a rights-recognition thesis that would be more aligned with the universal status of human rights in Africa than theses that rely on culturally particular ontologies of personhood. Gaus (2006) argues that rights that are recognised do a better job in providing a moral compass than any structured set of rights can ever do. Martin (2001: 50) says Green's description of a right has two principal elements: '1. The requirement for social recognition, and 2. The idea of a common good' (see Harris & Morrow 1986).

Based on this reading of rights, Martin (2001) argues that human rights are ways of acting or being treated that are considered active only if: 1. they are morally accredited (judged by moral standards, all bound into a list of rights, each of which should benefit people); 2. they enjoy significant, effective social recognition; 3. they are officially recognised in law and in the actions of courts (or they are situated in legally supported, regulated social and economic institutions); 4. they are uniformly upheld; and 5. they are protected by government oversight and enforcement.

The African rights-recognition theory of human rights I propose follows this formula. It is in tune with an Afro-communitarian ethos, in which rights are communally acknowledged and do not take a devil-take-the-hindmost, individualistic approach. Instead, it is rooted in a celebration of community as an overarching value in and of itself. These rights originate from the community solidarity so typical of sub-Saharan Africa; they are grounded in socially recognised practices.

Towards an African recognition theory of human rights

Apart from his well-known contributions to ontology and his moderate communitarian account of human rights in Africa, Gyekye's (1992b) work offers valuable insight into traditional practices of social consensus that constitute the moral basis for human rights in Africa. Particularly important in this regard are Gyekye's thoughts on traditional political ideas and their relevance to development in contemporary Africa. He draws attention to the relativist view on development in Africa shared by most Africanists, who believe that exploring traditional African values should be central to any project that seeks to bring development to the continent—they call it 'building on the indigenous' (Wiredu 1990; Gyekye 1992b; Ake 1993; Odhiambo 2002). Bohler-Muller (2015: 31) also advances this position, arguing that changes that *add* to the existing sociocultural arrangements stand a far better chance of being supported and carried out by the community than those enforced from the top.

Gyekye (1992b: 242) insists that the success of any attempt to reconcile traditional custom with democratic rights in Africa—where chieftaincy has long been the dominant feature of the socio-political landscape—depends on thorough investigation into the status and nature of authority, and power relationships in social structures. Such inquiry will reveal the extent to which people are in consensus about traditional power relations between the chief and those he represents. In Gyekye's account, the authority of a traditional African chief is limited by custom and consensus, since his role depends on social recognition. I agree, at least in principle, that any attempt to reconcile traditional customs with democratic rights in Africa depends on the pursuit of such an inquiry. So, I submit that a recognition theory of human rights would avoid problems of cultural essentialism embedded in Afro-communitarian and Western concepts of personhood by, instead, eliciting and clarifying normative principles that guide African customary practices.

Gyekye (1992b) illustrates the principles of consensual democratic recognition in Africa using the example of Akan politics. He emphasises the point that the position of the Akan village chief in Ghana was hereditary; he was traditionally elected from the royal lineage, in consultation with members of the lineage, but he was chosen only if councillors deemed him acceptable, and with citizens' consent. Teffo (2004: 446) captures the same when he quotes the South African saying: *kgosi ke kgosi ka batho* (a chief is a chief through the people), meaning one remains a chief only as long as the people consent to it. Consensual democratic practice in the Akan political tradition described by Gyekye (1992b) can be compared to Wamala's (2004) account of the traditional consensus system of government as the heart of social and political organisation and ethos of the people of Buganda in Uganda. Both authors describe the limited nature of political power in traditional monarchical systems. This contradicts the widely held beliefs of absolute power being central to African monarchs, opening the door to corruption.[14] Historically, this was simply not true, at least not until colonialists came to distort African political culture. The system was democratic in its own traditional sense, with councillors listening to people's opinions in public villages and where anyone was free to express dissent until consensus could be reached (Gyekye 1992b: 242–244; Wamala 2004: 439–440).

Teffo (2004: 447) agrees with Gyekye and Wamala that a chief was compelled not to be dogmatic, but tolerant of the views of others. Decisions were never seen as being his, but as those of all the members of the council. The chief rarely took part in deliberations himself, since he was not allowed to prejudice the proceedings. His duty was to authorise and pronounce the decision of the council. If this argument is correct, then it is fair to conclude that the idea of a chief as an autocrat with absolute power is a misrepresentation of traditional African political thought, which had been democratic in principle. Both Gyekye and Wamala state that chiefs are controlled by customs and the consensus of councillors representing the citizens of a community. The chief is not to impose his ruling, but rather to secure and enforce the customary practices of the community represented by the council. Rights of citizenship, here, do not come from essential properties of personhood—such as dignity or the capacity for friendliness. Instead, social rights and customary norms are a result of practices that the community recognises and the chief represents.

Based on all this, and using the traditional African systems of governance found in the Akan and Buganda societies as guidance, it is clear that there is scope in African political thought for a recognition theory of human rights. The consensual nature of traditional African political thought converges with the African recognition theory of human rights I propose here, in that such rights gain their recognition only once sufficient consensus is reached and most people agree that such rights serve the communal good. In his critique of international human rights instruments, Ake (1987) reproaches African intelligentsia for accepting, uncritically, the Western notions of human rights, which he considers to be poorly integrated with African realities. Rights-recognition theory of rights claims its relevance to African cultures in relation to the status that people's rights hold in traditional African communities, thus helping better to articulate the Africanist critique of Western principles of human rights. Even though Gyekye (1997) understands rights as underpinned by attributes of individuals, his account of traditional government in Akan society shows some scope for a rights-recognition theory of human rights. The status of rights in this case does not derive from basic facts about what makes a person; instead, it derives from commonly recognised customary practices that are enforced by the authority of the chief, who is bound by precedent and consensus.

If human rights are to be understood as inherent to human nature, there will always be disagreement as to how to interpret them, because of the assumption that African and Western scholars hold different ideas about personhood. The Western individualist approach is more likely to support individual rights, while the African communitarian perspective is likely to uphold customary practices because of a general duty to collective wellbeing. I agree with Boucher (2011: 753), who says theories that associate rights with an ontology of the person are in fact 'convenient fiction'. Continuing a debate about the incompatibility between the African communitarian and Western individualist ethos takes us nowhere. I also agree with Metz (2012b) in that, if contemporary African political philosophy is to develop in fresh directions, we have to look to new ideas instead of revising old debates. An African rights-recognition theory provides a good alternative, since it does not ground rights in essential properties of personhood, but rather in customary recognition within communities' moral framework. In practice, all human rights are codified in international customary law. As such, criticism of Western prejudice in international human rights law should not look to notions of personhood, but to the conflict between customary practices.

Conclusion

I have articulated and argued in this chapter that a credible approach to the human rights discourse may be given in an African moral theory—by developing a recognition theory of rights that does not ground rights on essential human properties, but on customary recognition in living, historical and moral communities. The account is not comprehensive, but it points in a direction in which such a theory could be developed—namely through close reflection on traditional African political thought, such as that given in Gyekye's account of the Akan political environment and in Wamala's discussion of traditional good governance in Buganda society. African theories of rights unnecessarily complicate the debate about human rights by linking it to a universal theory of human nature. By doing so, they only prolong the long-standing discussion about incompatibilities between the African and Western understanding of the concept of personhood. Rights-recognition theory avoids such an extraneous and pointlessly complicating approach and helps reconcile rights with lived customary practices as they evolve over time. Given the dynamic nature of culture (Odhiambo 2002: 7), the normative foundations of rights-recognition theory seem adequate for integrating compatible elements of various cultural practices in modern-day industrialised and globalised society.

Acknowledgement

This chapter was made possible thanks to financial support from the Centre for Leadership Ethics in Africa at the University of Fort Hare.

Notes

1 Afro-communitarianism is an intellectual movement that owes its source to nationalist politics of the 1960s. It claims that the values of community override individuals' rights and autonomy. It was brought to light through the writings of politicians often referred to as pioneers of Africa's intelligentsia (Masolo 2004: 488).

2 For a unique African understanding of human rights based on an indigenous African identity, see Ake (1987), who says the dominant Western notion of human rights, which, for instance, is endorsed in the Universal Declaration of Human Rights (1948), stresses rights that are incompatible with African realities. Ake argues that, if the idea of human rights is to make any sense in an African context, we need to domesticate these rights and redefine them to fit African conditions. See also Wiredu (1990), who seems to agree with Ake. Wiredu argues that a contemporary project is to develop a system of politics that will reflect traditional African thinking, while remaining responsive to the developments of the modern world, particularly with regards to the issue of human rights.

3 Metz (2012b: 61) says the political theory from sub-Saharan Africa that has been most widely analysed in the past 20 years has been Gyekye's moderate communitarianism. See also Metz (2011) for further discussions on how the old Menkiti-Gyekye debate on personhood should be given new attention, taking into account three distinct senses of 'person', a concept introduced by Behrens (2013).

4 Wiredu (2008) applauds the post-independence leaders of Africa such as Nkrumah, Senghor, Nyerere, Awolowo, Kaunda and Sekou Toure for devoting considerable attention to the philosophical bases of their programmes. He argues that, not only did these leaders understand that the colonial systems needed to be reviewed from an African perspective, they further understood that any such review had to be philosophical and he thus called them 'philosopher kings' (p. 332).

5 For Oyowe (2014: 337), the idea that collective and individual features mutually constitute the human person is hard to articulate, at least in the abstract. He cites the example of compensatory justice, as it is applied in South Africa, where the rights of a white male who applies for a job that is an equal opportunity position are potentially at risk, since it conflicts

with policy, which favours members of previously disadvantaged groups, typically black members of the population (p. 338).

6   I do not agree with Matolino's criticism, because I do not think it is legitimate to construe a thinker's view as being extreme simply on the basis of the argument that the exercise of rights should be in an appropriate social context. An alternative view, which follows later in the chapter, holds that rights do not exist independent of the society. In rights-recognition theory, the emphasis is on the fact that each right is recognised by the community and that it is justified by its contribution to the common good.

7   There are many other scholars who have criticised Gyekye's moderate communitarianism, but I will limit myself to the above discussed because my aim is not to discuss the criticism but simply to highlight the challenges Gyekye's account faces for attempting to derive human rights from the theory of human nature, based on equality between individuality and community.

8   See Oyowe (2013) for an insightful criticism of Metz's conception of human rights.

9   See also Oyowe (2014).

10   Here, I refer to international human rights instruments as declared in the Universal Declaration of Human Rights (1948).

11   British Idealism is a philosophy that dominated Britain towards the end of the 19th and the beginning of the 20th century with an emphasis on the intrinsic interdependence between society and individuals. It developed as a political philosophy structured around the key concept of the commitment to the 'common good', spreading through the English-speaking world with the writings and influence of TH Green, FH Bradley, B Bosanquet, E Caird, H Jones, A Seth, DG Ritchie, JS Mackenzie, W Wallace, JME McTaggart, J Watson, JH Muirhead, RG Collingwood and M Oakeshott (PSA).

12   They propose an elaborate scheme concerning the philosophical foundations of politics that reconcile rights-recognition thesis with customary international law. The implication is that, since there is no governance at the international level to enforce a universal constitution, establishing which rules are genuinely universally binding is a discursive activity. This, in turn, is underpinned by customary rules of interpretation that are evidentially based on the practices of states, precedent and the opinions of jurisprudents.

13   For a detailed argument on the limits of foundational ethics as grounds for a theory that will operate effectively at international level, see Boucher (2009).

14   For instance, Gyekye (1992b) argues that it is liberal democracy, with its underlying philosophical framework of individualism that has been imposed on Africa, that has created distance between government and the governed. This in turn has engendered attitudes of indifference and insensitivity to the affairs of the state. This attitude opened the floodgates of bribery, corruption, carelessness about state enterprise, and unethical and antisocial behaviour.

References

Ake C (1993) Building on the indigenous. In P Fruhling (Ed.) *Recovery In Africa*. Stockholm: Swedish Ministry of Foreign Affairs

Ake C (1987) The African context of human rights. *Africa Today* 34: 5–12

Behrens K (2013) Two 'Normative' Conceptions of Personhood. *Quest* 25: 103–118

Bohler-Muller N (2015) Ubuntu as a 'receptor' for human rights: How rights can be understood as relationships. Paper presented at the Beijing Forum on Human Rights, Beijing (16–17 September)

Boucher D (2009) *The limits of ethics in international relations: Natural law, natural rights, and human rights in transition.* Oxford: Oxford University Press

Boucher D (2011) The recognition theory of rights: Customary international law and human rights. *Political Studies Association* 59: 753–771

Cobbah JAM (1987) African values and the human rights debate: An African perspective. *Human Rights Quarterly* 9: 309–331

Famakinwa JO (2010) How moderated is Kwame Gyekye's moderate communitarianism: Thought and practice. *Journal of the Philosophical Association of Kenya (PAK)* 2: 65–77

Gaus GF (2006) The Rights Recognition Thesis: Defending and Extending Green. In M Dimova-Cookson and WJ Mander (Eds), *T. H. Green: Ethics, Metaphysics, and Political Philosophy.* Oxford: Clarendon Press

Green TH (1917) *Lectures on the Principles of Political Obligation.* London: Longmans.

Gyekye K (1992a) Person and community in African thought. In K Wiredu and K Gyekye (Eds) *Person and community: Ghanaian philosophical studies.* Washington DC: Council for Research in Values and Philosophy

Gyekye K (1992b) Traditional political ideas: Their relevance to contemporary Africa. In K Wiredu and K Gyekye (Eds) *Person and community: Ghanaian philosophical studies.* Washington DC: Council for Research in Values and Philosophy

Gyekye K (1997) *Tradition and modernity: Philosophical reflections on the African experience.* New York: Oxford University Press

Harris P and Morrow J (Eds) (1986) *T. H. Green, Lectures on the Principles Political Obligation and Other Writings*, Cambridge University Press

Martin R (1993) *A System of Rights.* Oxford: Clarendon Press

Martin R (2001) TH Green on individual rights and the common good. In A Simhony and D Weinstein (Eds) *The new liberalism: Reconciling liberty and community.* UK: Cambridge University Press

Masolo DA (2004) Western and African communitarianism: A comparison. In K Wiredu (Ed.) *A companion to African philosophy.* USA: Blackwell Publishing

Matolino B (2009) Radicals versus moderates: A critique of Gyekye's moderate communitarianism. *South African Journal of Philosophy* 28: 160–170

Menkiti A (1984) Person and community in African traditional thought. In AR Wright (Ed.) *African Philosophy: An Introduction* (3rd ed.). New York: University of America Press

Metz T (2010) Human dignity, capital punishment, and an African moral theory: Toward a new philosophy of human rights. *Journal of Human Rights* 9: 81–99

Metz T (2011) Introduction: Engaging with the philosophy of DA Masolo. *Quest: An African Journal of Philosophy/Revue Africaine de Philosophie* 25: 1–238

Metz T (2012a) African conceptions of human dignity: Vitality and community as the ground of human rights. *Human Rights Review* 13: 19–37

Metz T (2012b) Developing African political philosophy: Moral-theoretic strategies. *Philosophia Africana* 14: 61–83

Metz T (2014) African values and human rights as two sides of the same coin: A reply to Oyowe. *African Human Rights Law Journal* 14: 36–321

Odhiambo ESA (2002) The cultural dimensions of development in Africa. *African Studies Association* 45(3): 1–6

Oyowe OA (2013) Strange bedfellows: Rethinking ubuntu and human rights in South Africa. *African Human Rights Law Journal* 13: 103–124

Oyowe OA (2014) An African conception of human rights: Comments on the challenges of relativism. *Human Rights Review* 15: 329–347

Teffo J (2004) Democracy, kingship, and consensus: A South African perspective. In K Wiredu (Ed.) *A companion to African philosophy*. USA: Blackwell Publishing

Wamala E (2004) Government by consensus: An analysis of a traditional form of democracy. In K Wiredu (Ed.) *A companion to African philosophy*. USA: Blackwell Publishing

Wiredu K (1990) An Akan perspective on human rights. In AA An-Na'im and FM Deng (Eds) *Human rights in Africa: Cross-cultural perspectives*. Washington DC: Brookings Institution

Wiredu K (2008) Social philosophy in post-colonial Africa: Some preliminaries concerning communalism and communitarianism. *South African Journal of Philosophy* 27(4): 332–339

6 | Post-conflict rehabilitation of the child: Psychology and the law in Africa

Azubike Onuora-Oguno and Sigrid Shaanika

The deep-rooted state of violence in many countries in Africa can be traced back to activities of the colonial powers, who used brutal practices to conquer the continent (Khapoya 2013). Post-colonial Africa has grown into a bedrock of violence, especially with the emergence and interference of the military in governance (King & Lawrence 2005). Most African states have experienced a civil war at one point or another in their history; the Central African Republic (CAR) and the Democratic Republic of the Congo (DRC) continue to experience violent conflicts, Boko Haram in Nigeria keeps on institutionalising ardent attacks on the girl child, while the activities of the Lord's Resistance Army (LRA) in Uganda continue to cause psychological trauma to children who are either conscripted as child soldiers or subjected to sexual violence (Schauer & Elbert 2010; Beard 2011), and desensitised through exposure to brutal acts. While violence exacerbates the challenges facing African states, the poor state of governance and disregard for the rule of law do not help.

In conflict situations, children often experience physical and emotional violence, sexual abuse, rape and exploitation (UNDOC 2014). Many boys are conscripted as child soldiers and are made to commit offences that adversely affect their emotional wellbeing (Schauer & Elbert 2010); girls are often used as sexual objects and domestic labourers in areas of conflict. The alarming rate of sexual violence, among other crimes, culminated in the Rome Statute of the International Criminal Court (ICC)—the world's first permanent criminal court—coming into effect in 2002. The Rwandan Tribunal and the Special Court for Sierra Leone are two ad hoc African tribunals that have been set up to investigate the aftermath of the violent conflicts that ravaged these countries. Both tribunals and the ICC emphasised the need to take cognisance of the integrity of the child, whether as a victim of or a witness to violence (Onuora-Oguno 2010). The greater vulnerability of the girl child has been emphasised by the United Nations Children's Fund (UNICEF) West Africa, which reports that the girl child remained the prime target of abductions during conflicts (UNICEF 2005). Mazurana and Carlson (2006) add that girl children's vulnerability was often exacerbated by forceful separation from the family as a result of an early and forced marriage. Given these facts, Madzima-Bosha (2013) called for greater focus on children in post-conflict rehabilitation processes.

Post-conflict rehabilitation includes psychological counselling and social reconstruction when conflict comes to an end. Psychological counselling is important for helping victims and survivors of crimes, especially rape victims, reorganise their lives and overcome their traumatic experiences (Ayinde 2008). Ayinde (2008) specifically emphasises the significance of psychotherapy in helping victims/ survivors of sexual offences reintegrate into society. Various psychotherapeutic approaches are proposed to help victims on both physical and mental levels.

Legal frameworks within which post-conflict rehabilitation takes place should be premised on a human-rights-based approach. For instance, to drive development as envisaged in the 2063 African Union (AU) agenda, effective healing processes must be well integrated and embedded into the legal frameworks of whichever organisation(s) undertake such work. Agenda 2063 is a policy document that stipulates seven broad aspirations of the AU. It speaks of inclusive growth in Africa, and this should include the emotional and mental wellbeing of each individual. The human rights ethos positions the individual at the centre of development processes and related policies.[1] Consequently, for development to be beneficial to people, structures, projects and policies that do not take into account human rights should be jettisoned, including policies and practices in the post-conflict rehabilitation process. Non-recognition of a rights-based approach in a post-conflict psychological process could amount to a breach of fundamental human rights, especially the rights to life and a habitable environment. The direct link between adequate psychological rehabilitation and the right to life is made by reason of a stable state of mind being a prerequisite for wellbeing. The right to life is not a right that stands on its own. A traumatised person often loses the ability to live a trauma-free life or to secure their livelihood.

This chapter uses a desktop study to interrogate legal frameworks that could contribute to the post-conflict rehabilitation of the African child. Among these are the Protocol of the African Charter on the Rights and Welfare of the Child (ACRWC) (1990), the Protocol to the African Charter on Human and Peoples' Rights (ACHPR) on the Rights of Women in Africa, better known as the Maputo Protocol (2003), and the Child Rights Convention (CRC) (1989). The purpose of this analysis is to find out the extent to which these existing documents enshrine the psychological protection of the African child in the aftermath of conflict situations. We query whether legal frameworks that protect the rights of the child take the psychological disposition of victims into account. Finally, we call for psychology to play a greater role vis-à-vis the human rights framework in Africa. We contend that this is necessary to achieve positive outcomes for the child victim, and in line with the continent's 'the Africa we want' aspirations.

In this chapter, we draw on the ecological theory of Bronfenbrenner (2004), which broadens our understanding of the influence of the child's sociocultural background on their development. The theory focuses on individual experiences, and thus falls within the ambit of the human-rights-based approach. This places the individual at the centre of the process of human development, the objective being to protect and promote the person's rights. The analysis in this chapter likewise places the individual at the centre of the various phases of post-conflict recovery. It explains the impact of the community[2] on the mental wellbeing of a child by recognising the interconnectedness and mutual influence of the individual and the community in conflict formation and/or post-conflict rehabilitation. And healing and psychological recovery can take place only when both the individual and their environment are targeted (Bronfenbrenner 1994).

First, we examine the protection of the child at global and African regional levels, then we make a case for a psychological approach to post-conflict rehabilitation, pointing out the challenges of using psychological counselling in rehabilitation and accountability processes in Africa. We conclude by recommending a pragmatic approach to the better rehabilitation of the child in a post-conflict African context.

Protecting the psychological wellbeing of the child as part of a post-conflict rehabilitation: A global perspective

Recognising the vulnerability of the child in international law led to the United Nations (UN) establishing the Convention on the Rights of the Child (CRC) in 1989. The preamble of the treaty says, 'it is essential for every child to grow up in a loving family environment for the full and harmonious development of his or her personality.' The Convention emphasises the need for UN states parties 'to recognise the right of every child to a standard of adequate living for the child's physical, mental, spiritual, moral and social development.'[3] The CRC enshrines several provisions geared towards the best interests of the child, for example the right to be safe and the right to health and education services, among others. To ensure that the rights of the child are well protected, the CRC was put in place to receive complaints against states; to report on the situations of the child in the different states; and to mandate states to provide alternative interventions in improving the protection of the rights of the child.

To this effect, the CRC has issued general comments that further clarify the issue of the protection of the rights of the child (Detrick 1999). Article 19 of the CRC is of particular interest to the focus of this paper:

1. [UN states parties] shall take all appropriate legislative, administrative, social and educational measures to protect the child from all forms of physical or mental violence, injury or abuse, neglect or negligent treatment, maltreatment or exploitation, including sexual abuse, while in the care of parent(s), legal guardian(s) or any other person who has the care of the child.

2. Such protective measures should, as appropriate, include effective procedures for the establishment of social programmes to provide necessary support for the child and for those who have the care of the child, as well as for other forms of prevention and for identification, reporting, referral, investigation, treatment and follow-up of instances of child maltreatment described heretofore, and, as appropriate, for judicial involvement.[4]

The words 'to protect the child from mental violence' are particularly noteworthy. In our view, the need exists for clear guidelines on the post-conflict mental rehabilitation of children. And such guidelines must take a victim-centred rather than a system-centred approach.

The Rome Statute of the ICC captures the protection of the victim as follows:

> The Court shall take appropriate measures to protect the safety, physical and psychological wellbeing, dignity and privacy of victims and witnesses. In so doing, the Court shall have regard to all relevant factors, including age, gender ... and health, and the nature of the crime, in particular, but not limited to, where the crime involves sexual or gender violence or violence against children. The Prosecutor shall take such measures particularly during the investigation and prosecution of such crimes. These measures shall not be prejudicial to or inconsistent with the rights of the accused and a fair and impartial trial.[5]

To further promote best practice, the ICC continues to develop guidelines that support the protection of the best interests of victims in the criminal justice system.[6] While these may not be perfect, it is commendable that the psychological wellbeing of victims is protected in rehabilitation processes (Onuora-Oguno 2010; Ingadottir, Ngendahayo & Sellers 2015). Recounting experiences of prosecution in the International Criminal Tribunal for Yugoslavia (ICTY), Wald (2001: 108) says:

> It is not possible to recount in any shorthand way the victims' experiences: the physical or emotional horrors they lived through; the ruination of their lives, families, and communities; and the residues of hate, hopelessness and despair.

Two gaps exist when it comes to protecting victims: first, constant direct threats to the victim and family members; and second, protracted trials of perpetrators, which inevitably means the victim's psychological trauma is prolonged. Wald (2001: 109) explains:

> One witness openly pled with the court to stop the accused from threatening her with his eyes. At other times, watching and listening, it seems to me that the witness grows impatient with the trial process. Some express a humbling confidence that we will bring justice to their suffering. Others seem to find their courtroom experience with its stress on legal subtleties anti-climactic and frustrating.

While the law makes definite attempts to alleviate the situation, Wald's findings point to a gap that calls for attention. Oosterveld (2005) agrees, saying protecting the child psychologically does not necessarily ensure a victim's mental stability.

Protecting the psychological wellbeing of a child in a post-conflict context: An African perspective

Protecting children remains a major concern in Africa. Because of this, various regional treaties that specifically provide for the protection of the child have come into effect. Among the many provisions contained in the treaties are the protection of victims of trafficking and other dangerous child-related occurrences (Ebobrah 2010). The girl child is considered more vulnerable, and therefore receives special protection; the AU's Protocol to the African Charter on Human and Peoples' Rights on the Rights of Women in Africa, or the Maputo Protocol of 2003, calls on states parties to ensure programmes intended to rehabilitate female victims are implemented.[7] The parties to the Protocol are thus required to provide

... necessary support to victims of harmful practices through basic services such as health services, legal and judicial support, emotional and psychological counselling, as well as vocational training to make them self-supporting.[8]

It is important that post-conflict rehabilitation is executed efficiently so that a positive result can be assured for the African child. So, it is necessary to adopt psychological intervention models that are context-appropriate and use multidisciplinary approaches (Pells 2012). Unfortunately, the use of inappropriate counselling methods continues to dominate rehabilitation processes on the continent, resulting in calls for reform (De Bethune 2009). In post-conflict Liberia, for instance, trauma counselling has been recommended as a core component of the reintegration programme, along with psychological support, so that sustainable peace, security and human development may be achieved (Awodola 2009: 19). Positive results are possible, provided both psychological and legal interventions take into account local contexts.

The AU's 1990 African Charter on the Rights and Welfare of the Child (ACRWC) does not make specific mention of the post-conflict rehabilitation of the child, though it does allude to what is expected of states parties in case of armed conflicts. It is discouraging that the charter does not mention the psychological protection of the child. However, Article 5 stipulates that states parties should ensure, to the greatest extent possible, the survival, protection and development of the child.[9] The interpretations of the words 'survival' and 'development' could be interpreted as covering the rehabilitation of the child, which would allow for synergy between law and psychology. We are of the view that the process of psychological rehabilitation should primarily ensure that a child who has been a victim of armed conflict is able to find a way to survive and seek further development. Structures are needed that will ensure access to quality education as well as other services that will allow effective community reorientation and positive integration.

Mental health and stability will be further fortified by adequate housing. Article 24 of ACRWC says that 'all peoples shall have the right to a general satisfactory environment favourable to their development.'[10] It is necessary to take psychological factors into account and to cater for the mental development and wellbeing of the African child if the continent is to achieve its Agenda 2063 aspirations.

The case for a psychological approach to post-conflict rehabilitation

In the opening paragraph of the Preface to the AU Policy on Post-Conflict Reconstruction and Development (PCRD) adopted in Banjul in 2006, Djinnit says Africa has done commendable work in resolving the continent's conflicts. Yet, an alarming number of Africans are still victims of conflict. He said:

By the turn of the 21st century...it was also obvious that the peace achieved was fragile and could not be sustained in the long term so long as the underlying causes and the needs of the affected populations were not effectively addressed.[11]

Conflict that breeds violence in Africa extends to intra-community, interfamily, intertribal, domestic and interpersonal violence, terrorism, the omission of state and community to respond to human rights violations, pre- and post-election violence, prejudicially stimulated conflicts such as interreligious conflicts, attacks on minority groups such as lesbian, gay, bisexual, transgender, and/or intersex (LGBTI) people, as well as physical abuse and sexual violence targeted at other vulnerable groups (Jimenez 2012; Rudolph 2015).

Post-conflict reformation and reconstruction, along with the recovery and rehabilitation of victims of violence, should be prioritised, especially when considering the extent to which individual and societal wellbeing and development are intertwined. The relationship between a victim and their community can either help or hinder their condition, and interaction between individual and community is the pillar on which community stability rests (Haferkam & Smelser 1992; Bloomfield, Barnes & Huyse 2003). A psycho-legal framework is needed to inform post-conflict rehabilitation. To this end, the PCRD recommends that AU states parties adopt policies that establish structures and processes that would comprehensively and decisively meet the recovery and reconstruction needs of countries and communities emerging from conflict. For instance, parties to the policy document are encouraged to pursue integrated approaches to the repatriation, resettlement, reintegration and rehabilitation of refugees and the internally displaced, as well as ex-combatants and their families, paying close attention to child victims of violence.[12]

The need to sustain protection of the rights of the child has also been flagged as a major issue. The AU, furthermore, encourages parties to the policy document to design programmes that address the specific needs of the girl child, along with programmes that target victims of sexual abuse and gender-based violence, among other measures.[13] States also need to develop programmes that provide psychosocial support and allow families to reunite.[14] The PCRD has established benchmarks and standards for humanitarian/emergency activities, which include appropriate medical-care services, trauma counselling and legal assistance for the girl child, women and other vulnerable groups.[15] Children who have suffered and continue to suffer from the effects of violent conflict must receive special attention.[16] The Maputo Protocol highlights the need for states parties to provide accessible, accurate and relevant services for victims of gender-based violence, while the African Youth Charter (AYC) of 2006 recommends that states parties take appropriate measures to promote the physical and psychological recovery and social reintegration of young victims of armed conflict. The Protocol further recommends that the state provides access to counselling and rehabilitation services to victims who have suffered or continue to suffer abuse and sexual harassment; the state should also integrate gender sensitisation and human rights education at all levels of education, including at teacher training level.

The AU's African Charter on Human and Peoples' Rights (ACHPR) distinguishes the African cultural and human rights system from systems existing elsewhere. It embraces the importance of collaborative intervention between the individual, the community and the state when promoting, protecting and preserving the lives and human rights of people subjected to violence.[17] This indicates an acknowledgement of the principle that the healing and psychological recovery in a post-conflict situation needs to target both the individual and their environment. A person's sociopolitical context affects their perception of self and influences expectations about the future and the healing process needed to attain balance in their affective, cognitive and spiritual inner functions (Nancy & Cole 2001: 25–26). Not only will child victims of conflict benefit if communities mobilise to support their recovery and reintegration into society, but so will the entire society, with the social, economic and political networks it consists of (Nancy & Cole 2001: 24). Greater benefits follow when a healed individual begins to contribute meaningfully to the community. This has an impact on the group's resource development, especially in times when the main goal is the reconstruction of the community. Research has found that the collective reconstruction of a community has the power to unite members as they heal (Nancy & Cole 2001: 32), because the community, as the locus of recovery and reintegration, gives a sense of belonging to war-affected individuals (Nancy & Cole 2001: 24).

Given the significance of the connection between the individual and their sociocultural background, a combination of approaches is needed to meet the complex and unique needs of a conflict-traumatised child (Kaminer & Eagle 2010). Flexibility, eclecticism and multidimensional thinking would characterise a complex, victim-centred approach to rehabilitation. It would also need to be tailored to the needs of a given cultural system. After his missionary experiences in various parts of Africa, Juma (2011: 39) wrote:

> It seems as if there are two distinct ways in which people deal with illness. One class, mainly the educated and middle class, emphasises pharmacology or Western medically oriented approaches, while the vast majority of traditional Africans predominantly use traditional healing.

Speaking particularly of South Africa, he observed:

> The kind of healing that most South Africans are inclined to embrace is one that relates to the ubuntu worldview, a collective existence as opposed to the imported European ethos on the principle of individual survival. Most Africans in their cultural and religious beliefs would embrace a counselling approach that makes their family members (extended relations, deceased or alive), their belief systems and nature around them part and parcel of the healing process and the solution to their problem. (Juma 2011: 9)

Nancy and Cole (2001: 19), similarly, argue that the individualistic approach to trauma treatment may not be culture-appropriate in African countries, considering the communal nature of African societies. So, it is not just the individual that needs to be healed in the African society, but the family and community as a whole. Many Western-style interventions have been found inadequate for the needs of African societies (Juma 2011: 10). Because Western rehabilitation techniques do not recognise the multicultural diversity within the African context, they cannot effectively respond to the diverse needs of the people. The indiscriminate use of Western rehabilitation methods adversely affects the quality of services offered to victims of violence (Juma 2011: 4). The rehabilitation and restoration of physical and mental health within African cultural systems clearly lie within the social, cultural and historical context of each affected community (Juma 2011: 50). Not only may failure to consider the sociocultural context and belief systems lead to misunderstandings and misdiagnosis, they may, in fact, work against healing (Juma 2011: 6). The inference drawn here is that incomplete healing processes could possibly even result in the absence of positive change in the society. This may include, but not be limited to, lapses in structure, and interpersonal and group relationships. A positive and holistic healing process in African communities must take into account individual as well as group healing (Nancy & Cole 2001: 27).

Challenges to post-conflict rehabilitation in Africa

Having established the link between the individual and the community in the healing process, we have to consider some unique challenges in the ecological approach to post-conflict rehabilitation in Africa. Many challenges hinder psychological intervention among Africans, none as pervasive as the culture of silence and shame when it comes to sexual violence within families, communities and social institutions such as schools and churches. The veil of silence obstructs the implementation of state and regional mechanisms that exist to protect the victims of violence. For instance, it still remains difficult lawfully to prosecute perpetrators of domestic violence (Onuora-Oguno 2010). As a result, family members who need protection are subjected to prolonged trauma.

Another obstacle is the general disregard for psychology, which is considered a Western concept (Juma 2011; Daniel 2013). As a result, existing legal frameworks engaged in post-conflict rehabilitation rarely take advantage of the discipline. Introducing psychology into education systems would help demystify the discipline and grow the cohort of adequately trained professionals.

A further challenge involves the religious beliefs of African societies. Religion champions forgiveness, mostly at the expense of the individual's psychological wellbeing. Typically, a victim is coerced into demonstrating forgiveness towards the perpetrator, disregarding the victim's state of mental and emotional trauma, and neglecting to provide the appropriate psychological help that could eventually lead to forgiveness. Unresolved trauma can therefore shatter an individual's sense of belonging, their spiritual wellbeing and their purpose in life. Such unresolved trauma has been described as a 'survivor's mission' (Herman 2001).

Conclusion

This chapter examined the post-conflict rehabilitation of the African child and the extent to which legal systems accommodate psychology in this regard. We established that laws existing within African human rights systems, along with universal human rights laws, have mechanisms to protect child victims. However, we discovered several obstacles to applying the laws to bring about traumatised children's psychological wellbeing practically. Furthermore, we learnt that an overreliance on the Western approach to mental health is not appropriate in the African context, within which a more communal and holistic approach would conform better to the structure and functioning of African societies. That said, taking the recommended ecological approach brings its own set of cultural and religious challenges when it comes to the post-conflict rehabilitation of African children.

Recommendations

Based on our findings, we make the following recommendations:

1. African victims of violence need contextualised rehabilitation treatment delivered by well-trained psychologists who understand the specific cultural needs of African people. The academic curricula for psychology training programmes should be overhauled to target the conditions and realities of the victims of violence in Africa.
2. To complement the efforts of formal reform and rehabilitation structures, establishing grassroots community centres and focus groups could present a good start. Leaders and instructors in schools, religious communities and other social contexts should engage in progressive training on how to identify signs of emotional dysfunction in individuals of all ages (Nancy & Cole 2001).
3. Considering the devastating effects of conflict on entire communities, a collective understanding of what is going on and the mutual agreement among community members about their future should help rebuild a destroyed sense of togetherness (Nancy & Cole 2001: 28).
4. Integrating rehabilitation processes into social spaces such as schools, places of worship, the media, and music and literature will increase awareness and lead to a greater acceptance of psychology as a means to mental wellbeing.
5. The expertise of individuals directly and indirectly involved in working with victims of conflict and trauma should be ensured. We recommend that psychology modules be made compulsory in law and paralegal education.

Notes

1   Paragraph 14 of the United Nations Declaration on the Rights to Development.
2   For the purposes of this work, community is described as a group of people with a 'shared notion of togetherness, united by common history of goal sharing and participating in activities, culture, ideology and communication' (Nancy & Cole 2001: 25).
3   Article 27 (1) of the Child Right Convention (1989).
4   Article 19 of the Child Right Convention (1989).
5   Article 68 of the Rome Statute of the International Criminal Court.
6   Article 43 (6) of the Rome Statute of the International Criminal Court.

7   Article 4(e) of the Maputo Protocol (2003).

8   Article 5(c) of the Maputo Protocol (2003).

9   Article 5(2) of the African Charter on the Rights and Welfare of the Child (1990).

10   Article 24 of the African Charter on the Rights and Welfare of the Child (1990).

11   Preface to the African Union Policy on Post-Conflict Reconstruction and Development (2006).

12   §25(a)(ii) of the African Union Policy on Post-Conflict Reconstruction and Development (2006).

13   §25(d)(iv) of the African Union Policy on Post-Conflict Reconstruction and Development (2006).

14   §25(d)(v) of the African Union Policy on Post-Conflict Reconstruction and Development (2006).

15   §30(f) of the African Union Policy on Post-Conflict Reconstruction and Development (2006).

16   §44 of the African Union Policy on Post-Conflict Reconstruction and Development (2006).

17   Article 29 of the African Charter on Human and Peoples' Rights.

References

ACHRR (African Charter on Human and Peoples' Rights) (1986). Accessed October 2015, www.humanrights.se/wp-content/uploads/2012/01/African-Charter-on-Human-and-Peoples-Rights.pdf

ACRWC (African Charter on the Rights and Welfare of the Child) (1990). Accessed October 2015, www.unicef.org/esaro/African_Charter_articles_in_full.pdf

AYC (African Youth Charter) (2006). Accessed November 2015, www.thepresidency.gov.za/docs/african_youth_charter.pdf

Awodola F (2009) Trauma counselling and psychological care for former Liberian child soldiers. In W Vandenhole and Y Weyns (Eds) Rehabilitation and reintegration of war-affected children. Conference report. Accessed October 2015, www.law.kuleuven.be/linc/nieuws/RRWAC_Conference_Report.pdf

Ayinde OA (2008) Psychological techniques in helping rape victims. *Edo Journal of Psychology* 1(1): 128–136

Beard M (2011) The children of northern Uganda: The effects of civil war. *Global Majority E-Journal* 2(1): 4–18

Bloomfield D, Barnes T and Huyse L (Eds) (2003) *Reconciliation after violent conflict: A handbook*. Sweden: International IDEA

Bronfenbrenner U (1994) Ecological models of human development. *International Encyclopedia of Education* (Vol 3) (2nd edition). Oxford: Elsevier

De Bethune S (2009) Challenges to rehabilitation in war-affected settings. In W Vandenhole & Y Weyns (Eds) Rehabilitation and reintegration of war-affected children. Conference report. Accessed October 2015, www.law.kuleuven.be/linc/nieuws/RRWAC_Conference_Report.pdf

Daniel K (2013) Analysis of the importance of psychology today in Africa. *Global Journal of Human Social Science: Arts, Humanities and Psychology* 13(3): 21–25

Detrick S (1999) *A commentary on the United Nations Convention on the Rights of the Child.* Netherlands: Martinus Nijhoff Publishers

Ebobrah S (2010) Human rights developments in African sub-regional economic communities during 2009. *African Human Rights Law Journal* 10(12): 233–253

Egbewole WO and Onuora-Oguno AC (2014) Impunity and justice in Nigeria: Weeping for the innocent, extra-judicial killings on the rise. *University of Benin Law Journal* 15(1): 63–77

Haferkamp H and Smelser NJ (Eds) (1992) *Social change and modernity.* Berkeley: University of Berkeley: California Press

Herman JL (2001) *Trauma and recovery* (3rd revised edition). New York: Pandora Basic Books

Ingadottir T, Ngendahayo F and Sellers PV (2015) The International Criminal Court the victims and witnesses unit (article 43.6 of the Rome Statute). Discussion paper. Accessed November 2015, www.vrwg.org/downloads/publications/02/PICTVWUMar2000.pdf

Jimenez X (2012) *Gender perspectives in United Nations peacekeeping operations.* Williamsburg: Peace Operations Training Institute

Juma JO (2011) *African worldviews: Their impact on psychopathology and psychological counselling.* Accessed November 2017, http://uir.unisa.ac.za/bitstream/handle/10500/5760/thesis_juma_mhm_.pdf?sequence=1

Kaminer D and Eagle G (2010) *Traumatic stress in South Africa.* Johannesburg: Wits University Press

Khapoya VB (2013) *A new book: The African experience.* Oakland State University: Pearson

King G and Lawrence V (2005) *Africa, a continent in crisis: The economic and social implications of civil war and unrest among African nations.* Accessed October 2015, web.stanford.edu/class/e297a/Africa,a%20Continent%20in%20Crisis%20-%20The%20Economic%20and%20Social%20Implications%20of%20Civil%20War%20and%20Unrest%20Among%20African%20Nations.doc

Lansdown G (2011) *Every child's right to be heard: A resource guide on the UN committee on the rights of the child.* London: Save the Children UK

Madzima-Bosha T (2013) The effects of conflict are felt hardest by women and children. Accessed January 2017, www.insightonconflict.org/blog/2013/05/effects-conflict-women-children/

Mazurana D and Carlson K (2006) The girl child and armed conflict: Recognizing and addressing grave violations of girls' human rights. Accessed January 2017, www.un.org/womenwatch/daw/egm/elim-disc-viol-girlchild/ExpertPapers/EP.12%20Mazurana.pdf

Nancy F and Cole JB (2001) Community as a context of healing: Psychological recovery of children affected by war and political violence. *International Journal of Mental Health* 30(4): 19–41

Onuora-Oguno AC (2011) My witness becomes hostile: National and supra-national criminal justice systems examined. *Madonna University Law Journal* 1: 70–93

Onuora-Oguno AC (2010) Personal liberty and domestic violence: Any legal respite in Nigeria. *University of Ilorin Law Journal* 6: 18–31

Oosterveld V (2005) Gender-sensitive justice and the International Criminal Tribunal for Rwanda: Lessons learned for the International Criminal Court. *New England Journal of International and Comparative Law* 12(1): 119–133

OHCHR (Office of the High Commissioner for Human Rights) (2015) Committee on the rights of child reporting. Accessed November 2015, www.ohchr.org/EN/HRBodies/CRC/Pages/CRCIndex.aspx

PCRD (Policy on Post-Conflict Reconstruction and Development) (2006). Accessed October 2016, www.peaceau.org/uploads/pcrd-policy-framwowork-eng.pdf

Pells K (2012) We have life without living: Addressing the legacies of genocide for Rwanda's children and youth. Accessed November 2015, www.law.kuleuven.be/linc/nieuws/RRWAC Conference_Report.pdf

Rome Statute of the International Criminal Court (2002). Accessed October 2015, www.icc-cpi.int/nr/rdonlyres/ea9aeff7-5752-4f84-be94 0a655eb30e16/0/rome_statute_english.pdf

Rudolph JR (2015) Encyclopedia of modern ethnic conflicts. Accessed November 2015, www.docslide.us/documents/encyclopedia-of-modern-ethnic-conflicts.html

Schauer E and Elbert T (2010) The psychological impact of child soldiering. Accessed October 2015, www.usip.org/sites/default/files/missing-peace/The%20psychological%20impact%20 of%20child%20soldiering%20-%20Schauer.pdf

The Maputo Protocol: Protocol to the African Charter on Human and People's Rights on the Rights of Women in Africa (2011). Accessed October 2016, www.achpr.org/files/instruments/women-protocol/achpr_instr_proto_women_eng.pdf

UNICEF (United Nations Children's Fund) West Africa (2005) The impact of conflict on women and girls in West and Central Africa and the UNICEF response. Accessed January 2017, www.unicef.org/emerg/files/Impact_conflict_women.pdf

UNDOC (United Nations Office on Drugs and Crime) (2014) *Strengthening crime prevention and criminal justice responses to violence against women.* New York: UN. Accessed October 2015, www.unodc.org/documents/justice-and-prison-reform/Strengthening_Crime_Prevention_and_Criminal_Justice_Responses_to_Violence_against_Women.pdf

Wald PM (2001) The International Criminal Tribunal for the former Yugoslavia comes of age: Some observations on day-to-day dilemmas of an international court. *Journal of Law & Policy* 5: 87–118

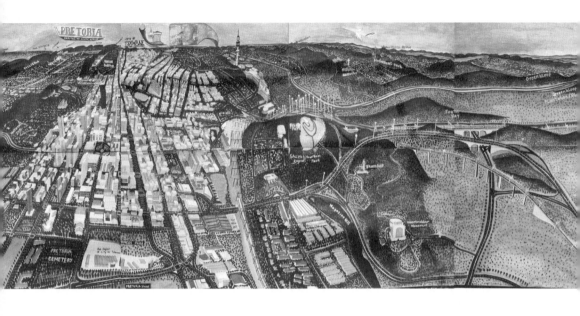

PART 3

AN AFRICA WITH A STRONG CULTURAL
IDENTITY, COMMON HERITAGE,
SHARED VALUES AND ETHICS

7 | Political leadership and cultural identity

Natasha Katuta Mwila

An Africa with a strong cultural identity, common heritage,
shared values and ethics

– Aspiration 5, Agenda 2063: The Africa We Want
(AUC 2015)

The fifth aspiration of the African Union Commission's Agenda 2063: The Africa We Want focuses on the benefits to be gained from Africa's unique attributes in culture and heritage, based on a system of shared values and ethics. These attributes are envisioned as being critical to uniting the continent strategically. This chapter asserts that achieving the other six aspirations of the African Union's Agenda 2063 hinges on the achievement of Aspiration 5.

Agenda 2063: The Africa We Want

Aspirations

Aspiration 1: A prosperous Africa based on inclusive growth and sustainable development

Aspiration 2: An integrated continent, politically united, based on the ideals of Pan-Africanism and the vision of Africa's Renaissance

Aspiration 3: An Africa of good governance, democracy, respect for human rights, justice and the rule of law

Aspiration 4: A peaceful and secure Africa

Aspiration 5: An Africa with a strong cultural identity, common heritage, shared values and ethics

Aspiration 6: An Africa where development is people-driven, unleashing the potential of its women and youth

Aspiration 7: Africa as a strong, united and influential global player and partner

With the history of the continent being as diverse as it is, much of the unification in culture, heritage, values and ethics would have to start at country level before Aspiration 5 can be achieved.

The question of the roles that culture and heritage play in Africa's sustainable development has never been more prominent. Several scholars and policymakers have attempted to answer this question, putting forward several conclusions that strong culture and a preserved heritage contribute meaningfully to sustainable development (Nurse 2006; Owuor 2007; Breidlid 2009). The questions that have consequently emerged on the cultural front are: How is cultural identity formed? And what supports and what threatens the development of a strong cultural identity? This chapter reflects on these questions through a historical narrative analysis of cultural development in Zambia.

The literature on social identity suggests that cultural identification forms an integral part of individual identity processes (Ennaji 2005; Pratt 2005). There are vagaries in how individuals come to identify with the various elements of culture. One proposition is that influential personalities in society have the capacity to mould the culture of their followers. One such group of personalities is political leaders.

Scholars are of the view that a strong association exists between cultural development and factors such as changes in political climate, economic trends, business development and education (James 2015). These factors may, in turn, be influenced by political leadership. It would follow, then, that stable patterns of political leadership, economic and business growth, and supportive education would lead to strong cultural identification. The inverse would, of course, also be true—namely that sporadic changes in political leadership, economic and business downturns, and poor educational frameworks would lead to the fragmentation of cultural identification and a consequent weak cultural identity. The cultural fabric of common heritage, shared values and ethics comes under threat where cracks in cultural identity emerge. Because policies about the economy, business development and education flow from political echelons, this chapter presents a political perspective on the second scenario, in which political instability results in a weak cultural identity.

Much of Zambian society has been historically paternalistic in its culture (Borrego & Johnson III 2011; Falola & Jean-Jacques 2015). Male individuals are identified not only as the 'head of the house' but also as 'fathers', 'providers' and 'teachers'. These monikers have found their way into political leadership and will be interrogated to unpack their impact on cultural development. I will explore how various Zambian political leaders have enacted these identities in politics, the economy, business development and education over various eras of political leadership. The political leaders included in this chapter are those who held the title of 'President of the Republic of Zambia' during the first 50 years of Zambia's independence, from 1964 to 2014. The chapter does take into account the fact that presidents have not been solely responsible for cultural development in the country; other political leaders such as ministers and permanent secretaries in various ministries have played their part in this respect. I focus on presidents because they are most visible in the implementation of national decisions affecting cultural development and, more often than not, they appoint the political leaders who serve alongside them.

The rise of the 'head of the house' in pre-independence Zambia: In-group versus out-group cultural development

Northern Rhodesia, as Zambia was known before independence, came into being in 1911 as a protectorate of the British Government (Brownlie & Burns 1979). The relatively few European settlers who occupied the country introduced race-based class distinctions that were instrumental in the development of an 'us (Africans) versus them (Europeans)' narrative. The 'colour bar' consisted of a number of divisive, race-based practices that included the *chitupa* (a requirement for Africans to have a pass when moving anywhere across the country), lower wages for Africans, job reservation in favour of Europeans, separate shopping and public transport facilities, residential areas, and health and education systems (Tembo 2012). This form of race-based separation was not unique to Northern Rhodesia. It was commonplace in many British territories in Africa at the time, including South Africa, Southern Rhodesia (present-day Zimbabwe), British East Africa (present-day Kenya) and South-West Africa (present-day Namibia). Prior to this era, tribal divisions were also commonplace in Northern Rhodesia, but when the settlers arrived, tribal differences appeared to be set aside. The cultural identity of the country's indigenous people was rooted in the shared heritage of being black Africans and sharing the hardships of territory loss and the limited freedoms that the colonial era brought. Race-based class distinctions had a distressing effect on culture, an issue analysed later in the chapter.

Mining exploration led to the development of towns in the mineral-rich regions of the country (Limpitlaw 2011). This greatly changed not only the economic landscape, but also economic activities needed for survival in the new economic climate, which, in turn, created a new class among the indigenous population. The new class emerged as indigenes moved from their rural, agrarian communities to work in the mines and developing towns for wages (Burdette 1984; Goudie & Neyapti 1999). This wave of migration compelled the rural-urban migrants to adopt some of the cultural cues of the perceived upper-class Europeans. These cultural cues included the English language, British education, Christian religion, English first names, and British dress codes and etiquette (Tembo 2012). These cues were not simply adopted to establish a sense of belonging; they were a prerequisite for participation in the new economy. Indigenous individuals who adopted these cues gained an identity as belonging to an urban upper class. Some members of the new class emerged from a cohort of Africans sponsored for education abroad. Exposure to foreign places, cultures and people further permeated the distinction of these individuals from their rural counterparts. This, in turn, resulted in the development of greater inferiority complexes in the identities of the rural indigenous population, as the educated sought more rights for themselves as an esteemed class (Abdi et al. 2010).

The new African elite became the figures of hope for a better future. They became the resource for advice and direction for the rural populace, sometimes replacing traditional leaders as authorities. African representation in government largely comprised individuals from this new class, further reinforcing their social identity as 'the head of the house'—those in charge of setting the agenda for the rural population.

The self-identity of a few indigenous Africans as belonging to the class of the African elite inspired participation in political life, enterprise and education. Many members of the new class responded to their role as 'the head of the house' and felt it was their responsibility to establish their own churches and political parties in opposition to European rule. Religion and politics became characteristic of the culture at that time.

It was during this era that Kenneth David Kaunda emerged as a political leader.

Kenneth David Kaunda: Transitioning towards humanism and 'One Zambia, One Nation'

Kaunda, whose father was a Christian missionary and a teacher, inherited access to the elite class of Africans in Northern Rhodesia, with the requisite cultural cues for class distinction, namely religion, language and education. He went on to become an upper-primary school teacher and eventually headmaster in his career, and a choirmaster at church. His extensive participation in African politics and overseas travel to meet with renowned leaders of freedom move-ments like Martin Luther King Jr solidified his identity as the nation's founder, or the 'father of the nation'. He led the country to independence in 1964, when it became known as Zambia.

As the 'father of the nation', Kaunda was looked to as the reconciler of the divided indigenes and provider of the Zambian people's needs. As a reconciler, he promoted an ideology of humanism with the motto 'One Zambia, One Nation' presented to the Zambian people in 1969 (APRM 2015). This ideology is still considered an important feature of what Zambian culture ought to be. It reduced perceptions of class gaps and bridged the differences among Zambia's many tribes.[1] It embraced the philosophy of extending help to others, consistent with which Kaunda supported several African nations in their fights for independence. Kaunda's institutionalising a one-party state, in which his party was the only one not outlawed, was also aligned with the 'One Zambia, One Nation' motto. His father persona meant his actions went largely unopposed. In his role as provider, Kaunda decided on a planned economy and went about reclaiming economic assets from foreign controllers (Abdi et al. 2010). The business landscape was characterised by parastatal entities, and government was the largest employer. Other features of the business environment included price controls and food subsidies—all targeted towards making the cost of living affordable for Zambians.

Kaunda believed in education as a pathway to true liberation and reprised his role as teacher through heavy investment in education systems and institutions across the nation. Zambian participation in the education sector blossomed during this period and academic aspiration became a feature of Zambian culture.

While the human development of Zambians significantly improved in this era compared with the last, this period is associated with a culture of Zambian people's overreliance and dependence on government and its political leadership. This era was all about entitlement, with most people feeling they had suffered enough before independence and now was the time to enjoy their freedoms and be well provided for by the government.

Many of Kaunda's achievements were enabled by nationalisation policies that unfortunately coincided with the economic downturn of the 1970s (Juang & Morrissette 2008). The Zambian economic slump resulted in high levels of dissent and dissatisfaction among citizens as their 'father' had failed to provide for their needs in a manner to which they had become accustomed. Several economic stakeholders of Zambia blamed Kaunda's authoritarian approach to governance for the downturn, advocating instead multi-partisan politics.

Many Zambians believed that Kaunda had secret informants, the *shushushu*, who would report any thought of disloyalty to his government, and that ruthless action would be taken to silence dissenters (Sardanis 2014). Allegations of manipulation, intimidation and violence against any opposition created an environment of distrust. 'One Zambia' became divided yet again.

Frederick Jacob Titus Chiluba: Transitioning to multi-partisan democracy

Chiluba represented the Movement for Multi-Party Democracy as presidential candidate in the first multi-partisan elections, winning in 1991 and signalling the end of the Kaunda era. He was largely regarded as a hero who was able to fend off the Kaunda forces and emerge victorious. He led a cultural shift in the Zambian perspective of liberation rooted in democratic principles and political freedom.

These principles also applied to liberalising the economy, a process characterised by mass privatisation (Houngnikpo & Kyambalesa 2012). What unsuspecting Zambians did not know was that this would end in the loss of jobs and state benefits, which characterised the Kaunda era. This unfamiliar level of discomfort created further distrust in the already shaky system. Many people regarded Chiluba's philosophy as one that discouraged a dependence on the state and advocated individual hard work. Critics ascribed the motto 'every man for himself, God for us all' to Chiluba's cultural perspective. This ideology is also thought to be the underlying cause of the high levels of corruption and bribery associated with the Chiluba era. And, while it is credited with having stimulated an independent business culture, it is unclear whether independent business activity emerged through conscious innovative efforts, or simply in response to the uncertainties about employment. Whatever the cause, business participation, particularly at the informal level, today still characterises Zambian culture.

In the mid-1990s, Chiluba declared Zambia a Christian nation (Phiri 2003). This proved to spark a degree of unity among people who were conflicted about three issues—they were happy to be in a democratic environment, resentful over the lack of improvement in their welfare despite democracy, and in doubt as to whether they should have given the father of the nation another chance to resolve the country's problems. The religious position reinforced religious affinity in the colonial era and has been carried through to present-day cultural identity. However, it has been a subject of contention in as far as having it spelled out in the country's constitution (Van Klinken 2015). Critics fear that a religious declaration will undermine the strides made towards tolerance and unity in Zambia, because it takes a strong and aggressive position on human rights issues such as homosexuality. Furthermore, it does not acknowledge religions other than the Christian doctrine.

The Chiluba government made little effort towards maintaining and improving educational standards, and many educational institutions and reforms of the Kaunda era became dilapidated or fell into disuse. Many Zambians saw this as the outcome of having a leader who was a school dropout himself. The value of education seemed lost on most university graduates, who previously would have been assured employment in the Kaunda administration, but were now confronted with joblessness regardless of their level of education.

In contrast to the Kaunda era, during which political leadership was seen to be conservative and benevolent to the poor when it came to personal spending, Chiluba spent lavishly while the country descended into ever-greater depths of poverty. It was clear to many that those in political power were taking as much as they could while at the helm, because the newly gotten political uncertainty (in the age of plural politics and democracy) meant leadership wasn't guaranteed come election time. Rampant corruption soon followed across all spheres of Zambian life, including the non-politically affiliated. Uncertainty and a culture of corruption seemed to go hand in hand.

Motions for a third term of office for Chiluba, beyond the constitutional allowance of two terms, were met with heavy criticism and opposition, resulting in Levy Patrick Mwanawasa emerging as the new leader of the Movement for Multi-Party Democracy and his election as president of the country in 2002.

Levy Patrick Mwanawasa: Zero tolerance to corruption

Mwanawasa, a trained lawyer, was respected as a legal strongman during the days of opposition to Kaunda. He served as vice-president in the Chiluba adminis-tration and earned a reputation for integrity by quietly retreating from political life after a failed contest against Chiluba for party leadership. Chiluba's later endorsement of Mwanawasa as his successor seemed to reinforce Mwanawasa's good reputation, despite accusations made against the Chiluba government of manipulating the 2001 presidential elections, from which Mwanawasa emerged as president. Others, again, suspected that Mwanawasa was endorsed so that he could be used as a political puppet by the Chiluba regime—an opinion that would later be publicly debunked.

Mwanawasa quickly dissociated himself from the taint of corruption that had coloured the preceding administration by appointing several members of the opposition to his cabinet. This was a welcome initiative in the politically divided camps of Zambian society. The move also encouraged tribal unity, since Mwanawasa's cabinet did not appear to favour any one tribal group over another. He also launched a full-scale attack against his predecessor, Chiluba, for issues regarding corruption, even supporting calls to strip the former president of his immunity and subject him to court trials.

At a time when very few African leaders did so, Mwanawasa also openly criticised Zimbabwe's Robert Mugabe, a move that further established his reputation as a man of principle who is also without fear. With a slogan proclaiming that 'no one is above the law', Mwanawasa's zero-tolerance approach to corruption restored a level of trust among Zambians (Nchito 2015).[2] This boosted investor confidence and led to a revival in business. Although he attempted to revive the economy through reducing the national debt and addressing inflation growth, he did not make much progress in addressing the worsening poverty levels in the county. He also made little contribution to education. This disciplinarian did not succeed in satisfying Zambians' expectations of him as a 'provider' and neither would his successor, Rupiah Bwezani Banda, who assumed power upon Mwanawasa's death in office in 2008.

Rupiah Bwezani Banda: Undoing the 'good work'

Banda's extensive political experience and reputation as a successful diplomat and statesman in all three preceding administrations meant that Zambians had confidence in his capabilities as the country's leader. However, his leadership was characterised by frequent travel, personal business investments and allegations of abuse of office, corrupt practices and a plunder of national resources and revenue (Mbao 2011).

The Banda era commenced with a cloud of suspicion over the president's honesty and motives. He first assumed power as an interim president following the death of Mwanawasa. The transition period caused a great deal of anxiety and distrust for Zambians, who had heard rumours about Mwanawasa's hospitalisation in Paris while Banda had kept on reassuring people of their leader's good state of health.

Public sentiment holds that, even after being elected into power, Banda's inaction in any part of the country's development was noticeable. The profits from supposed government business deals did not reach the poor. Banda's friendship with Chiluba further dissatisfied the people, who believed he was undoing the good governance set in motion by Mwanawasa. What is more, they believed that Banda influenced Chiluba's acquittals on charges of corruption (Mbao 2011). The sun of accountability had apparently set on Zambia bringing a new dawn of corruption.

The continuing poverty set the stage for the emergence of a populist leader who promised to restore the dignity of Zambians through improved welfare. This personality was Michael Chilufya Sata, who became president of Zambia in 2011.

Michael Chilufya Sata: The 'man of action'

Michael Chilufya Sata has been dubbed a 'man of action' for his visible works in his role as Lusaka's District Governor during the Kaunda era (Larmer & Fraser 2007). Among other things, he was instrumental in overseeing several works of construction in the capital. Sata served in the Chiluba government, leaving an indelible mark on every portfolio for which he was responsible and earning himself the nickname King Cobra (Nchindila 2008). Eventually, he formed his own political party, the Patriotic Front.

Sata was revered as a servant of the Zambian people. His servant persona was rooted partly in his humble beginnings, which resonated with Zambians, most of whom lived in abject poverty. The fact that he had had a difficult start in life and had not advanced very far in his education made him relatable to sections of the population that may otherwise have felt sidelined. His pro-poor policies were well received domestically, even though they made him a figure of controversy in the international arena as he tabled radical resolutions to the state of poverty the country found itself in at the time (Mills & Herbst 2014).

Sata was lauded for his resilience, evident in his contesting the presidential seat repeatedly despite three consecutive defeats. His eventual win, on his fourth attempt, saw the dawn of a number of reforms in language and education that had implications for the cultural development of Zambia.

The official language of Zambia is English, a reminder of the country's British colonial past. However, an estimated 72 indigenous languages are spoken in the country. Sata sought reforms in language targeted at celebrating the indigenous heritage of Zambia's people. For Sata, and many other Zambians, language was an important part of cultural identity and essential in resolving the complexes inherited from the country's colonial past. He went about this by moving a motion to have a local languages policy in which indigenous languages would be the official languages of instruction at public schools (Sardanis 2014). Reactions towards this reform were mixed. Some felt that this was a retrogressive step, since students would not be able to compete on a global front where the English language continues to be a popular language of communication. For others, the debate revolved around the practicalities of educating not only students, but also the educators in using a different language of instruction. The need to translate educational material into the various indigenous languages complicated the matter even further.

From a cultural standpoint, a greater debate emerged—one with far-reaching consequences. With the country having a large number of languages and ethnic groups, many parts of the country do not have a dominant or common language that is understood by most inhabitants. Debates arose in Zambia's ten provinces over which language should be the official indigenous language for each geographic sector of the population. These debates escalated into turmoil in regions where some tribes have historically been at odds with one another. In the North-Western Province, for example, the question of which language should be the official indigenous language between Lunda and Luvale was a source of some upheaval. Rather than enhance a unifying cultural identity, the question of language reignited the flames of historical tribal divisions (Papstein 1989). This worked against the 'One Zambia, One Nation' philosophy the country had worked hard to uphold.

So, despite his reputation as the 'man of action', Michael Sata achieved very little prior to his death in office in 2014. His short legacy as president was evidenced only by his countrywide 're' exercise, namely renaming, redistricting and reprovincing (Chisala 2013),[3] which, in many ways, sought to unify the people by acknowledging iconic Zambian people and places. However, critics called this a sleek cover-up, by means of distraction, of his failure to deliver on his numerous pre-election promises.

The cultural evolution in Zambia

Looking at how the political environment in Zambia unfolded over the years teaches us that the national culture is prone to change where strong leaders are absent. It is particularly difficult to have one established national culture when so many ethnic groups exist in Zambia. Historically, fragmentation has been a characteristic of the Zambian cultural landscape. Cultural identity of Zambians was further undermined during the colonial era. Several cultural compromises had to be made because of socioeconomic pressures that required people to abandon their ways of life and adapt to new economic realities. As mentioned earlier, this economic survival entailed neglecting—in some instances, totally abandoning—the very essence of culture, language, religion, dress and other nuances of a way of life. This survival also necessitated resettling from rural farming areas to the growing mining towns. Studies have shown that resettlement can have a devastating effect on culture as it

> tears apart communities and disperses the fragments, disrupts patterns of social interaction and interpersonal ties, destabilises and renders useless integral reciprocal help networks, and scatters kin and other social groups…it destroys communities. The result is widespread…loss of cultural identity. (Fisher 1999: 29)

Fisher (1999) says cultural identity is rooted in historical geographical heritage. Moving away from their historical geographical sites has an impact on people's cultural identity. Since cultural identity is part of the individual, it moves with them when the person relocates. However, separation from the natural historical geographical site where the identity is formed also results in a change of the identity—even more so when the person is separated from like-minded people and is unable to practise the culture in the new environment.

The race-based class distinctions and accompanying oppression that featured during the colonial era caused psychological distress and mental health problems for the African population in Zambia (Rollock & Gordon 2000). This may account for the collective inferiority complex that prevailed at the time (King 2004), and sometimes still does to this day. An inferiority complex can make people discard their own culture in favour of the supposed superior one. Searching for favourable identification and trying to overcome a sense of inferiority, many Africans in Zambia turned to new religions and politics.

In their obsession with religion and politics, many Zambians saw Kaunda as a demigod; the biblical Moses of the era, there to deliver people from the hands of the Pharaoh—in this instance, the colonialists. Zambians believed that Kaunda could do no wrong. When he emerged as a founding father, the people may have taken the title 'father' too far, not least because he did what fathers generally do, namely provide for their children. Kaunda's socialist-driven largesse gave Zambians a sense of economic freedom, which they craved.

Some aspects of Kaunda's approach were worthwhile, especially the unifying legacy of his era. However, the economic legacy brought a descent into a lackadaisical comfort zone. One did not have to work too hard. Kaunda took care of all the basics—he reduced food prices and provided affordable primary education, among others. Zambians looked to Kaunda for education, employment and overall welfare—over-dependence became symptomatic of the culture.

The economic discomfort that followed the crash in copper prices in the 1970s—copper being Zambia's largest export earner—was all it took to set cultural growth on a different path. The economic downturn was characterised by severe food shortages. The passive Zambian woke up when their tummy rumbled. Distrust in the system soon followed and fragmentation occurred. The cultural transition was towards political pluralism and free market economics, heralding the Chiluba era. For the free market to benefit Zambians, they needed an entrepreneurial mindset to take the economy into their own hands. But this was not what the education of the Kaunda era enabled. The education system created potential employees, not potential employers—a characteristic that still prevails in the nation today. Doubly catastrophic for Zambians was when the free market and privatisation took away the security of guaranteed state employment. At this juncture, it became clear that neither the president nor the government was any Zambian's father, and that people would have to learn fast how to become self-reliant.

Any positives that may have been attributable to Chiluba's government were overshadowed by the damage caused by corruption. Chiluba supporters laud him for his privatisation efforts, which, they argue, minimised the inefficiencies of the economic system. Some scholars argue that privatisation sets the stage for corrupt practices (Sandholtz & Taagepera 2005) while others view corruption as a cultural outcome (Nye 1967; Husted & Instituto Tecnologico y de Estudios 1999; Paldam 2002).

When Mwanawasa came to power, the dirty laundry of the Chiluba era came out to be aired. This had a unifying effect, because it brought a sense of justice for the poor who had been robbed by the selfish actions of the preceding leadership. Zambian confidence in the leadership was back on track and ready for unity to be rebuilt. However, restoring unity was tripped up by inattention to the economic plight of the people, which caused agitation.

Banda's time worsened matters as people's agitation escalated. The unfortunate consequence of this spate of bad leadership was that corruption reared its head yet again. This time around, it was not the preserve of the higher echelons of political leadership only; it trickled down to the basic functions of everyday life.

Sata's election to power demonstrated an important change in Zambian cultural development. For the first time, people were able to resonate with a political leader—here was a leader who shared a background of poverty, one who was intimately familiar with people's personal hardships. This was in stark contrast to the political realities of earlier eras, represented by a highly educated and an internationally accomplished African elite. Selecting leaders was largely aspirational—people picked those to whom they could aspire. With a series of disappointments in this cohort, it was not surprising that people turned to the 'common man'. All they wanted, after all, was change. The untimely death of Sata, before the completion of even a single term in office, makes it difficult to determine his impact on Zambian culture.

Zambia's cultural transition

Zambian culture has passed through several phases, and some features of the cultural transition worked well together while others did not.

Colonial era: A national inferiority complex, religious fanaticism, political romanticism, socioeconomic divide

Kaunda era: Tolerance and unity, laissez-faire work ethic, overreliance on leadership for day-to-day solutions, blind trust, academic aspiration, sense of entitlement

Chiluba era: Scepticism, democracy, oriented towards enterprise rather than employment, informal entrepreneurship, religious intolerance, joblessness, corruption

Mwanawasa era: Rule of law, improved business environment, rebuilding of trust, abject poverty

Banda era: Corruption, distrust, lack of accountability, further abject poverty

Sata era: Representative leadership, hero-seeking

These features have occurred in a continuum across the eras. As young as independent Zambia is, some generations have lived through all the transitions and their cultural identity is therefore a complex suite of characteristics from each wave of cultural evolution. What can be concluded is that the state of Zambian culture is largely intertwined with the economic pulse of the nation.

The Zambian political story demonstrates a reciprocal relationship between the country's political leaders and the cultural influence that those leaders have on the people who elected them. People choose leaders they believe will best address their interests. The power and influence that come along with leadership mean that leaders can set the agenda and bring about shifts in cultural positions. It is vital, then, that the people have a solid understanding of what their cultural values are and should be. This is critical in ensuring that the leaders who serve them espouse and reinforce these values and, in so doing, enhance their cultural identity.

Conclusion

An old adage has it that 'if you do not know who you are, I will tell you who you are.' Another says, 'if you do not stand for anything, you will fall for everything.' These could not be more apt to conclude this chapter. Zambia's cultural evolution appears to be closely linked to and hampered by the inability of its people to establish who they really are and to define what they want from their leadership. Some blame can be attributed to the inferiority complex brought about by colonialism, which tore at the fabric of people's cultural identity. The long period of dictatorship could also be partly responsible, since it resulted in a population of a docile people who waited to be told what it meant to be Zambian.

Colonialism ended more than 50 years ago and dictatorial rule 25 years ago—yet, to this day, one crucial issue keeps Zambia from forming a strong national identity, with common heritage, shared values and ethics. The elephant in the room is the economic disparity that exists among Zambians. Most of them know the expression, 'Zambians think with their stomachs'. This goes to show how important economic welfare is for Zambians of all walks of life. As serious economic and political questions about corruption, the abuse of office and non-existent welfare go unanswered, the gap between the haves and the have-nots is widening. Class distinctions have never been more pronounced, prompting divergent perspectives on cultural values. The national identity of Zambians continues to be weak under poor political leadership.

Notes

1   Zambia Tourism (n.d.) Tribes in Zambia. Accessed October 2017, www.zambiatourism.com/about-zambia/people/tribes.

2   Nchito M, Transnational organised crime, its expansion into diverse areas of criminality and the role of the prosecutor. *International Association of Prosecutors*, 6 July 2015.

3   Chisala C, Michael Sata, the 'Re' President, *Zambian Watchdog*, 14 April 2013.

References

Abdi AA, Shizha E and Ellis L (2010) *Citizenship education and social development in Zambia: Research on education in Africa, the Caribbean and the Middle East*. Charlotte: Information Age Publishing

APRM (African Peer Review Mechanism) (2013) *APRM Country Review Report No 16—Republic of Zambia*

AUC (African Union Commission) (2015) *Agenda 2063: The Africa We Want*. Accessed December 2017, http://www.un.org/en/africa/osaa/pdf/au/agenda2063.pdf

Borrego E and Johnson III RG (2011) *Cultural competence for public managers: Managing diversity in today's world*. Boca Raton: CRC Press

Breidlid A (2009) Culture, indigenous knowledge systems and sustainable development: A critical view of education in an African context. *International Journal of Educational Development* 29(2): 140–148

Brownlie I and Burns IR (1979) *African boundaries: A land diplomatic encyclopaedia*. London: C Hurst & Co

Burdette MM (1984) The mines, class power, and foreign policy in Zambia. *Journal of Southern African Studies* 10(2): 198–218

Ennaji M (2005) *Multilingualism, cultural identity, and education in Morocco*. Berlin: Springer Science and Business Media

Falola T and Jean-Jacques D (2015) *Africa: An encyclopedia of culture and society*. Santa Barbara: ABC-CLIO

Fisher WF (1999) Going under: The struggle against large dams. *Cultural Survival Quarterly* 23(3): 29–32

Goudie A and Neyapti B (1999) *Development centre studies: Conflict and growth in Southern Africa* (Vol 3). Paris: OECD Publications

Houngnikpo MC and Kyambalesa H (2012) *Economic integration and development in Africa*. Farnham: Ashgate Publishing

Husted BW and Instituto Tecnologico y de Estudios (1999) Wealth, culture, and corruption. *Journal of International Business Studies* 30(2): 339–359

James P (2015) Despite the terrors of typologies: The importance of understanding categories of difference and identity. *Interventions: International Journal of Postcolonial Studies* 17(2): 174–195

Juang RM and Morrissette N (2008) *Africa and the Americas: Culture, politics, and history: A multidisciplinary encyclopedia* (Vol 3). Santa Barbara: ABC-CLIO

King RH (2004) *Race, culture, and the intellectuals, 1940–1970*. Washington DC: Woodrow Wilson Centre Press

Larmer M and Fraser A (2007) Of cabbages and King Cobra: Populist politics and Zambia's 2006 election. *African Affairs* 106(425): 611–637

Limpitlaw D (2011) Nationalization and mining: Lessons from Zambia. *Journal of the Southern African Institute of Mining and Metallurgy* 111: 737–739

Mbao MLM (2011) Prevention and combating of corruption in Zambia. *Comparative and International Law Journal of Southern Africa* 44(2): 255–274

Mills G and Herbst J (2014) *Africa's third liberation*. Westminster: Penguin

Nchindila BM (2008) Honest by chance: An investigation into Bemba music in Zambian politics. *Muziki* 5(2): 298–322

Nurse K (2006) Culture as the fourth pillar of sustainable development. *Small States: Economic Review and Basic Statistics* 11: 28–40

Nye JS (1967) Corruption and political development: A cost-benefit analysis. *American Political Science Review* 61(2): 417–427

Owuor J (2007) Integrating African indigenous knowledge in Kenya's formal education system: The potential for sustainable development. *Journal of Contemporary Issues in Education* 2(2): 21–37

Paldam M (2002) The cross-country pattern of corruption: Economics, culture and the seesaw dynamics. *European Journal of Political Economy* 18(2): 215–240

Papstein R (1989) From ethnic identity to tribalism: The Upper Zambezi region of Zambia, 1830–1981. In L Vail (Ed.) *The Creation of Tribalism in Southern Africa.* Berkeley: University of California Press

Phiri IA (2003) President Frederick JT Chiluba of Zambia: The Christian nation and democracy. *Journal of Religion in Africa* 33(4): 401–428

Pratt N (2005) Identity, culture and democratization: The case of Egypt. *New Political Science* 27(1): 69–86

Rollock D and Gordon EW (2000) Racism and mental health into the 21st century: Perspectives and parameters. *American Journal of Orthopsychiatry* 70(1): 5–13

Sandholtz W and Taagepera R (2005) Corruption, culture, and communism. *International Review of Sociology: Revue Internationale de Sociologie* 15(1): 109–131

Sardanis A (2014) *Zambia: The first 50 years.* London: I.B. Tauris

Tembo MS (2012) *Satisfying Zambian hunger for culture: Social change in the global world.* Bloomington: Xlibris Corporation

Van Klinken A (2015) Sexual orientation, (anti-)discrimination and human rights in a 'Christian nation': The politicization of homosexuality in Zambia. *Critical African Studies,* DOI:10.1080 /21681392.2015.1056315

8 | Visioning the Africa we want: Post-Africanism and the art of Titus Matiyane

Pfunzo Sidogi

During a lecture presented at the University of South Africa in 2012, which I had the privilege to attend, famed Nigerian playwright Wole Soyinka questioned what aliens would think of the various cultures of the world if they were to flick through world cinema. What would they think of Africa if they had to encounter African visual culture in all its forms, Soyinka wondered? Many scholars, myself included, may as well be those aliens when we look at 21st century African art, asking ourselves what kinds of images African artists depict and which Africa these images communicate to their African audiences and the rest of the world. The big question is, in what ways are contemporary artists imagining the Africa we want now and envisaging it for (or in) 2063? Do the precepts of Agenda 2063, especially Aspiration 5, correspond with the many images produced by African artists about the African experience? This chapter contends that statements such as that of Aspiration 5, however noble, are at odds with the socioeconomic and cultural trajectory of an increasingly industrialising, globalising and urbanising Africa, as illustrated and foretold by Titus Matiyane and other artists.

Aspiration 5 of Agenda 2063: The Africa We Want wants 'An Africa with a strong cultural identity, common heritage, shared values and ethics' (AU 2014: 8). This chapter questions whether it is even possible on the increasingly urbanising continent, where more than 60 per cent of the populace is projected to be city-based by 2050 (UN Habitat 2010). I assert that Aspiration 5 is not in keeping with the realities of 21st century urbanised African spaces—also known as Afropolises—where difference and heterogeneity are the constant.[1] A significant portion of the chapter flags the difficulties inherent in attempting to engineer a homogeneous African identity, as implied by Aspiration 5. On the face of it, Aspiration 5 seems to encourage the diversity of African cultures in their multicoloured beauty. However, and regrettably, those who champion it, i.e. the political and intellectual African elite, are not open to dissident expressions of self—which are for the most part performed in African urbanisms—that unsettle these stable notions of being African. As a critique of Aspiration 5, and viewing the issue from a Post-Africanist and, to a lesser degree, Afropolitanist perspective, I examine the work of Titus Matiyane, who shows an Africa where Aspiration 5 is an improbable outcome.

The fallacy of a singular African identity

The advent of cosmopolitanism and urbanisation across Africa has all but eroded the possibility of realising the idyllic notion of a reified African identity.[2] Freire et al. (2014: 1) suggest that urbanisation, above any other factor, has become the 'main policy narrative for Africa'. In the contemporary mind, urbanisation happens in parallel with the emergence of the metropolis and megalopolis, which Kilbridge et al. (1970: v) say 'are the new order in the organisation of human settlements'. At the risk of oversimplifying a complex and ever-changing process, urbanisation relates to the continuous movement of diverse people into industrialised towns, cities and megacities. At a very basic level, this process is motivated by the socioeconomic opportunities presented by cities that are organised mostly along neo liberal capitalist lines[3] (Harvey 1975). Individuals tend to resettle in urban spaces because they believe they will enjoy higher standards of living and overall economic advantages in modern cities. This reality is more pronounced in African cities where the disruption of rural and village livelihoods necessitated the mass movement of people to the African city.

Recent dynamic transformation of the old colonial cities into African-flavour metropolises that can be observed on the continent has resulted in the birth of the so-called Afropolises—emerging African urban centres that are vastly different from those in the Global North, ones that 'are blending their postcolonial structures with postmodern influences and ultimately also supplanting them' (Von Ruckteschell in Pinther et al. 2012: 11). Another term that describes these evolving African cities is 'Afropolitanism', which conveys the ideas of 'self-definition and self-articulation' among Africans living on the continent as well as those in the diaspora (Hassan 2011: 15). Of particular significance is the fact that Afropolitanism aims to crystallise the experiences and heterogeneous identities of Africans residing in Afropolises; 'it speaks of cosmopolitanism and a sense of belonging to the metropolis' (Hassan 2011: 18). Therefore, the Afropolitan framework encourages Africans to think of themselves as citizens of the world, shaping and being shaped by the global processes. But, perhaps most importantly, Afropolitanism calls for a more fluid formulation of 'being African', where 'Africa awakens to the forms of multiplicity (including racial multiplicity) which are constituents of its identity' (Mbembe 2005: 29). The differences in the nature of being African best play out in urbanised cityscapes.

This pragmatic truth has not slowed continued calls for a shared African identity, which resurfaced in Agenda 2063. Aspiration 5 of Agenda 2063 says 'culture, heritage and a *common identity* and destiny will be the centre of all our strategies' (African Union 2014: 8; emphasis added). At the core of this pronouncement is the desire to attain a single African identity. Such Afrocentric and Pan-Africanist aspirations were probably best articulated by Cheikh Anta Diop (1989: x)—a contemporary of Julius Nyerere, Chinua Achebe, Ngugi wa Thiong'o and Kwame Nkrumah—when he wrote that his anthology, *The cultural unity of black Africa*, 'tried to bring out the profound cultural unity still alive beneath the deceptive appearance of cultural heterogeneity'. Prominent scholars such as Hall (2000: 22) have supported the search for a shared cultural identity: 'We should not, for a moment, underestimate or neglect the importance of the act of imaginative rediscovery that this conception of a rediscovered essential identity entails'. Hall's argument is valid insofar as this collective African consciousness and 'imaginative rediscovery' fuelled the many African resistance and decolonisation campaigns during the early to mid-21st century. But its limitations are glaringly obvious in a contemporary Africa that has to contend with an ever-changing demographic and sociopolitical morphology, where a distinct African identity is unattainable.[4] In a discussion of race relations in South Africa, Boswell (2014: 13) contends that 'it is no longer feasible to imagine that identity is fixed'.

The xenophobic violence in South Africa in 2008 and more recently in 2015 indicates just how fallacious and questionable the idea of a homogeneous African identity is. Because of its relatively advanced industrialised centres and associated economic opportunities, South Africa has become home to Africans of various nationalities and ethnicities. The cities of Johannesburg,[5] Cape Town, Durban and Pretoria—among others—are quintessential Afropolitan spaces. Notwithstanding several campaigns and policy injunctions by the South African government since 1994 for oneness among Africans, the xenophobic antipathy persists among black South Africans against other black Africans. Unsurprisingly, these conflicts are ascribed not to the inherent divisionism, economic competitiveness and destructive tendencies within humans, especially when they mingle in great numbers in overcrowded urban spaces, but to colonial and imperialist legacies. For Diop and his followers such as Amadiume, for example, the deceptive heterogeneity within Africa is a result of the foreign contamination of African civilisation: '...these differences are externally imposed. They derive from colonial heritage' (Diop 1989: x). Seminal cultural institutions in South Africa went as far as blaming apartheid for the xenophobic attacks, saying 'apartheid used the notions of "tradition" and "culture" in a deliberately exclusivist manner, which sought to entrench division among blacks...' (Freedom Park 2011: 211) Even though there is some truth to these arguments, I find the rhetoric of blame counterproductive because it shifts the discussion away from the real issues, in this case the real ethnic, linguistic and cultural differences among Africans, and how these dissimilarities have to be consistently negotiated within a multicultural, urban setting.[6] Unfortunately, as Stevens argues (2011), Africans are not naturally inclined to deal with ethnic differences.

The politics of representing diverse African identities

The image is the most widespread mode of communication in modern society, whether in industrially advanced, developing, or deeply challenged societies (Hall 1997: 5). The dynamics and mechanics of Africa's visual culture are both intriguing and complicated. The same goes for producing art—on the one hand, it has benefit-ed from, and on the other it has been the victim of, the dramatic sociopolitical and economic changes that have spread through Africa since the start of the decoloni-sation process. While there is ample space for improvement, one cannot deny that the number and scale of festivals, fairs, exhibitions and various other platforms for art appreciation have grown exponentially since the 1950s, albeit in a handful of African states. Similarly, and regrettably, most of the African countries have seen a strangely negative, near-militant attitude of their governing bodies towards artists who do not toe the political or cultural line. South African artists Zanele Muholi and Brett Murray were both chastised by the political elite for producing images deemed inappropriate, or more accurately, for producing art that challenged the cherished ideal of a homogeneous African identity, either subliminally or overtly. More disturbingly, these artists were also attacked for crafting art that was deemed un-African in the sense that it defied the restrictive prevailing philosophies of what it means to be African, ideals that are implicitly reinforced by Aspiration 5 of the Agenda 2063 declaration.

In 2009, female photographer Zanele Muholi tested the legitimacy of the 'common heritage, values and ethics' truism by presenting a series of photographs showing lesbian African couples in intimate poses. The exhibition, which included the work of nine other female South African artists, was titled *Innovative Women* and hosted at Constitution Hill, the very centre of South Africa's democratisation project. Muholi's work dealt with the sensitive theme of same-sex relationships in Africa and broke new ground by portraying black lesbian couples as ordinary individuals immersed within the various tiers of South African society. The crunch came when then Minister of Arts and Culture[7] Lulu Xingwana, who was scheduled to open the exhibition, lambasted Muholi's images and left the exhibition in disapproval.[8] A subsequent press statement released by Xingwana's spokesperson, Lisa Combrink, defended the minister's abrupt exit as follows: 'Our mandate is to promote social cohesion and nation building. I left the exhibition because it expressed the very opposite of this. It was immoral, offensive and going against nation building.'[9]

The 'social cohesion and nation building' the minister was supposedly upholding was that of a singular African identity that disregards difference, in this case homosexuality.[10] In an interview with *Mail & Guardian* Editor Verashni Pillay[11] several months later, Xingwana further justified her actions by saying

> To my mind, these were not works of art but crude misrepresentations of women (both black and white) masquerading as artworks rather than engaged in questioning or interrogating—which I believe is what art is about. Those particular works of art stereotyped black women.

Such misguided and blatantly homophobic opinions about images that aesthetically engage with pertinent issues, in this instance sexual identity in contemporary Africa, should be read against the backdrop of essentialist and stereotyped understandings of African-ness that tend to demonise anything that goes against the so-called African character—the very shackling ideals, dare I say, that Aspiration 5 tacitly endorses.

Two years later, in 2011, another row broke out in South Africa, this time over a painting that depicted President Jacob Zuma with his penis exposed. This was a crass, in-your-face illustration, dubbed 'The Spear', produced by erstwhile resistance artist Brett Murray, and a pastiche of a Vladimir Lenin propaganda poster designed by Victor Ivanov in 1967. Freschi[12] describes the image as a signifier of gender and sociopolitical issues relating to power. He goes on to argue that Murray's whole exhibition was essentially one-dimensional, dealing through coded icons with the ruling party's flagrant abuse of authority and wealth. This quarrel revealed how the idea of African-ness is expediently deployed to protect the interests and reputations of those in authority. Instead of reading the artwork as a critique of unrestrained hegemonic leadership in Africa, various supporters of President Zuma, such as the then president of the South African Students' Congress, Ngoako Selamolela, branded it as a culturally inappropriate image and 'an attack to the very value and moral systems of the majority African people....'[13] Also speaking on the apparently un-African disposition of the artwork, members of the Zuma family commented that

> As far as we are concerned, in our society it is only animals that stand naked, not human beings. It's the most disgusting thing that has ever been published or said about the president. As a family, we are still in shock, because in our culture the parading of private parts is something that is a shame and is considered as showing disrespect to that person and others.[14]

What many displeased commenters stopped short of saying was that, as a white South African, Brett Murray had no right to represent a black South African in the manner he did.[15] Race relations in Africa are an ever-present topic and, as Boswell says (2014: 2), 'racism not only continues...it is simply reproduced and maintained'. The feeling among many black South Africans was that Murray's painting was an act of racism. This was echoed by art critic and education officer at the Pretoria Art Museum, Mmutle Kgokong (2012), who argued that 'The Spear divided the nation along racial lines....' This was not the first time a white artist was slated for representing black Africans in a manner that dissatisfied the subjects themselves. Oguibe's (1997) sharply worded critique of Candice Breitz's *Rainbow Series* (1996) also referred to the artist's European heritage and the fact that her subject matter was mostly black African females shown in ways considered un-African. Oguibe's (1997: 71) unapologetic assessment of Breitz's work reads

> Breitz's art is not a critique of hatred and violence: it is an art of hatred and violence. She places black women at the centre of her work, but only as racial signifiers through which she may act out a barely concealed and particularly intense impulse of hateful violence.

This was a direct reprimand to white [South] African artists not to objectify and cannibalise black culture, or more directly put, it cautioned them to not represent the black African in any form or manner not consistent with the innate African spirit.[16] Enwezor (1997: 39) raises alarm regarding this policing strategy by stating

> I question the wisdom of enacting any kind of representational corrective through a recourse to 'positive' images of blackness. For identity must never be turned into a copyright; an antinomy in which ethnicity through group reckoning stages its authenticities and retains exclusive user rights of its images. To do so would be to fetishise identity, to render it into a totem, a token of mythology, an ideological fantasy.

It can be argued that Aspiration 5 tries to 'fetishise' African identity by keeping it stable and communal. It is of course impractical and near impossible to supervise what type of images about Africa are produced on the continent—this is clear from the continued appropriation of the black body by African artists, independent of race. Artists should be afforded the space to appropriate this body as their creativity demands, and more so if their artworks challenge established notions of being African.

My concern, as shown in the two instances above, is how visual culture has been attacked by some African leaders, both in the political and intellectual domains, to maintain a skewed view of a fixed African identity or African-ness that is diametrically opposed to the developmental trajectories of a continuously changing and urbanising Africa. Referring to the persistent homogenisation of knowledge production, Thabo Mbeki,[17] former president of the Republic of South Africa and foremost advocate of the African Renaissance project, suggests that, in modern-day Africa, 'knowledge has become less democratised... [as] contemporary society faces the frightening reality of the capacity of a small but powerful minority of humanity to determine what society should "know", and what passes as "knowledge"'. This predicament can also be related to the desire by certain influential Africans to determine what society should see and how they should read what they see, especially regarding, but not limited to, visual art.

African visual culture is under the persistent gaze of the ruling political and intellectual class. Any African artist who dares to depict an Africa where cultural differences are openly embraced, deconstructed, questioned and celebrated is constrained and censored by those who continue to pursue the unattainable utopia of a singular African cultural identity centred on shared values and worldviews, as suggested by Aspiration 5. Commenting on the situation in South Africa, Peterson (2015: 6) confirms that 'artists enjoy a less-admired status and are, increasingly, becoming the target of censure and derision.' As Africa continues its march into a globalised era, where cosmopolitan urban centres proliferate on the continent, it becomes less and less likely that a coherent African-ness will ever become a reality. This then questions the expediency of Aspiration 5, which aims to create the unity, which in turn inadvertently retains restrictive views of sexuality and African identity. Ndlovu-Gatsheni (2010: 281) summarises the problem succinctly:

> The central challenge in the struggle of forging stable African identities remains that of how to negotiate and blend together diversities of race, ethnicity, religion, gender, class, region, language, culture, generation as well as how to deal with the phenomenon of degeneration of plural and civic forms of nationalism into nativism, xenophobia and even genocides in recent years. These issues need serious and unsententious consideration at this juncture when African leaders are busy toying with and implementing the mega-project of establishing the United States of Africa.

It can be argued that such Pan-Africanist ideals, repeated in Agenda 2063, are non-pragmatic constructs that work only as theoretical thought experiments. Speaking on Africa's present-day problems, Ugwuanyi (2014) believes that 'addressing these challenges through the ideology of Pan-Africanism without the effort to understand, engage and productively negotiate African differences will be counter-productive.'

Post-Africanism: Beyond a common African identity

The first part of this chapter explored the overriding preoccupation of Aspiration 5 and its deficiencies. This section presents a brief introduction to Post-Africanism (Ekpo 1995, 1996, 2004, 2005a, 2005b, 2010a, 2010b, 2014), a fresh, African-based[18] philosophy that promotes a more democratic and forward-thinking understanding of African identity. Post-Africanism critiques Afrocentric, anti-West inclinations found in African literature and visual culture, suggesting instead that Africans synthesise and pragmatically assimilate the best of what the rest of the world has to offer, impartial to any philosophical or cultural tenet, whether African or otherwise (Ekpo 2010a: 183). In other words, significantly, Post-Africanism calls for a fluid African identity and therefore artistic expression, both of which are allowed to transform continually depending on context and need.

Since the publication of the first Post-Africanism essay in *Textual Practice* (Ekpo 1995), quickly followed by another in *Third Text* (Ekpo 1996), both prominent journals in circulation across the African continent, few African scholars have responded to the theory in academic publications over the past two decades. Van Haute was the first to engage with Post-Africanist thought in relation to contemporary South African art during a South African Visual Art Historians (SAVAH) colloquium at the University of Witwatersrand in 2011.[19] Two years later, the Tshwane University of Technology (TUT) invited Denis Ekpo, the progenitor of Post-Africanism, to deliver a keynote speech at a conference steeped in Afrocentric rhetoric.[20] Following the symposium, during his three-week stay at TUT, Ekpo presented a series of lectures at the Faculty of the Arts and shared the motivations that led him to this nuanced deconstruction of being African, much of which is captured in his article 'Any European around to help me talk about myself? The white man's burden of black Africa's critical practices' (Ekpo 2005a).

Since Ekpo's visit to South Africa, a slight fad has developed of artists and curators appropriating the term 'Post-African' to explore themes directly related to Africa's destiny and its multilateral identities. The biggest event showcasing the trend was a group exhibition hosted by the Goodman Gallery and curated by Tegan Bristow in Johannesburg in May and June 2015, called *Post-African Futures*.[21] Bristow said at the time, 'the exhibition [was] an exploration of multiple "African cultures of technology" that have unique sociopolitical and economic histories'.[22] The show was described as 'a critique of both globalised media practices and romanticised Africanisms' (Goodman Gallery 2015). Another smaller exhibition titled simply *Post African* was held at Mzansi Gallery, also in Johannesburg. Both these shows interrogated how African artists are depicting in art the ambiguities of African experiences.

During my many conversations with Ekpo, he revealed that he sees South Africa as both a schema and a light at the end of the tunnel for the rest of Africa when it comes to showcasing fluid, non-sectarian African identities that take into account global realities. Ekpo has devoted much of his energy to the subject of modernity and Africa's apparent schizophrenic attitude towards it. However, Post-Africanism's value for African creative expression is that it stimulates diversity in the ways Africa is depicted that are not imprisoned by one-dimensional ideals of African-ness as put forward in Aspiration 5. Through Post-African rehabilitation, the current and coming generations of African artists can continue to reposition their thinking away from ideas of a narrow African identity, towards a more pragmatic and open pronouncement of being African. Ekpo (1995: 134) speaks about the Post-African mind as follows:

> The Post-Africanist mind can retrieve all its power and creative potentials by repossessing himself of the Western logos and using it as a power tool rather than being possessed and bewitched by it and forced into either a romantic search for an impossible Afrocentricity or the depressive rhetoric of perpetual accusation of the West.

Using the ideas proposed by Post-Africanism, African artists must take advantage of artworks' communicative power to reimagine Africa. They should act as guardians in the articulation of the Africa we want and 'play midwife to a redeemed future' of unconstrained realities (Ekpo 2010a: 186).

Panoramas of multiple identities: The art of Titus Matiyane

One artist whose work embodies Post-African ideals is Tshwane-/Pretoria-based artist Titus Matiyane. Born in Atteridgeville on the outskirts of Pretoria in 1963, Matiyane has produced art since the early 1980s. His initial works were unlike the politically laden images of his contemporaries; instead, Matiyane was obsessed with recreating miniature models of some symbols of Western modernity and scientific advancement such as the *Pan Am 747* (1983), a Boeing jet, the *Challenger* (1985), the spacecraft, and the *Concord* (1985), the supersonic jet. Using found materials such as wire and pieces of scrap metal, Matiyane crafted slightly crude but recognisable replicas of the most advanced vehicles of transport. Matiyane's attachment to these machines of progress—mostly foreign to him—also exposed the artist's wish for a modern and comfortable lifestyle (Younge 1988).

Matiyane's creative endeavours led to moderately successful shows at the Durban Art Gallery and the South African National Art Gallery in 1985 and 1986, respectively. Later, Younge (1988: 41) mentioned Matiyane in one of the seminal publications on black South African art,[23] bluntly stating that the artist had 'stopped making things'. However, Matiyane resurfaced during the early 1990s with a fresh and even bolder approach, illustrating the results of capitalist-driven Western modernisation by producing large mixed-media drawings of cities; he started with the *Panorama of Pretoria* (1992), which was shown at the National Arts Festival in Grahamstown, followed by the *Atteridgeville Panorama* (1993), *Panorama of Western Cape* (1995) and many more. These panoramas proved to be the creative breakthrough that catapulted Matiyane's career and enabled him to enjoy the objects of Western modernity which he had fantasised about and depicted in his earlier works.

Matiyane has since become synonymous with, and world-renowned for, large portrayals of international megalopolises and carefully selected Afropolises. During 2007 and 2008, he went on a travelling exhibition with his collection titled *Cities of the World*; he visited the Netherlands, Germany, Mali and South Africa, and examined some leading cities of the globe, including London, New York, Rotterdam, Amsterdam, Hong Kong, and several urban centres in South Africa.[24] Matiyane's fascination with cities is fitting, since half of the world's population currently live in urban spaces; the United Nations (UN) projects that this number will rise by as much as 84 per cent by 2050 (UN 2009). This applies to Africa as well, and one of the plausible results of this mass urbanisation will be the development of societies that are even less homogeneous across the continent. In fact, because of Africa's favourable climate and increasing economic opportunities, it is likely that more people from other regions of the world will continue to relocate to the emerging Afropolises, which will further erode and compromise the seemingly fallacious idea of an authentic African identity.

Matiyane's representations of cities are massive and ambitious, firstly in terms of the physical size of his panoramic mixed-media artworks—which can stretch to 45 metres in width—and the sheer tenacity in taking on such elaborate works, and secondly, because Matiyane's landscapes attempt to crystallise and capture in one image the history, with all its triumphs, tragedies, progress and setbacks that would characterise any major city of the world. In fact, Matiyane's depiction of cities is a kind of leveller, where individual identity is free to be imagined and performed without fear of persecution. Commenting on his show, *Panoramas of the BRICS Capitals*,[25] curator Elfriede Dreyer (2015) writes:

> There are superficially neither perceivable binaries of have and have not, poverty and wealth, nor anxieties, losses or racial discrimination. East meets West meets Africa in a global blueprint of urban patterning.

Although some might disagree, urban centres create the likelihood of greater social and cultural integration and tolerance, because individuality and difference can coexist.

Matiyane's aerial portraits of cities force us to think differently about promoting a unified and shared African value system, because such uniformity is implausible in urban settings. Responding to Thabo Mbeki's famous 'I am an African' speech presented to the South African Parliament in 1996, Ndlovu-Gatsheni (2010: 287) says, 'What is clear in his definition is that African identity is a product of a tapestry of interwoven histories and migrations, some tragic and others heroic.' It is this tapestry of complex and diverse people living in a communal space that becomes evident in Matiyane's rendition of African urban centres such as Gauteng province in South Africa. Matiyane allows us to view the African landscape from a perspective unfamiliar to most Africans. Another critical and perhaps overlooked mind-shift created by Matiyane's representation of African cities is that it shows Africans, and indeed the rest of the world, that Africa does in fact have industrialised urban spaces. In a book that documents how Americans imagine Africa, Magee (2012: 6) concedes that she is often baffled by 'photographs of African urban areas, for it is commonly thought that Africans live in grass houses in jungle villages.' Thus, Matiyane's informal visual treatment of African cityscapes reminds us that Africa is part of, and partly shaped by, global processes.

Both Matiyane and Post-Africanism in general make us look at the big picture rather than micro-analysing events and spaces, broadening our view in a pragmatic and holistic manner. Matiyane's bold representations are a perfect visual embodiment of Post-Africanist discourse, in which he aesthetically recolonises the landscape, in much the same way as Ekpo urges Africans to repossess their African identity from the prison of Afrocentric archetypes.

Conclusion

The prominent African art critic, scholar and curator, Okwui Enwezor (1997: 39), laments that 'the predicament into which one is thrown, then, is how to imagine identity in the present tense ...'. African identity is a coalface of contention, the central concern being, who stands to benefit from the limited understanding of being African that is projected by Aspiration 5? Based on how political and intellectual elites have reacted to differing portrayals of contemporary Africa by artists like Zanele Muholi, it seems that they have a vested interest in maintaining a lopsided idea of African-ness. Although the advent of democracy has afforded artists the space to challenge convention and put forward alternative realities, many are influenced by the commonly held notions of Africa and the identity of African people. Therefore, we have a duty to critically evaluate calls such as those laid out in the 'Agenda 2063: The Africa We Want', and to thoroughly examine whether these principles are in line with the complex realities of 21st century Africa.

My cynical final analysis is that declarations like Aspiration 5, 'An Africa with a strong cultural identity, common heritage, values and ethics' (African Union 2014: 8), play into the hands of those in power, who manipulate the masses and benefit the most from a homogeneous definition of being African. My other misgiving about this, and other goals set out in Agenda 2063, is that they essentially encourage African artists to continue to create images driven by the anticolonial, anti-imperial discourse, which reduces African creativity to one-dimensional image-making.

It is my conviction that Post-Africanism can credibly remedy this crisis, and that artists like Titus Matiyane, whose bold, dynamic and progress-favouring representations of African landscapes, both figuratively and in the abstract, are leading the way in depicting an alternative Africa, one different from that pushed by Aspiration 5 of Agenda 2063. Not only does Matiyane's art empower Africans to reshape their destiny, but it also permits Africans to transcend the existing constrained understanding of what it is to be African on a psychological level, so that they can fashion more diverse and inclusive identities.

Notes

1 Georgiou (2013) argues that modern cities are sites of difference.

2 I must emphasise that I do not oppose the rationalisation of African identity as constituted through African experiences, traditions and values. The problem arises when these traditions and values become a hegemonic force that opposes other radical expressions that do not conform to it.

3 Scargill (1979: 1) argues that, besides cultural and social factors, modern cities are characterised by international economic forces such as neo liberal capitalism, which determines the physical formations of cities. Masilela (2013: 336) agrees: 'There can be many alternative modernities on the cultural plane or epiphenomenal level but there can be only capitalist modernity at the infrastructural level.'

4 This distinct or one-dimensional African identity is fallacious on two fronts: first, because it advances an essentialist notion of what it means to be African; and second, this essentialist conception of being African is imposed onto the whole African continent, as large and undulating as it is.

5 South Africa is seen by many as the quintessential Afropolitan site, with Mbembe (2005: 29) going as far as labelling Johannesburg 'the centre of Afropolitanism par excellence' on the African continent.

6 An interesting case is that of the Royal Bafokeng Nation and to a lesser extent the resurgence of nostalgia among the Vhavenda for the Republic of Venda Homeland, a divisive apartheid-era construct. Although these two groups do not denounce being South African—for the obvious security and socioeconomic advantages linked to being a citizen—they have articulated their own identity as being separate, premised on the uniqueness of their cultures, and these individualised identities are showcased unapologetically among other ethnic groups in the country.

7 Ironically, the Department had partially funded the exhibition to the tune of R300 000.

8 In 2012 I presented a paper titled 'African Visual Culture: Stagnant or evolving?' at a Language, Literature and Society Conference hosted by the University of Botswana. To my shock, many of the African academics at the conference derided Muholi's images, commenting during the question-and-answer session that the minister was justified in her actions, since the photos promoted something unnatural that had been brought to Africa by Westerners.

9 Smith D, South African minister describes lesbian photos as immoral. *The Guardian*, 2 March 2010.

10 This incident was more alarming considering the fact that South Africa is by far the most lenient and accepting African country for openly gay and lesbian individuals, both legally and culturally. Puzzlingly, Xingwana was removed from her position as minister of Arts and Culture only to become the first minister of the newly formed Department of Women, Children and People with Disabilities.

11 Pillay V, Xingwana: But is it art? *Mail & Guardian*, 4 March 2010.

12 Freschi F, Opening address for the South African Visual Art Historians Conference, University of South Africa, 4–7 July 2012.

13 News24, Zuma *Spear* 'an attack on African culture'. Accessed June 2012, www.news24.com/SouthAfrica/Politics/Zuma-Spear-an-attack-on-African-culture-20120521.

14 News24, Zuma painting 'sadistic' – SACP. Accessed June 2012, www.news24.com/ SouthAfrica/Politics/Zuma-painting-sadistic-SACP-20120520.

15 Interestingly, another visual artist, Ayanda Mabulu, also depicted President Jacob Zuma with his genitalia exposed in a much cruder and more direct style. Among similar works, his paintings titled *Ngcono ihlwempu kunesibhanxo sesityebi* (Better poor than a rich puppet) (2010) and *Spear down my throat* (2015) show Jacob Zuma in highly sexualised, near-pornographic scenes with his penis as the focal point.

16 On the other side of the argument, scholars like Ekpo (2005a: 115) consider Oguibe's 'mesmeric overreactions to the artistic trifles of white people' as a sophisticated continuation of the Afrocentric, anticolonial position.

17 Mbeki T, We have a right to know. *Sunday Times*, 22 January 2012.

18 Unlike concepts such as Pan-Africanism and Afro-futurism, imported into Africa from the diaspora, Post-Africanism evolved from within.

19 Ironically, Van Haute's presentation was my first encounter with Ekpo's ideas. However, Ekpo had prior online exchanges with another prominent South African art historian, Mario Pissarra, via his Africa South Art Initiative, founded to encourage greater interaction among South African scholars dealing with art and their counterparts elsewhere in Africa.

20 The conference was themed 'The Arts and Indigenous Knowledge Systems (IKS) in a Modern[ising] Africa' and took place between 25 and 27 September 2013. It was hoped that the colloquium would catalogue and celebrate the role the arts play in preserving, developing and exploiting African IKS in a continuously modernising Africa. The conference convener, Rudi de Lange, saw Ekpo as the voice of dissent needed to invoke meaningful debate and robust academic engagement.

21 The show exhibited the work of 20 artists and collaborators from South Africa, Kenya, Democratic Republic of the Congo, Tunisia, Central African Republic and Nigeria. These artists use digital media platforms in their creative pursuits.

22 Van Niekerk G, Black to the future. *City Press*, 5 June 2015.

23 Regrettably, Younge misspelt Matiyane's surname as Moteyane. This editorial oversight by a white scholar writing about black art is consistent with what Van Robbroeck (2006: 4) sees as an 'un-nuanced view of the South African art world'. This condescension reared its head again in *The collector's guide to art and artists in South Africa* (The South African Institute of Artists & Designers 1998), in which his name was incorrectly spelt as Matinyane.

24 A book cataloguing this travelling show (De Kler 2007) is unfortunately the only credible and authoritative reading of Matiyane's work.

25 The *Panoramas of the BRICS Capitals* show had six panoramas, five of them showcasing the BRICS countries' capital cities, with the last being a depiction of the whole African landscape condensed into one panel.

References

AU (African Union) (2014) *Agenda 2063: The Africa We Want* (2nd edition). Addis Ababa: African Union Commission. Accessed October 2017, archive.au.int/assets/images/agenda2063.pdf

Boswell R (2014) Black faces, white spaces: Adjusting self to manage aversive racism in South Africa. *Africa Insight* 44(3): 1–14

De Kler A (Ed.) (2007) *Titus Matiyane: Cities of the World*. Rotterdam: 010 Publishers

Diop CA (1989) *The cultural unity of black Africa: The domains of patriarchy and of matriarchy in classical antiquity*. London: Karnak House

Dreyer A (2015) Titus Matiyane: Panoramas of the BRICS capitals. University of Johannesburg Art Gallery, 7 October–11 November

Ekpo D (1995b) Towards a Post-Africanism: Contemporary African thoughts and postmodernism. *Textual Practice* 9: 121–135

Ekpo D (1996) How Africa misunderstood the West: The failure of anti-West radicalism and postmodernity. *Third Text* 10(35): 3–13

Ekpo D (2004) *Neither anti-imperialism nor the white man's tears: An anti-postcolonial discourse*. Ikot Ekpene: Iwoh and Sons

Ekpo D (2005a) Any European around to help me talk about myself? The white man's burden of black Africa's critical practices. *Third Text* 19(2): 107–124

Ekpo D (2005b) The abortion of Africa's modernity. *Third Text* 19(4): 423

Ekpo D (2010a) From Negritude to post-Africanism. *Third Text* 24(2): 177–187

Ekpo D (2010b) Speak Negritude but think and act French: The foundations of Senghor's political philosophy. *Third Text* 24(2): 227–239

Ekpo D (2014) Redemption from Afrophilia: Considering post-African solutions to Africa's problems. Paper presented at the African Unity for Renaissance Conference, South Africa, Human Sciences Research Council, 22–24 May 2014

Enwezor O (1997) Reframing the black subject: Ideology and fantasy in contemporary South African Representation. *Third Text* 11(40): 21–40

Freedom Park (2011) *Tools, time and place: Looking over our shoulder for forward movement*. Pretoria: Freedom Park

Freire ME, Lall S and Leipziger D (2014) *Africa's urbanisation: Challenges and opportunities*. Washington, DC: The Growth Dialogue

Georgiou M (2013) *Media and the city: Cosmopolitanism and difference*. Cambridge: Polity

Goodman Gallery (2015) Post-African futures: Curated by Tegan Bristow. Accessed November 2015, www.goodman-gallery.com/exhibitions/560

Hall S (1997) Representation and the media. Accessed June 2010, www.mediaed.org/assets/products/409/transcript_409.pdf

Hall S (2000) Cultural identity and the diaspora. In N Mirzoeff (Ed.) *Diaspora and visual culture: Representing Africans and Jews*. London: Routledge

Harvey D (1975) Review of BJL Berry's The human consequences of urbanisation. *Annals of the Association of American Geography* 65: 99–103

Hassan SM (2011) Rethinking cosmopolitanism: is 'Afropolitan' the answer? *Reflections* 5: 3–29

Kilbridge MD, O'Block RP and Teplitz PV (Eds) (1970) *Urban analysis.* Boston: Harvard University

Kgokong M (2012) Neo resistance art and its fallacy. Accessed November 2015, mmutleak.com/2012/05/23/neo-resistance-art-and-its-fallacy/

Magee C (2012) *Africa in the American imagination: Popular culture, racialized identities, and African visual culture.* Mississippi: University of Mississippi Press

Masilela N (2013) *An outline of the new African Movement in South Africa.* Cape Town: Africa World Press

Mbembe A (2005) Afropolitanism. In S Njami (Ed.) *Africa Remix: Contemporary art of a continent.* Johannesburg: Jacana

Ndlovu-Gatsheni SJ (2010) Do 'Africans' exist? Genealogies and paradoxes of African identities and the discourses of nativism and xenophobia. *African Identities* 8(3): 281–295

Oguibe O (1997) A brief reflection on the work of contemporary women artists. In HM Salah (Ed.) *Gendered visions: The art of contemporary Africana women artists.* Trenton: Africa World Press

Peterson B (2015) Achebe, art and critical consciousness. In J Ogude (Ed.) *Chinua Achebe's legacy: Illuminations from Africa.* Pretoria: Africa Institute of South Africa

Pinther K, Förster L and Hanussek C (Eds) (2012) *Afropolis: City media art.* Johannesburg: Jacana

Scargill DI (1979) *The form of cities.* London: Bell & Hyman

Stevens FL (2011) *The African philosophy of self-destruction.* Cape Town: 3dP New Media

The South African Institute of Artists and Designers (1998) *The collector's guide to art and artists in South Africa.* Claremont: Twenty Two Press

Ugwuanyi LO (2014) From Pan-Africanism to Pro-Africanism: A critical review of the ideology of Pan-Africanism with a fresh proposal. Paper presented at the African Unity for Renaissance Conference, South Africa, Human Sciences Research Council, 22–24 May

UN (United Nations) (2009) *Urban and rural areas 2009.* Accessed November 2015, www.un.org/en/development/desa/population/publications/urbanization/urban-rural.shtml

UN Habitat (United Nations Habitat) (2010) *The state of African Cities.* Nairobi: UN Habitat

Van Haute B (2011) Post-Africanism and contemporary art in South African townships. Paper presented at the Annual South African Visual Art Historians Conference, South Africa, University of Witwatersrand, 12–15 January

Van Robbroeck L (2006) Writing white on black: Modernism as discursive paradigm in South African writing on modern black art. DPhil thesis, University Of Stellenbosch

Younge G (1988) *Art of the South African Townships.* London: Thames and Hudson

9 | Preserving an intangible cultural heritage: Indigenous songs of the Naro of Botswana

Matheanoga Fana Rabatoko

The 2003 United Nations Educational, Scientific and Cultural Organisation (UNESCO) Convention for the Safeguarding of the Intangible Cultural Heritage defines intangible cultural heritage (ICH) as

> practices, representations, expressions, knowledge, skills—as well as the instruments, objects, artefacts and cultural spaces associated therewith—that communities, groups and, in some cases, individuals recognize as part of their cultural heritage. This intangible cultural heritage, transmitted from generation to generation, is constantly recreated by communities and groups in response to their environment, their interaction with nature and their history, and provides them with a sense of identity and continuity, thus promoting respect for cultural diversity and human creativity. (UNESCO 2003, Article 2)

Five areas through which ICH can be expressed are listed in the Convention, namely a) oral traditions and expressions, including language; b) performing arts; c) social practices, rituals and festive events; d) knowledge and practices concerning nature and the universe; and e) traditional craftsmanship (UNESCO 2003). Researchers in many countries have acknowledged the importance of preserving cultural heritage in the form of indigenous songs. Corn (2012: 231), for example, raised awareness about the crisis threatening Australia's indigenous music. Kang (2010: 77–78) observed a similar threat in Korea, where the adoption of Western culture has replaced Korean cultural practices to such an extent that Korean music has begun to disappear. It is important to bear in mind that, in African countries, the documentation of performances predates the arrival of the Europeans or sound recordings. 'Oral traditions served to preserve in dynamic ways the aspects of performances that people wanted to remember' (Stone 1998: 7). However, with the arrival of the 21st century, the importance of analysing and transcribing indigenous songs to preserve traditional musical arts came to be recognised. And it is this process that could pave the way for the inclusion of indigenous songs into curricular blueprints and the formal education system.

In this chapter, I study the indigenous songs[1] and dances of the Naro of D'Kar—a village in the Ghanzi district in the western part of Botswana—as a form of ICH embedded in oral traditions and expressions, social practices, rituals and festive events, as well as the performing arts. It is important to note that the current state of Naro music cannot be deemed 'purely indigenous', because the songs and dances of the group have been exposed to and influenced by other cultures and bear traces of the interplay of social, economic and political factors that have had an impact on the life of the group.

I undertook the study with the objective of collecting and analysing some songs of the Naro, intending to find out how appropriate they would be for inclusion in Botswana's music education curricula. Two research questions guided the evaluation and analysis of the songs: (1) In terms of the structural, stylistic and textual elements of Naro indigenous songs, to what extent and in what ways are they suitable for inclusion within Botswana's music education curricula? And (2), in terms of the performance context, to what extent and in what ways are Naro indigenous songs suitable for inclusion within Botswana's music education curricula?

Background

Botswana is a heterogeneous society with diverse cultures. The indigenous people of Botswana include, among others, the San with their 12 respective ethnic language groups; the Bakalanga of the central and north-east; the Wayei and the Hambukushu of the north-west; the Subia of the north, as well as the Bakgalagadi of the Kweneng and Kgalagadi regions. San culture, like other indigenous cultures around the world, is threatened by extinction as a result of cultural assimilation into more dominant cultures, discrimination against minority groups, and the trends of modernisation and globalisation (Nyathi-Ramahobo 2008; Chebanne 2010a; Nyathi-Saleshando 2011; Solway, 2011; Boikhutso & Jotia 2013; Toivanen 2013).

The San are Southern Africa's first indigenous peoples (Ketsitlile 2012). Today, about 107 000 San people live in Angola, Botswana, Namibia, South Africa, Zambia and Zimbabwe (Barume 2010: 163). The name 'San' is a part of the word KhoiSan, which Chebanne (2010b: 93) defined as '[being] generally accepted as a common reference for the combined Khoe (those speaking Khoekhoe languages) and San (those speaking non-Khoekhoe languages)'. In Southern Africa, Botswana has the greatest ethnic and linguistic diversity of KhoiSan communities (Chebanne 2008; 2010a).

According to Brezinger's model, as presented by Visser,[2] the KhoiSan are divided into 12 language groups—an assertion maintained by both Marshall (1989) and Schadeberg J (2002) *The San of the Kalahari*. Pretoria: PrePress Images. However, Chebanne (2008: 95) asserts that only five groups are to be found in Botswana, distributed across the Central Kalahari, Eastern Kalahari and Northern Kalahari. The D'Kar Museum identifies 12 language groups across five regions of Botswana. They are: Central KhoiSan, who speak eight ethnic languages, namely Khwedam, Naro, //Gana, G/wi, Tsua, Shua, Kua, and /Xaise; south-eastern KhoiSan, who speak #Hua (Sasi); northern KhoiSan, who speak Ju/'hoansi; and southern KhoiSan, who speak the !Xoo language, and one area remains unconfirmed where people speak the N/U language. This study focused on the Naro speakers whose number in Botswana, as reported by Chebanne (2008: 105), can be estimated at five to ten thousand people.

Much research has been done among the local San groups in fields such as anthropology, linguistics and sociology (Lee 1979; Tanaka 1980; Chebanne 2010b; Ketsitlile 2012). As far as music goes, there is an urgent need to study and document the different types of traditional musics[3] of Botswana (Phibion 2003: 250), and particularly to preserve the culture and music of the San (Rabatoko 2013: 65).

Approaches to preserving intangible cultural practices, and particularly music, vary. Strategies for preservation include popularisation through media and technology; inclusion in educational curricula; archiving, documenting and publishing; re-contextualising musical arts; and emphasising the plight of cultural practices through research (Nzewi 2003; Van der Meer 2005; Lin & Lajinga 2011; Emmanuel 2013). This chapter focuses on documenting and analysing the indigenous songs of the Naro of D'Kar, as well as understanding the symbolic content of their music to determine its suitability for inclusion in the music education curriculum of Botswana. I designed the research around the premise that a positive result of understanding a particular culture can be arrived at by studying both the past and current music of the society involved within its context, and looking at the ways in which both have changed over the course of time—an idea advanced by Campbell (2004). This scholar believes that an understanding of the role music plays at 'the intersection of both culture and identity may enhance the overall understanding of the music itself' (2004: 216). In this study, Naro songs have been analysed in terms of their structure, style and text. The analysis included an exploration of the performance contexts of the songs that corresponded with eight thematic areas of Naro cultural activity, in which music plays an important role. These activities are ritual healing, thanksgiving, entertainment, social commentary, initiation, hunting, children's play, and worship (Rabatoko 2013: 2). I also explored the contextual uses and age groups of people performing different songs. Practices associated with these songs, as well as the seasons or special times of the year during which different types are performed, were investigated as well.

Considering the pluralistic nature of Botswana's society, Gay's (2005: 223) call for 'systemic changes [that] must occur that affect policies, programmes, personnel, pedagogy, and power at the institutional level', along with Chebanne's (2010a: 102) advice for Botswana to 'review its national and institutional policies that have a bearing of multiculturalism and multilingualism and ensure that all ethnic and linguistic groups are taken on board' guide this chapter.

Music education in Botswana

Music education is included at all levels of the Botswana education system. Botswana's basic education spans a period of ten years from Standard 1 to Form 3. The Creative and Performing Arts (CAPA) category caters for music teaching in primary schools, both at the lower and middle levels (Standards 1 to 4), as well as at the upper level (from Standards 5 to 7). The content of the subject aims to aid students in developing their creativity, aesthetic skills, psychomotor skills and love for the arts. The rationale behind including music as a subject in the Botswana education syllabus is the fact that it has the potential to contribute to the preservation and transmission of the cultural heritage of Botswana. The secondary school programme content is organised around two broad areas—core and optional. Music education is included in the latter. It was introduced into the junior secondary schools in 2007 following a pilot programme developed in response to the recommendation of the Revised National Policy of Education (1994) to include music as an optional subject in junior secondary schools. At the tertiary level, music education is offered at colleges of education, the University of Botswana (UB) and the Botswana College of Distance and Open Learning (BOCODOL). At colleges of education, music is offered as a minor subject in both the Diplomas in Secondary and Primary Education. UB offers music education as an elective, optional, or core course for practical specialisation in teaching. Furthermore, pre-service teachers from various UB departments are also eligible to enrol in music education (Phuthego 2007: 4).

Conceptual framework

The content and context of this research is situated within the area of Indigenous Knowledge Systems (IKSs). Morris (2005: 1) defines IKS as 'local knowledge, as opposed to what might be termed global knowledge, or, in a colonial context, metropolitan (or "Western") knowledge'. In a broader context, Odora-Hoppers (2011: 76) describes IKS as the 'combination of knowledge systems encompassing technology, philosophy, social, economic, learning/educational, and legal as well as governance systems'. It therefore includes records of folklore and traditional beliefs, ceremonies, customs, dances, music, folk recipes, veld foods and medicines, indigenous ecological knowledge, oral history and living history (Morris 2005).

Using IKSs as a conceptual framework, I analysed the indigenous music of the Naro—and its educational relevance—through a culturally sensitive lens. The study and preservation of the Naro indigenous songs dovetail with the attributes of IKS, as observed by Odora-Hoppers (2011: 77), who was of the opinion that indigenous knowledge could be 'preserved, transferred, or adopted and adapted elsewhere'. Moreover, Mbatha (2013: 172), after Nonaka (1996), emphasised the significance of IKSs, arguing that IKSs had been widely used by communities to preserve knowledge by capturing, storing, processing, retrieving and disseminating it. Mbatha (2013: 171) contended that IKSs recognised, generated, transferred and managed tacit knowledge across time and space. IKSs also represent people's heritage and are 'a national resource which should be protected, promoted, developed, and where appropriate, conserved' (Odora-Hoppers 2011: 76).

Research methodology

The research was designed as an ethnographic study in a village of D'Kar in the Ghanzi district. To gain an understanding of the social and cultural systems of the people of the village, my focal point for three consecutive years was the complete immersion into the Naro community living there, consistent with the principles of conducting ethnographic research developed by Leedey and Ormrod (2006). I collected qualitative data through observations and semi-structured interviews and focus group discussions with representatives of the Naro of D'Kar. Purposive sampling was used to select participants for the study, with the focus on a group of elderly members of the community and the primary school learners. These interactions allowed the exploration of attitudes, values, perceptions, opinions, feelings and behaviours of the participants. Curriculum developers and implementers from the formal education system were also interviewed.

Focus group discussions with the elderly members of the community included two interactions over two years with 40 adults belonging to a traditional dance group called Giraffe. Semi-structured interviews were conducted with selected members of the group, including the trance master and his assistant. As for the primary school pupils, 18 children from Standards 1 to 7 participated in the study in the first year, while in the third and final year, learners from Standard 7 were not included on account of their being unavailable. Five music teachers as well as the principal education officer (PEO) were consulted once in a focus group forum. Participants were protected by means of Agawu's (2003: 85) rules on conducting ethnographic research. Appropriate letters of intent were issued, and the right permissions were sought from relevant authorities. The issues of validity and reliability were dealt with through the use of triangulation, which helped 'see the same thing from different perspectives and thus to be able to confirm or challenge the findings of one method with those of another' (Laws, Harper & Marcus 2003: 281).

Regarding the music material, 45 songs were collected, but only 19 were analysed for the purposes of the study. All songs were recorded on both CD and DVD, and they were also transcribed.

Interpretative philosophy, which focuses on the meaning and symbolic content of qualitative data (Nieuwenhuis 2007), was used to analyse the collected songs. The symbolic meanings were identified using three levels of analysis: (1) structure, style, text and performance context; (2) scales, ranges, metres, ostinatos, melodic and rhythmic patterns; and (3) the thematic areas in which Naro music is used.

Findings and discussion

Analysis in terms of structure, style, text and performance context

Form and structure is essential to music; without form, music will descend into chaos. The music of the Naro is essentially antiphonal.[4] The predominant call and response in the songs of the Naro give them a unique and distinguishing characteristic of AB. It is imperative to note that this call and response is different from the Western idea of tension and release. In the songs and dances of the Naro, there are two phrases: the first phrase takes the listener in one direction and the second phrase brings them back home. While the arrival is usually clear, gentle and in recognisable cadences, points of departure are, mostly, controversial and deceptive. But, most importantly, there is a recognisable element of symmetry in the dance. Continuous variation—an aspect of music in which melodic, rhythmic and harmonic elements undergo continuous change and development during the course of a piece of music—is common in Naro music. This aspect manifests in the various topics discussed in a song, as well as in the form of transition from one mode to another within a musical performance.

While the Naro perform their songs in their 'indigenous' context, they constantly add harmonies to a single melodic line. And this continuous addition is done communally with the whole group participating. This feature is common to many other musics in Africa, as observed by Carver (2002: 56):

> African musics are frequently made within the context of the community. The role of the individual is far less dominant and to a very large extent the musics are performed by more than one person. In this sense, African musics reveal a sensibility that is profoundly pluralistic and one that is centred in the humanistic context of communal participation.

When it comes to the topics of music and language, and music and communication, a close observation of the relationship between the speech patterns of Naro language and their musical lyrics can lead one to conclude that the Naro language itself is a type of music. Discussing the relationship between music and language, Agawu (2001: 8) states that, to come up with a clear analysis of African music, one must take into account the distinct function a particular piece of music is meant to serve. It follows then that, to some extent, one may generalise and say that African musics may be classified as some form of text.

As far as the music of the Naro goes, it is clear that, while all musical types are meant to serve a clearly marked function, the textual element of the song is metaphorically more deeply embedded in the dance. The Naro songs are characterised by short syllables—*Ayee-uyee aye-uweee-ayee-uwee*—cyclically repeated. A similar cycle of repetition can be also found in dance patterns, especially those performed by men. It is easier to interpret the message of the song by following the *ad libitum* or improvised cycle of those syllables, since they demonstrate both the context and the meaning of the song pictorially. Most of the song titles are drawn from the names of wild animals and birds for reasons known only to the Naro people. The only domestic animal mentioned in songs was the horse (*Bii*); it did not belong to the Naro but to the white farmers who settled in the area. Interestingly, more than three songs may bear one name; for example, various songs may be referred to as *tcibi*, which means a dove. The differences in various *tcibi* songs may be presented textually in a recitative cycle by one singer, while a larger number of distinguishing characteristics may be demonstrated by the dance patterns symbolically illuminating the text sung or recited.

While the spoken word is used minimally in the Naro songs, the role of the recitation and the dance itself are critical leads to understanding the song's text and the music content as well as the context in which the song is set. Paying close attention to the whole performance, one could easily come to agree with Agawu's (2001: 9) view about the concept of African music and text that

> to be properly understood, African music must be approached at the level of musical language domesticated in various 'compositions' and at the level constituted by a supplementary but necessary critical language. Performers are able to reach their audiences directly and even carry out an internal dialogue among themselves

without investing heavily in spoken language. The linguistic and metalinguistic dimensions of an African composition are so thoroughly intertwined that their separation, even in theory, would seem difficult if not impossible.

Although some people (outsiders) easily dismiss the repeated syllables of the Naro songs as being 'nonsensical', rich meaning—consistent with the sociolinguistic patterns of the Naro language—resides within the flow of such syllables in the music. The manner in which the high, medium and low tones are articulated in those *Ayee-uyee ayee-uweee-ayee uwee* song syllables endorses Agawu's assertion that African music is naturally influenced by the nature of African languages, which are tonal in context.

Generally speaking, the music of the Naro people can serve multiple functions, depending on people's activity. However, this does not imply that Naro music is worthless outside its social role. While some scholars have dismissed African music as meaningless because of its cyclic and repetitive nature, Euba (1970: 121) recognises that 'knowledge of the speech language of the ethnic group to which the piece belongs is crucial to an understanding of the musical language'.

Finally, the meaning of both performance and text in Naro music can be inferred by observing visual expressions that accompany the song. These add an artistic side and dramatic element to it, adding a dimension to the musical component that would be missed if an audience only listened without looking. The Naro performance shows that musical sounds can acquire textual meaning that goes beyond the literal and the obvious.

Analysis in terms of scales, ranges, metres, ostinatos, and melodic and rhythmic patterns

In her endeavour to identify a musical education philosophy based on African music, Carver (2002: 47) suggests holism as a possible approach, in line with the premise that 'music is embedded in a social and, thus, cultural matrix'. From the African perspective, the symbiotic relationship between music and culture is incontrovertible. Therefore, since culture should be perceived as a whole, rather than as 'surface patterns' on their own (Blacking in Carver 2002: 47), African music must also be approached holistically. That system of analysis stands in contrast to the Western method of looking at musical aspects embedded in culture (ranges, form and structure, metres, ostinatos, and melodic and rhythmic patterns) as separate music elements. Below, I analysed those aspects in the music of the Naro from a Western perspective. However, they do not function as separate entities, but rather as a composite.

The music of the Naro can easily confuse the casual music theorist who listens without paying closer attention to starting points. Most of this music has its root in modes of various degrees. San music is modal, since it tends to lack clear starting points, the attribute similar to the musical mode as defined in *Music Theory*.[5] This manual describes a musical mode as an ordered series of intervals that relate to a starting note, the absolute pitch of which is not specified. Discussing the difference between a mode and a scale, this work maintains that the mode is abstract for its lack of a definite starting pitch.

Music Theory[6] argues that the moment you 'specify the starting note by its absolute pitch and apply the definition of the mode, you obtain a scale'. In an analytical sense, once the starting note is pointed out, the scale automatically becomes the melody of the mode[7].

While this explains the basic pattern of the Naro music to some extent, the music mostly ends up taking the absolute form of either a major or minor scale, notwithstanding its having started from an unspecified note. However, it has become evident that the dominating scale in both instrumental and a cappella songs is pentatonic (having five notes per octave), while heptatonic (having seven notes) and hexatonic (having six notes) scales were picked up, especially in the instrumental music (for example in pieces played on *tantadiri* and *dqoma*[8]). In the Western theory of music, the total range of available musical sound covers more than seven octaves.

The human voice and most musical instruments operate within a segment of the musical space described above. Music of the Naro, usually within the same range, at times differs when it comes to the pitch range, especially with regard to the upper voices used during Naro performances. The highness or lowness of sound within the Naro music can mesmerise the listener—surprisingly, women's voices can reach higher than the second octave note 'A' on the treble clef. When it comes to scoring, alternation is between three parts—soprano, mezzo-soprano and men's voices (upper, middle and lower voices).

A large number of the Naro songs and dances are set to simple, duple, triple, or compound metres. A proper understanding of the Naro songs and dances must be guided by the examination of the relationship between its metric groups and the tempo, sources of beats, and the emphasis of those beats. The music of the Naro can be characterised by regular quality of movement based on equal metric groups and well-emphasised beats. This emphasis is mostly executed by women clapping. Most Naro songs maintain a steady and moderate pace, but vigour grows gradually as a result of the cross-rhythmic patterns brought about by the dancers. The cross beats brought into the performance by the dancers, especially the men with their ankle rattles or *dquri*,[9] can easily bamboozle the uninitiated ear into thinking that the Naro songs and dances are polymetric. It is not uncommon in Naro performances to see two or three dancers, each executing his group of beats into a single metre in one song.

Ostinato patterns (continually repeated musical phrases or rhythms) are observable throughout the musical performances of the Naro, in both instrumental and a cappella renditions. Instrumentalists often sing as they play, and it is common for the instrumental part to be based on cycling ostinatos and for the song to have its own independent melody, which may enter at a different point and vary as the song develops. Examples of this were seen in all instrumental performances that used the *dhengo*, *zoma*, *tantadiri*, and *djoma*. Among the Naro, the instrumental ostinatos provide the rhythmic and harmonic foundation for the song and often contain the outline of the song's melody, especially in compositions using the *tantadiri* and *dhengo*. As for a cappella performances, songs may be ad-libbed based on a set of stock phrases that can be rearranged, broken up, and presented in a new way to add variety throughout the same performance. This is especially common within the healing music, where the songs can be very long, at times lasting around 30 to 45 minutes per performance.

When it comes to melody, the Naro songs are cyclic in nature, and repetition is unavoidable as an organising principle on top of which improvisation is built. The melody and rhythm within the Naro songs are interwoven, always navigating the terrain towards a sense of completeness on top of form and structure, and the metre of each performance. To understand the exploitation of melody in the Naro songs, one needs to appreciate a technique known as hocket, where different performers sing individual notes of a melody alternately. This technique sees a single melody being shared between two or more alternating voices—when one voice sounds, the others are quiet. Just like the interlocking rhythmic patterns produced by dancers, hocketing is the process of combining simple interlocking parts to create a complex whole. The hocketing technique of the Naro must not be confused with Western organum (a form of early polyphony based on existing plainsong in medieval music[10]). As an aspect of melody among the Naro, the hocket technique occurs when a second melody is added in parallel with the main melody. However, the added melody does not support the main melody, duplicating it instead at an interval of either a fourth or fifth down or up. This was especially clear in songs of social commentary, where performers recited laments in instrumental ensembles of *tantadiri*, *zoma*, and *dhengo* to highlight acts of repression.

Rhythm is contentious, but probably the most interesting aspect of Naro music. While the measurement of musical time from the Western perspective takes place according to an idea or plan in the composer's mind, in Naro music, the rhythmical measurement of time is determined by the mood and emotions of the performers. Hence, to a large extent, the Naro songs and dances are cross-rhythmic. Generally speaking, Naro songs are polyrhythmic, which means that two or more conflicting rhythms not readily understood as deriving from one another or as being different manifestations of the same metre can be used simultaneously. These polyrhythmic patterns happen as a result of common cross beats and syncopated notes produced by both women's clapping and men's dancing.

Analysis in terms of thematic areas in which Naro music is used

The music of the Naro of D'Kar currently uses eight thematic areas. These are music for healing, entertainment, in thanksgiving, as social commentary, for hunting, during initiation, in worship, and in children's play. However, research participants and two trance masters—69-year-old Mr Xgaiga Qhomatca and 64-year-old Mr Xhara Qoma—all emphasised the importance of the historic use of music for healing purposes.

Qhomatca mentioned that he first heard music being used in his community 'when I was still a small child. I found my parents and grandparents singing and dancing to cure illnesses' (Qhomatca interview, 28 November 2015). Qoma had similar experiences: 'My grandparents were dancing when I was still young and they used the song for curing illnesses and to drive away evil spirits' (Qoma interview, 28 November 2015). It became evident while collecting data that different activity areas were rooted primarily in the music of healing; even music for children's play could be associated with it, as the healing trance dances would be spontaneously triggered by children's play songs. The interview with Qoma further revealed that any form of music could 'kill him' and result in him starting to heal. The 'killing' refers to the trance state and the process of getting into that altered state of consciousness. The state of trance is described in the Naro language with the expression *cii sa x'oo*, which means 'to die because of a song' or 'death by song'. Qoma claimed that he could 'die' anytime, even during social dances, depending on how he connected with the song and dance at any given moment. Hence, 'I never dance during church services on Sundays, because I will die inside the church' (Qoma interview, 28 November 2015).

Carver (2002: 60) argues that much traditional music originated from healing ceremonies; therefore, the context in which a song occurs should be respected. When trying to categorise the collected songs of the Naro according to themes, it is apparent that some thematic areas overlap others, to the point of it becoming impossible sometimes to attribute a particular song to a theme. This complex, symbiotic web of relativity is the result of all the songs originating from music used for healing and their being later customised to different thematic areas. To solve the synoptic problem, I decided to divide the mentioned eight thematic areas into four broad categories, all of which emanate from healing songs and dances.

Figure 9.1 *Broad thematic areas*

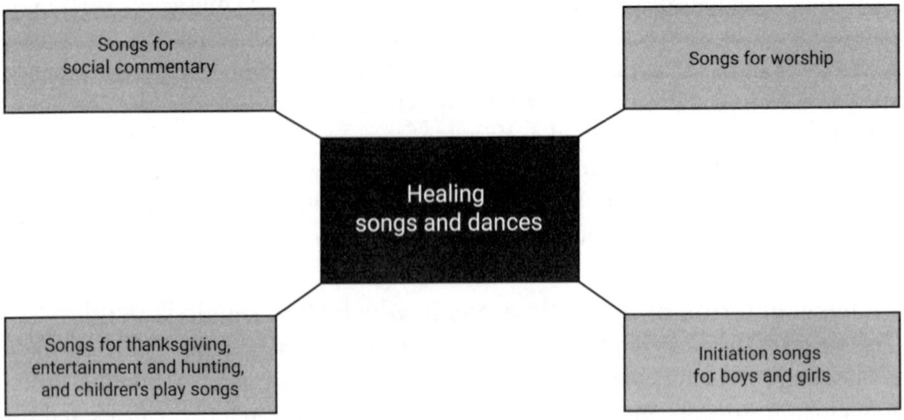

In the initiation songs category, various songs apply specifically to boys and girls at their different stages of transition from childhood into adulthood. *Zoma*, a musical instrument, is also the word used to refer to the initiation of boys. Numerous songs and dances are classified under *zoma*. Girls' initiation is called *duu*, meaning eland, and multiple songs and dances fall under this category. Initiation songs are in a category of their own, because Qhomatca had made it clear that music for those activities are never performed outside such ceremonies (Qhomatca interview, 28 November 2015).

The songs for worship are not common and are mostly accompanied on instruments like *zoma*, *tantadiri*, *dhengo* and *dqoma*. Usually these songs are solo performances, with the exception of those accompanied on a *tantadiri* by a women's ensemble of at least six at a time. Qoma, who is a master player of the *dhengo*, uses the instrument to worship God; maintaining the correct beat, tempo and tune, he accompanies people who sing or dance (Qoma interview, 28 November 2015). When the song reaches a climax, he throws the *dhengo* aside and joins the dance. In the process, he may go into a trance and begin to heal.

Music for social commentary predominates in the Naro musical repertoire. The songs mostly blame the government for the current predicament of the San people, and the uncertainties that threaten them because of political interference in their lifestyle. In one *tantadiri* group performance, the lead singer lamented the sufferings of the San people, who 'know many things in their own way'—a reference to the indigenous knowledge of the group. The song alluded to the San people's knowledge of indigenous medicines, hunting techniques and musical arts. In a nutshell, the Naro's music of social commentary can be termed music of a San nationalism.

Songs for thanksgiving, entertainment, hunting and children's play depict happiness and joy, and ultimately the belief in unending life. The source of that life is associated with the 'greater God residing in the eastern sky', according to Qhomatca. The songs are ceremonial in nature and directed at God, since 'we are nothing alone, but rely on Him to provide us with wild berries, wild animals, and more rains,' said Qoma.

Conclusion

The music of the Naro is primarily polyphonic and polyrhythmic, and it is essentially performed to serve specific communal functions. Taking into consideration that the songs remain valid and current within their thematic areas for the San communities, their suitability for inclusion into Botswana music education curriculum is unquestioned. When looking at elements such as structure, style, text, scales, ranges, metres, ostinatos, as well as melodic and rhythmic patterns of Naro music, it can be argued that the songs of this group can easily be incorporated at any level of the curriculum that deals with the music fundamentals of theory and practice. Furthermore, the performance contexts as well as the thematic areas of the songs correspond well with other traditional musics of the world, so they can complement music education as a part of world music history. This is especially important as an element of multicultural music education.

The role music plays in the development of human beings is fundamental to bringing about educated societies. Music provides people with a sense of collectivity through the process of cultural, personal and social expression. Preserving Naro music by including it in educational policy and the curriculum corresponds with the role education plays in ensuring continuity within societies and the preservation of cultural values, ideas, beliefs and skills. Botswana's 'quality' education should guarantee the protection of the achievements, knowledge and cultural heritage produced by all of society.

Given the pluralistic nature of Botswana society, a multicultural music education approach should be considered for the country's music education curricula. Such an approach would ensure equal footing in education for the diverse cultures in the country and thus contribute towards an inclusive and sustainable society. Moreover, it would acknowledge the role the cultural and social context play as an integral part of the lifestyles and identities of the multiple groups in Botswana, including the Naro of D'Kar. Accordingly, including Naro music into the school curriculum would serve as a way of preserving the ICH of this group.

Notes

1   The term 'indigenous' refers to 'the root, something natural or innate' (Odora-Hoppers 2011: 76). In the context of this study, 'indigenous music' refers to the traditional music of an ethnic group.

2   Coby and Hessel Visser, personal communication, 8 July 2014.

3   In ethnomusicology, it is commonly accepted to pluralise the term 'music' when referring to various cultural music genres of African origin to accommodate the limitation posed by the direct translation of the English word.

4   Alternate or responsive singing by a choir in two divisions. Accessed 30 August 2017, www.dictionary.com/browse/antiphony

5   *Music Theory. Advanced Level.* Accessed October 2016, www.beverlyteacher.com/Music%20 Theory%20-%20Advanced.pdf

6   *Music Theory. Advanced Level.* Accessed October 2016, www.beverlyteacher.com/Music%20 Theory%20-%20Advanced.pdf

7   *Music Theory. Advanced Level.* Accessed October 2016, www.beverlyteacher.com/Music%20 Theory%20-%20Advanced.pdf

8   Orchestration among the Naro of D'Kar is minimal. They use only five instruments: (1) *dhengo* (thumb piano), (2) *zoma* (guitar-like instrument with four strings), traditionally made of wood, (3) *dqoma* (mouth bow), (4) *tantadiri* (a large bow-like instrument with one string), and (5) *maskanda* guitar. The Naro have known about all of these instruments for a long time, and the thumb piano is the most common and popular among all the KhoiSan.

9   *Dquri* is considered part of attire.

10   Merriam-Webster Dictionary. Accessed August 2017, www.merriam-webster.com/
     dictionary/organum.

References

Agawu K (2001) African music as text. *Research in African Literatures* 32(2): 8–16

Agawu K (2003) *Representing African music: Postcolonial notes, queries, positions.* London:
     Routledge

Bakan MB (2013) *World music: Traditions and transformations* (2nd edition). Prepublication copy

Barume AK (2010) *Land rights of indigenous peoples in Africa.* Copenhagen: International Work
     Group on Indigenous Affairs

Berg BL (2004) *Qualitative research methods for social sciences.* New York: Pearson

Boikhutso K and Jotia LA (2013) Language identity and multicultural diversity in Botswana.
     International Journal of Lifelong Education 32(6): 797–815

Carver MA (2002) Unit standards for African musics in South Africa. MA thesis, University of
     Pretoria

Carver M (2012) *Understanding African music.* Grahamstown: International Library of African
     Music

Campbell PS (2004) *Teaching music globally: Experiencing music, experiencing culture.* New York:
     Oxford University Press

Chebanne A (2008) A Sociolinguistic perspective of the indigenous communities of Botswana.
     African Study Monographs 29(3): 93–118

Chebanne A (2010a) The Khoisan in Botswana. Can multicultural discourse redeem them?
     Journal of Multicultural Discourses 5(2): 87–105

Chebanne A (2010b) The role of dictionaries in the documentation and codification of African
     languages: The case of Khoisan. *Lexikos* 20: 92–108

Corn A (2012) The role of the national recording project for indigenous performance in
     Australia in sustaining indigenous music and dance traditions. *Canadian Society for
     Traditional Music* 39(1): 231–250

Emmanuel E (2013) The use of rhythms as a form of therapy from traditional African
     perspectives. Paper presented at a multicultural music education lecture series/conference at
     the University of Jyväskylä, Finland

Euba A (1970) Creative potential and propagation of African traditional music. In *Collection of
     conference proceedings papers on African Music.* UNESCO: Paris

Gay G (2005) Politics of multicultural teacher education. *Journal of Teacher Education*
     56(3): 221-228. Accessed November 2017, http://journals.sagepub.com/doi/
     pdf/10.1177/0022487105275913

Kang HH (2010) Towards an understanding of contemporary Korean-American choral music.
     Doctoral thesis, University of South Carolina

Ketsitlile L (2012) An integrative review on the San of Botswana's indigenous literacy and formal
     schooling education. *The Australian Journal of Indigenous Education* 41: 218–228

Laws S, Harper C & Marcus R (2003) *Research for development: A practical guide*. London: Sage Publications

Lee R (1979) *The !Kung San*. Cambridge: Cambridge University Press

Leedy P & Ormrod JE (2006) *Practical research: Planning and design*. Upper Saddle River, NJ: Pearson Education

Lin CP and Lajinga AA (2013) *An introduction to selected instrumental ensembles and folk songs of East Malaysia*. Kuching: Sarawak Institute of Teacher Education, Batu Lingtang Campus, Jalan College

Marshall ET (1989) *The harmless people*. New York: Vintage Books

Mbatha B (2013) Un-packing four sequential modes of knowledge conversion in managing indigenous knowledge. *Indilinga African Journal of Indigenous Knowledge Systems* 12(2): 171–187

Morris D (2005) Indigenous knowledge systems (IKS) and the teaching of history. Accessed June 2015, www.museumsnc.co.za/aboutus/depts/archaeology/pdf/IKS.pdf

Nieuwenhuis J (2011) Qualitative research designs and data-gathering techniques. In K Maree (Ed.) First *steps in research*. Pretoria: Van Schaik

Nketia JHK (1979) *The music of Africa*. London: Victor Gollancz Ltd

Nonaka I (1996) The Knowledge Creating Company. In K Starkey (ed.) *How Organizations Learn*. London: International Thomson Business Press

Nyathi-Ramahobo L (2008) Minority tribes in Botswana: The politics of recognition. Minority Rights Group International briefing. Accessed October 2016, www.refworld.org/pdfid/496dc0c82.pdf

Nyathi-Saleshando L (2011) An advocacy project for multicultural education: The case of the Shiyei language in Botswana. *International Review of Education* 57(5/6): 567–582

Nzewi M (2003) Acquiring knowledge of the musical arts in traditional society. In A Herbst, A Kofi & M Nzewi (Eds) *Musical arts in Africa: Theory, practice and education*. Pretoria: University of South Africa

Odora-Hoppers CA (2011) Indigenous knowledge systems and academic institutions in South Africa. *Perspectives in Education* 19(1): 73–85

Phibion OS (2003) Bakalanga music and dance in Botswana and Zimbabwe. DMus thesis, University of Pretoria

Phuthego M (2007) An evaluation of the integration of indigenous musical arts in the creative and performing arts syllabus and the implementation thereof in primary schools curriculum in Botswana. DMus thesis, University of Pretoria

Rabatoko MF (2013) Ritual music and healing dances of the Basarwa of Botswana in the Ghanzi Region. BMus Honours thesis, University of Pretoria

Schadeberg J (2002) *The San of the Kalahari*. Pretoria: PrePress Images

Solway J (2011) 'Culture fatigue': The state and minority rights in Botswana. *Indiana Journal of Global Legal Studies* 18(1): 211–240

Stone R (1998) African music in a constellation of arts. In R Stone (Ed.) *The Garland Encyclopaedia of World Music* (Vol. 1). New York: Garland Publishing

Tanaka J (1980) *The San hunter-gatherers of the Kalahari*. Tokyo: University of Tokyo Press

Toivanen P (2013) The Yoik: Indigenous music from the North. Paper presented at the Multicultural Music Education Seminar, University of Jyväskylä, Finland, 15 September

UNESCO (United Nations Educational, Scientific and Cultural Organization) (2003) Convention for the Safeguarding of the Intangible Cultural Heritage. Accessed October 2016, portal. unesco.org/en/ev.php-URL_ID=17716&URL_DO=DO_TOPIC&URL_SECTION=201.html

Van der Meer W (2005) The location of music: Towards a hybrid musicology. *Dutch Journal of Music Theory* 10(1): 57–71

Interviews

Ms Tumku Bob, participant in the study, D'Kar village, 28 November 2015

Mr Xhara Qoma, trance master, D'Kar village, 28 November 2015

Mr Xgaiga Qhomatca, trance master, D'Kar village, 28 November 2015

PART 4

AN AFRICA WHERE DEVELOPMENT IS
PEOPLE-DRIVEN, UNLEASHING THE
POTENTIAL OF WOMEN AND YOUTH

10 | Stokvels as small-business financiers in KwaZulu-Natal, South Africa

Matshediso Joy Ndlovu

Much has been written about South Africa's economic problems—the triple challenge of unemployment, poverty and inequalities, as well as the role the small business can play in alleviating these. Yet, with much research and resources devoted to small business, the sector remains stagnant. Using the definition provided by South Africa's National Small Business Amendment Act (26 of 2003), a small business is defined as a business entity managed by one owner or more, employing between 5 to 50 employees, with assets not exceeding R5 million, and a turnover of less than R32 million a year. For the purposes of this chapter, 'small business' refers to those on the lower scale of the categories, or those that employ fewer people, with limited assets and revenue.

Studies reveal that as many as 40 per cent of small businesses lack funds to launch or expand their businesses (Mutezo 2005). This is supported by a study undertaken by South Africa's Department of Trade and Industry, which indicated that access to finance was a serious consequence of the inequalities of the past and needed to be redressed urgently (DTI 1994). Bbenkele (2007) suggests that this is the result of many people seeing traditional banks as being unsuccessful in meeting the needs of small business owners. Rogerson (2008) agrees and believes that the lack of finance, together with poor skills and leadership training as well as inflexible regulatory training, will continue to be a problematic thread in the small business policy arena.

While various studies have confirmed the lack of finance as a major impediment to the growth of small business, and that the microfinance sector can be a potential solution to this challenge, very few studies have been conducted to determine the potential of the informal sector to fill this gap. The study conducted by Denis (2004) confirms this and highlights the fact that, although literature in small business finance has grown tremendously over the past decades, a large body of information still remains untapped. Several aspects of entrepreneurial finance have not yet been examined empirically, including the role of stokvels (informal community lenders) as financiers for small businesses. This absence of literature, and the fact that that stokvels are worth an estimated R25 billion, representing a growing sector in South Africa, motivated this study.

This chapter aims to determine whether stokvels in the KwaZulu-Natal (KZN) region can expand access to finance for small businesses by providing microloans. It introduces stokvels and investigates their role as financiers for small businesses.

Its findings, recommendations and conclusions further provide a framework with which stokvels can be elevated to play a greater role in providing much-needed finance. The sections below review the literature about stokvels in South Africa, describing and analysing components of stokvels as well as their impact on the establishment, expansion and sustaining of small businesses. A description and discussion of the methodology, data and the empirical results follows, with the last section offering a conclusion and recommendations.

Literature review

'Microfinance' is an all-inclusive term in South Africa, referring to institutions that lend to both personal and business entities. It is defined as the financial innovation of providing small loans for people who lack collateral, do not have a verifiable credit history, or do not qualify for traditional credit (NCR 2008). The country's microfinance landscape is made up of a number of institutions, from Section 21 (non-profit) companies cooperatives, trusts, close corporations and proprietary limited companies to informal lenders such as stokvels and relatives. Mondi (2007) places the South Africa's total credit industry at an estimated total of R362 billion, with the microlending industry representing five per cent of the overall credit industry. He believes the credit industry is made up of various organisations servicing different markets—from the formal (commercial banks and NGOs) to the informal (stokvels, family and associates). For the purposes of this study, microfinance will be looked at from an informal perspective, specifically referring to stokvels.

Stokvels have been in existence as informal township lenders for much longer than the formal microfinance sector (Skowronski 2009). They are customarily defined as community-based rotating credit or savings clubs—members of the club make regular, fixed and cyclical contributions to a common fund, which is then either given as a lump sum to one member in each cycle or reinvested in the fund (Townsend & Mosala 2008). They are known in South Africa by various names, depending on the language used, for example *mohodisana* (Sesotho), *makgotla* (Setswana), or *gooi-goois* (Afrikaans) (African Response 2012). The word 'stokvel' is the most common and will be used throughout this chapter.

Many studies have stated that the term 'stokvel' has its origins in the stock fair cattle auctions run in the 19th century by English settlers who pooled money to buy cattle on auction (Lukhele 1990; Townsend & Mosala 2008; Calvin & Coetzee 2010; African Response 2012; Ndalana 2014). Some argue that stokvels should not be reduced to a European phenomenon, but should rather be acknowledged as a South African initiative that took place long before the settlers arrived and has stood the test of time (Msibi interview, 13 February 2015, 18 July 2015). The stokvel has since evolved and is thought to be primarily about mobilising financial resources for the attainment of specific targets within a group of like-minded individuals (Calvin & Coetzee 2010).

Seven types of stokvels exist, as described by Ndalana (2014) and www.stokvella.com:

1. *Contribution stokvels*: These are customary savings schemes where members contribute a fixed amount on an agreed frequency and then receive the lump sum on a rotational basis.
2. *Basic stokvels*: Also known as events stokvels, these differ slightly from the contribution stokvel in that they function as a savings scheme that pays out sums of money for specific events, such as for a death, or at Christmas.
3. *Grocery stokvels*: The main aim of this stokvel is to collect members' contributions throughout a period for the purpose of purchasing groceries at the end of the agreed-upon period. The collected contributions are then distributed either as cash, or as cash coupons, or as groceries.
4. *Purchasing stokvels*: This form of stokvel collects contributions from members with the sole aim of assisting them to save for and purchase big items/assets.
5. *Family stokvels*: This type of stokvel is formed by families with the aim of saving to address and provide for the needs of the family.
6. *Party stokvels*: This type of stokvel is business orientated. The members are in the business of arranging events and then sharing the profits made from the event.
7. *Investment stokvels*: This stokvel collects contributions from members, then invest it for a period. At the maturity of the investment, the money is paid out and shared among members.
8. *Borrowing stokvels*: This stokvel lends money from its regular pool of money to members, sub-members and other community members at high monthly interest rates (between 20 and 50 per cent).

The study on which this chapter is based indicates that the most popular forms of stokvel remain the traditional ones such as the basic, contribution and grocery stokvels, although this is changing with the younger generation moving away from the traditional consumption-related stokvels to modern stokvels aligned with investment and saving (Ndalana 2014). The study by Kisaka-Lwayo and Obi (2013) supports this view. This chapter focuses on the borrowing and investment stokvel.

The literature indicates that, although stokvels are heralded as a success story in South Africa, large knowledge gaps exist when it comes to how stokvels do and can impact the establishment, expansion and sustainment of entrepreneurship. Questions that can close the gaps include:

- How many stokvels loan to small businesses?
- Why do stokvels who do not loan to small business not do so?
- How many stokvels plan to loan to small business?
- What can be done to encourage stokvels to invest?

Methodology

The study on which this chapter is based used a mixed-method research process for its ability to improve the validity and rigour of the study and to enhance research understanding (Hair et al. 2010). The concurrent, triangulation design used entailed collecting quantitative and qualitative data simultaneously. The quantitative data included a survey of 50 stokvels in the KwaZulu-Natal area and was complemented by qualitative in-depth interviews with key players. To qualify, a stokvel had to have been in operation for more than two years, be a borrowing/lending type of stokvel and be based in or servicing the KZN market. The quantitative data provided numerical data, making it easy to determine the magnitude and frequency of relationships, while the qualitative data provided additional information that enhanced interpretation and understanding, enabling in-depth analysis. The collected data was then compared and interpreted, and a model was developed that provided a multi-faceted and complete picture.

Probability sampling (simple random sampling), where every object has the same probability of being chosen, was deemed the most appropriate for the research that informed this chapter. This was because it enabled the study to draw externally valid conclusions about the entire population based on the sample. It was the simplest probability sampling technique, meaning time and resource savings were achieved. Moreover, it was thought to be the safest way to ensure that the total population was sufficiently represented by the sample and it was seen as relatively easy to interpret data collected in this manner (Yates, Moore & Starnes 2008).

Populations and sample

Jones (2015) places the total number of stokvel clubs in South Africa at between 400 000 and 800 000, and their worth at between R25 billion and R45 billion. KZN was estimated to have 10 per cent of that market (Ndalana 2014). Four provinces made up 70 per cent of the stokvel market: Gauteng has 24 per cent, Limpopo 20 per cent, the North West province 12 per cent and KZN 14 per cent (Badat 2012). Placing the total number of stokvels in the country at 800 000, the KZN stokvel population would therefore number 112 000. Before data collection could begin, an appropriate sample size had to be determined. Israel (2013) says that, for a researcher to achieve an appropriate sample size, various factors have to be considered. These include the aims and objectives of the study, the population size, the risk of choosing a 'bad' sample, the permissible sampling error, the level of precision, the level of confidence, and the degree of variability in the attributes being measured. All these were considered when selecting the sample size for this study. The sample was 50, an ideal size considering the suggestion of Sekaran and Bougie (2009) that a sample size greater than 30 and fewer than 500 is appropriate for most research.

The population and sample sizes breakdown for the research was as follows:

Table 10.1 *Population and sample sizes*

	Population	Sample
Quantitative (surveys)	112 000	50
Qualitative (interviews)	112 000	15
	TOTAL	65

Design

Van Wyk (2015: 4) says research design is an overall plan that describes theoretical research problems and connects it to field research. He further believes that it looks at the most cost-effective way to collect and analyse data. Mdluli (2006) defines it simply as the overall organisation and planning of the research. Two broad types of research design exist—quantitative and qualitative. Neuman (2000) defines quantitative research as research design that measures objective facts and tests hypotheses, while qualitative research measures and generalises data in an ad hoc, researcher-dependent method. He adds that it uses disciplines to distinguish between the two. Quantitative research stems from the physical sciences and is scientific, objective and reliable, while qualitative research is rooted in the social sciences and seeks to understand behaviours and social phenomena through direct engagement with the subjects (Neuman 2000).

Instruments

Many methods can be used to collect data for research—from literature review to interviews. These measurement tools are also referred to as instruments. Biddix (2015) suggests that research instruments are divided into two—those administered by the researcher and those administered by the respondent. Sekaran and Bougie (2013) believe each type of instrument has its own advantage or disadvantage. Based on the research questions and the need to balance advantages and disadvantages, instruments were selected from both categories.

Statistical analysis

The three-point Likert scale was used and each item was scored as illustrated in Table 10.2 below.

Table 10.2 *Response format and scoring in the survey*

Response format	Allocated score
Agree	3
Disagree	2
Not sure	1

The quantitative study involved sending 50 questionnaires to stokvel clubs in KZN. The aim was to determine scientifically whether stokvels could play a role as financiers of small businesses. Ninety-five per cent of the questionnaires were returned. The results are presented in Table 10.3.

The broad objective of the qualitative study was to add value to the quantitative results and gain additional insights into the stokvel sector. It was also useful in supporting the quantitative study, conducted concurrently, and entailed conducting phenomenological interviews with 15 key role players in the sector.

These individuals occupied management positions within their clubs, such as that of chairperson, deputy chair and treasurer—in other words, they had sufficient industry knowledge. The respondents were located throughout KZN.

Study outcomes

The research indicated the following:

Forms of stokvels
Eighty-five per cent of respondents belonged to traditional stokvels (contribution, basic and grocery stokvels). Ten per cent belonged to purchasing stokvels, and the remaining five per cent belonged to family, investment and borrowing stokvels. None of the respondents belonged to the party stokvel.

Membership of stokvels
The average number of members in a club was 23 and the average age was 45 years. None of the respondents had members younger than 35 years of age. Younger members tended to join basic (events) stokvels, while the older generations belonged to grocery and contribution clubs.

Contribution of members
Contributions tended to be minimal, ranging from R100 to R500, even in the higher Living Standards Measure (LSM) groups. Members were careful not to overcommit, with payment of the agreed fixed amount being on a monthly basis. Members who were keen to receive a higher return would normally borrow money from the club, then lend it to others outside the club at a higher interest rate. The more the members borrowed, the bigger the interest share they would receive. Members who did not provide microloans could expect to get only the amounts they had contributed. It was rare for members to get less than they had contributed, unless they owed the club money.

Loan provision
Seventy-five per cent of the respondents provided loans to members, sub-members and the community at large. A member who recommended a loan approval would stand as guarantor and would have to pay in cases of default. This was a risk that dissuaded members from taking loans and encouraging others to do likewise. The high interest rate normally charged did not make up for the high risk. The appetite for risk was generally low in these clubs. Members wanted at least a return of the money they had contributed.

Loans to small businesses (general, youth and women)
Fewer than 30 per cent of the respondents provided loans to small businesses. This number could be higher, since half of the respondents claimed that it was nearly

impossible to establish that with certainty, because they normally did not keep records or ask borrowers what they intended to use the money for. What they were primarily concerned about was the return date and interest amounts. Many confessed that, even though the need for funding was probably high for youth-owned entrepreneurs, they would not be inclined to provide them with loans because they considered them high risk.

Plans to lend to small businesses (general, youth and women)

More than 50 per cent of respondents were keen to change the direction of their clubs in the future. They felt that the investment and borrowing stokvels were well positioned to explore these opportunities and to attract the younger generation that had shunned the sector, considering it old and irrelevant.

Registration

Almost all (99 per cent) of the stokvels were neither registered credit providers, nor members of the National Stokvel Association or any other sector associations. They saw no benefit in formalising in this manner, and the general vision seemed to be short-term, with minimum to average return expectations.

Table 10.3 *Percentage of respondents scoring outcome measures with highest success*

Outcome measure	Percentage
Provides small loans	75
Lends to small businesses	25
Lends to women-owned small businesses	17
Lends to youth-owned small businesses	5
Plans to lend to small businesses	65
Plans to lend to women-owned businesses	54
Plans to lend to youth-owned small businesses	58
Registered loan provider	6

Most of the respondents were not convinced that their associations could play any significant role in the development of small businesses. It was a concept they were unfamiliar with, although some said they might play an indirect role.

The risk factor was a concern and something that most felt they could not dedicate time to managing and administering.

This study set out to determine whether the sector provided microlending to small businesses and, if it did, the level at which it occurred, and who the recipients of such loans were. The objective was to establish whether the stokvel sector could play a role of any significance as a financier for the small businesses. These objectives were met, as is evident from the discussion above.

Conclusion

This chapter indicates that, although investment and borrowing stokvels have been slowly gaining popularity and could play a significant role as a financier of small businesses in the future, the sector was not ready to take advantage of the opportunity. Ndalana (2014) points out that only five per cent of stokvels were invested in the stock market or in entrepreneurial activities. This is a low proportion, considering the size of the market. This study tried to establish whether the possibility existed of increasing this percentage and what it was that enabled or prevented these clubs from playing the financier role. Many raised risk as the major factor preventing them from going in that direction, citing the fact that most start-ups went out of business within two years of commencing operation. This emphasised just how risky a venture that could be for them.

Furthermore, the transition from traditional stokvels to borrowing and/or investing stokvels would entail investing in further resources such as administering the loans, registering as credit providers, and then ensuring compliance with various requirements. For many, this would be costly and time consuming.

Respondents to the study on which this chapter is based pointed out that their main reasons for joining or starting stokvels were to save money to satisfy and/or address a specific individual need, and not for entrepreneurial purposes. They felt strongly that these were two different issues that should be separated. Exploring the option further would be too much work and should be conducted by other parties such as the government, NGOs, the private sector and so on.

This is a disappointing result, because this type of thinking prevents many from making a real difference in the country and the KZN province. Because of it, stokvel members miss out on opportunities that could get real rewards and growth as a result of their contributions.

Recommendations

Although the findings of this research are not entirely conclusive—for example, a lot of uncertainty existed about the main reasons why people borrowed from the clubs and what the microloans were used for—they do highlight a number of issues and form a basis for the recommendations below.

Stokvel function

The way stokvels function and are managed should be reviewed. While more than 80 per cent had a guiding constitution, fewer than 20 per cent were registered or formed part of an association body, so institutional and external compliance was generally low. Many members wanted an informal and easy club that did not require additional effort from them. But where they do want growth, they would need to do more work around strategy and full compliance. Furthermore, where they want to remain sustainable, they would need to relook their purpose and how they operate, and tailor these to the needs of the younger generation, who consider the clubs outdated and irrelevant to current conditions.

Governance and compliance

The sector is known for low compliance and governance, and members want high returns with minimal effort. On occasion in the past, this had led to instances of consumer and member exploitation. For future growth and sustainability, much emphasis will have to be placed on governance and compliance.

Product and service overhaul

The sector does not provide its members with many alternatives. The offering remains basic and uninspiring, with many scholars and practitioners recommending an overhaul of the sector. Skowronski (2009) recommends that the sector's microfinance intermediaries (MFIs) investigate the possibility of offering additional financial services such as long-term savings and insurance products, since its market is particularly vulnerable and at risk of experiencing unexpected financial crises such as death, major health incidents and losses as a result of crime, to name a few.

Massive consumer education

Poor interface with the consumer was notable and acknowledged by many MFIs. Issues of trust, lack of microfinance knowledge and poor marketing featured strongly. Consumers were wary of the MFIs and did not have sufficient knowledge about the sector, while the sector was featured neither extensively nor positively in the media. This should be changed—the public should be widely educated about the sector, which should also be broadly marketed and specifically branded. MFIs must make efforts to meet the needs not only of the urban poor, but of rural people as well, since the need in far-flung areas is very high.

Funding and investors

Lack of funds is a major problem for the industry. The high risks involved and the fact that the sector is young makes it unattractive to potential investors and funders. Reportedly high corruption levels, low governance and unfavourable environmental factors further add up to weak funding attraction. Private–public partnerships (PPPs) can be entered into to provide MFIs with much-needed funding and to explore ways in which to build capacity.

Future research

Future research may explore how the sector can be educated about opportunities and how risks may be minimised. Further future research may include:
- Evaluating the real returns of lending to small businesses as opposed to borrowing for individual consumption;
- Conducting a comparison analysis between various forms of stokvel;
- Assessing funding models for the marginalised in South Africa, then comparing these with the offering of the stokvels; and
- Investigating why some groups of people were not keen to join and invest in the sector, and determining whether factors other than the high level of risks were at play.

Limitations

The study that informed this chapter had a number of limitations. These ranged from the lack of information on MFIs and stokvels in particular, to the lack of comprehensive prior research conducted on stokvels. Limited data is available in the public domain, since so few stokvels are registered, listed or banked entities that have the obligation to report to persons or institutions other than their members.

Despite these shortcomings, the quality and validity of the study was not compromised. Instead, the limitations highlight the need for more research. Future research should look at different variables and contexts, and it should be primary, not secondary, research. This study contributes to the existing literature and body of knowledge by providing a documented exploration of stokvels. It builds on existing theories and establishes that stokvels could be financiers for small businesses, given the correct environment.

References

African Response (2012) Stokvels–a hidden economy–unpacking the potential of South African traditional saving schemes. Accessed March 2015, www.africanresponse.co.za/assets/press/2012StokvelHiddenEconomy.pdf

Badat NY (2012) Not your gogo's stokvels. Accessed February 2015, www.iol.co.za/the-star/not-your-gogos-stokvels-1243875

Bbenkele EK (2007) An investigation of small and medium enterprises perceptions towards services offered by commercial banks in South Africa. *African Journal of Accounting, Economics, Finance and Banking Research* 1(1): 13–25

Biddix JP (2015) Research methodology. Accessed September 2015, researchrundowns.com/quantitative-methods/

Calvin B and Coetzee G (2010) *Review of the South African microfinance sector. Volume II Section IV: Special products.* University of Pretoria Centre for Microfinance. Accessed July 2015, www.up.ac.za/media/shared/Legacy/sitefiles/file/1/3841/volumeiisectionivspecialproducts.pdf

Denis DJ (2004) Entrepreneurial finance: An overview of the issues and evidence. *Journal of Corporate Finance* 10(2): 301–326

DTI (Department of Trade and Industry) (1994) Strategies for the development of integrated policy and support programme for small, medium and micro-enterprise in South Africa. Discussion paper. Pretoria: DTI

Hair JF, Money HA, Celsi MW, Samouel P and Page MJ (2010) *Essentials of business research method* (2nd edition). New York: ME Sharpe

Israel GD (2013) Determining sample size. Accessed November 2017, http://www.psycholosphere.com/Determining%20sample%20size%20by%20Glen%20Israel.pdf

Jackson P (2014) 3 reasons entrepreneurs fail to secure funding. Accessed August 2017, www.entrepreneur.com/article/234604

Jones G (2015) A stokvel by any other name is still empowering. Accessed June 2015, www.businesslive.co.za/bd/companies/financial-services/2015-05-11-a-stokvel-by-any-other-name-is-still-empowering/

Kisaka-Lwayo M and Obi A (2013) Econometric analysis of risk preference patterns among smallholder organic producers in South Africa. *Journal of Agricultural Science and Technology* 3(3): 171–181

Lukhele A (1990) *Stokvels in South Africa: Informal savings schemes by Blacks for the Black Community.* Johannesburg: Amagi Books

Mdluli TK (2006) Developing a research policy model for the South African local government health sector: A case study at the eThekwini Municipality. DBA Thesis, University Of Kwa-Zulu Natal. Accessed August 2017, researchspace.ukzn.ac.za/handle/10413/1308

Mondi L (2007) Mass banking and the micro-financing industry in SA's second economy. Paper presented at the Making Finance Work for Africa conference, Zambezi Sun Hotel, Livingstone, Zambia, 7–9 May 2007

Mutezo TA (2005) Obstacles in the access of SMME funding: An empirical perspective on Tshwane. MComThesis, UNISA. Accessed September 2017, www.uir.unisa.ac.za/bitstream/handle/10500/1803/dissertation.pdf;sequence=1

NCR (National Credit Regulator) (2008) *National Credit Regulator Report.* Accessed October 2015, www.ncr.org.za/documents/pages/Financial%20Statement/Financial%20Statements%20(1).pdf

Ndalana L (2014) Investment in stokvels gaining ground. Accessed June 2015, www.fin24.com/Savings/Get-Saving/Investment-stokvels-gaining-ground-20140709

Neuman WL (2000) *Social research methods: Qualitative and quantitative approaches* (4th edition). Boston: Allyn & Bacon

Rogerson CM (2008) Tracking SMME development in South Africa: Issues of finance, training and the regulatory environment. *Springer Science* 19(3): 61–81

Sekaran U and Bougie R (2013) *Research methods for business: A skill-building approach* (6th edition). Chichester: John Wiley & Sons Publishers

Sekaran U and Bougie R (2009) *Research methods for business: A skill-building approach* (5th edition). Chichester: John Wiley & Sons Publishers

Skowronski G (2009) The microcredit sector in South Africa: An overview of the history, financial access, challenges and key players. Accessed August 2017, www.gdrc.org/icm/country/za-mf-paradigmshift.pdf

Townsend S and Mosala T (2008) The stokvel sector: Opportunities and challenges. Accessed August 2017, www.sk.sagepub.com/cases/the-stokvel-sector-opportunities-and-challenges

Van Wyk B (2015) *Research design and methods, Part I: Post-graduate enrolment and throughput.* Cape Town: University of the Western Cape

Yates DS, Moore DS and Starnes DS (2008) *The practice of statistics* (3rd edition). New York: WH Freeman Publishing Company

Interviews

NP Msibi, Chairperson: Siyakhula Stokvel Club, Durban, 13 February 2015 and 18 July 2015

#Sowhat? Or a letter to new African thinkers

Olga Bialostocka and Vuyo Mjimba

As academics, we have an important role to play in seeking solutions to the many societal concerns of our times. In its purest form, our role is definitely not to seek glory, nor to appeal to popular opinion. Neither is it for us to use our skills, titles, degrees and expertise merely to shine on conference pedestals or university plinths, to out-talk radio or television presenters and catch the limelight each time it is within our grasp. No, we must be agents of change who use our understanding of various pieces of societal issues and their associated processes as it pertains to our discipline for the greater good.

Admittedly, we cannot be experts in everything and we should not pretend we are, especially on public platforms such as radio and television. In fact, these platforms of communication can project any information as being of a higher quality than it actually is, turning anyone in the studio into an expert of some sort. This is not surprising; after all, the media have their own agendas, usually governed by numbers, and are not necessarily astute when it comes to academic rigour and collective concerns. Thus, beware the lure of such platforms; we do not automatically become specialists simply by being given a national or even international platform to speak. We do not become scholars just because we were offered the label by institutions or individuals who, themselves, have no authority in granting us such a distinction. Nor do we become experts by joining renowned symposia or associations, where our name might proudly lurk next to that of a well-reputed academic. Expertise needs to be grown and systematically nurtured through years of meticulous research, hours of intense reading, and analysis of hundreds of scholarly works published by others. Experts grow from receiving robust mentoring and critiques from like and differently minded colleagues. Expertise is not built in a vacuum; instead, it matures on the back of the history of a particular field we deem our speciality.

The trend of instant experts is cause for concern, since it can put in jeopardy the integrity of high-level research. We need to resist the temptation of the shiny fruit of quick success because it can abruptly turn out to be not so sweet when we come face to face with real experts who may expose our ignorance, whether on purpose or inadvertently. We should be mindful of a desire for quick elevation to the top of the academic mountain by always being around influential people, in the right place and at the right time. A rapid rise is not always the best way to the top; at least not to the real top, where Socrates, with his famous 'all I know is that I know nothing', reminds us of the virtue of introspection.

Our research needs to serve people. Research for the sake of research, career advancement or egotistic self-development has no place in today's world with all its challenges. Neither are the financial means available to conduct scholarly work with just these objectives in mind. That is why, each time we embark on a new research journey, we should ask ourselves a simple question: So what? What do my results mean in the greater scheme of things? Where do they lead me? What practical and theoretical lessons do my research findings and conclusions offer?

During the 10th Africa Young Graduates and Scholars (AYGS) conference hosted by the University of Limpopo in March 2016, Dr Vuyo Mjimba asked the *#sowhat* question, which quickly became the catchphrase of the event. Focused on their respective presentations, participants were suddenly forced to look at the bigger picture and go to the core of the sense and purpose of their research, asking themselves: Why do I do what I do? Who do I serve? What guides me? What do I want to achieve and why? So, what did Vuyo mean when he asked the now famous *sowhat* question? Here is his explanation.

Vuyo: Very early in my life I developed a habit of questioning everything around me. This included interrogating the fact that I should eat at the same time as everyone else, even when I was not hungry. I often wondered why my father's car (and all other cars) moved forward and, at times, backward with such ease, when I struggled to walk backwards. I also asked myself why some minerals lay buried very deep underground while others did not. A few years ago, my mother reminded me about my habit of asking questions over and over again, much to her irritation. I faintly recall how this so-called quality sometimes got me into trouble, because I grew up in a culture where children had to be seen and not heard. During the 2016 AYGS conference, my inquisitive nature took over again. I asked the *so what* question after a young scholar delivered a presentation that examined the history of commercially rich, ancient African empires. My query was not intended to put the presenter on the spot, but rather to spark in the audience a deeper reflection on the implications of the findings of the paper they had just listened to: How can Africa's past glories be used to inform pathways to conquer present challenges? It may be heart-warming to hear that Africa played a great role in global commerce in ancient times—especially for an African—but it does not soothe the pains of the present-day afflictions that have caused the continent to maintain the label of the least developed in virtually all the measures of development. My *so what* question was related to the lessons that can be drawn from these ancient empires, and their contemporary application in the many poor, disease-ridden and politically mismanaged modern countries of Africa. The presentation was fascinating, but *so what*?

Research must have a purpose. It has to increase knowledge to solve the lingering problems of the contemporary world. The generation of credible knowledge dictates a need for robust research. Vital in this process are the conclusions drawn from the academic work. Meanwhile, when asked about conclusion(s) of their very well thought-out and articulated research problems and questions, complicated methodologies, and interesting results, emerging scholars usually provide summaries of their findings. Drawing conclusions from the latter seems to be a challenge for many young researchers. The *so what* question is an attempt to help and guide them towards reaching robust conclusions in their research, conclusions that would further translate into effective applications.

As standard practice, conclusions must exhibit the value of a piece of research. They emerge from completely developed arguments and thoroughly answered research questions. Solid conclusions come as a result of reflection; at the end of a paper, thesis or presentation, the readers or audience need to have a clear understanding of the benefits of the work completed. To this end, the conclusion has to achieve a number of objectives, which can be encapsulated in the following three rules of thumb:

1. The conclusion has to link the study findings to a larger context within which the research is located.
2. It should suggest the implications of the research findings, as well as their importance within the specific field.
3. It should ask questions and/or suggest ideas for further research.

The implications or importance of findings relate directly to the *so what* question; it is in the conclusions of research papers that researchers draw out the distinguishing features of study results. For example, in their monumental work on the effects of natural resources on economic development, Sachs and Warner (1995, 1997, 2001) demonstrate that, in almost all of the cases they had studied, economies with extremely abundant natural resources grew less rapidly for the period of 20 years between 1970 and 1990 than the economies with fewer natural resources. To explain the phenomenon, the scholars suggested that resource-rich countries tended to be high-price economies, which, as a consequence, might often miss out on export-led growth. Thus, Sachs and Warner conclude, since resource abundance has a tendency to retard economic development, industrialisation should be prioritised in countries that seek rapid economic growth. This conclusion was not a thumb suck; it was based on a thorough interrogation of the relevant literature, and resulted from the scholars asking themselves the *so what* question once their findings were clearly articulated and demonstrated. In this case, a negative correlation between resource abundance and economic growth and development was not sufficient as a conclusion to the study; an explanation of the paradox was needed. The essence of research is to draw lessons from findings. Sachs and Warner's lesson spoke to the folly of relying on natural resources to drive economic growth and development. And that was the conclusion of their research on this subject.

The economic history of industrialised and newly industrialised economies is well documented, highlighting cases of good and bad practices. The question is, what does it all mean to the contemporary Africa that tries to improve its economic, environmental and social conditions? *So what* for Africa, the continent presented as the cradle of civilisation that has hosted great and rich empires, and suffered from slavery, colonialism and neocolonialism? *So what*? If academics could answer this question in theory and in practice, perhaps the condition of many African countries could change for the better. This is the challenge for both emerging and experienced scholars, as well as practitioners in private and public spaces.

* * *

Research has to have a purpose and the publications that emerge from it must advance the field, either theoretically or empirically, and even practically. In essence, there must be some value added. This added value will be usually summarised in the form of conclusions at the end of the paper.

Anne Frank once wrote that 'paper is more patient than man'. Anything can be written on paper, and paper does not judge or resist. However, the reader brings a new dimension to academic writing in the form of opinions—acceptance or rejection of the publication. Thus, it is prudent for any academic to write only if they have something noteworthy to communicate. Do not yield to the pressure of academia to publish or perish, even when you have simply nothing to say. In other words, 'if you have nothing nice to say, say nothing at all'. It is true that a good track of publications can help secure funding for your future research and open the door to tenure at the universities. However, this pressure to write plentifully and strive to publish (even inadequately reasoned ideas) presents a hazard; you may end up killing your integrity as a scholar by disseminating substandard work under your name. Seek to strike a balance between quality and quantity. If you believe that you do have important and interesting insights on a topic to share with the public, communicate this through scholarly and rigorous writing in an accredited and highly regarded publication.

So, why are you publishing? Is it because it is a norm expected by the institution where you work? Do you consider it a good way of promoting yourself, reaching new heights in academia or business, or is it because of personal goals and aspirations? Or do you want to make a difference and have some impact on society? After all, this is what scholarly research is all about—to better explain the world so that we can all navigate life in a more humane way.

Academia will challenge you. Therefore, be authentic and know why you are doing what you are doing. Do not compromise your integrity by chasing numbers that do nothing to move the world forward. Publish only if you truly have something insightful to say.

References

Sachs J and Warner AM (1995) Natural resource abundance and economic growth. National Bureau of Economic Research (NBER) Working Paper No 5398. Accessed September 2017, www.nber.org/papers/w5398.pdf

Sachs J and Warner AM (1997) Sources of slow growth in African economies. Institute for International Development and Centre for International Development. Harvard University. Accessed September 2017, www.earth.columbia.edu/sitefiles/file/about/director/documents/jrnafec1297.pdf

Sachs J and Warner AM (2001) Natural resource and economic development: The curse of natural resources. *European Economic Review* 45: 827–838

Contributors

Volume editor

Olga Bialostocka (PhD) works for the Africa Institute of South Africa in the Human Sciences Research Council, South Africa. She is interested in the broad field of culture as a pillar of and a resource for sustainable development.

List of contributors

James Ojochenemi David is a PhD candidate in the Department of Anthropology and Development Studies, University of Zululand, South Africa. His research interests include security, development and indigenous knowledge systems.

Hlengiwe Dlamini (PhD) is a postdoctoral fellow of the University of the Free State, South Africa. In her research, she focuses on politics and the evolution of the rule of law in Swaziland.

Vuyo Mjimba (PhD) is a Chief Research Specialist at the Africa Institute of South Africa in the Human Sciences Research Council, South Africa. His research focus is sustainable development around issues of industrialisation, green economy and renewable energy.

Natasha Katuta Mwila (PhD) is a lecturer in the Department of Management at Monash University, South Africa. She is interested in transdisciplinary studies.

Matshediso Joy Ndlovu (DBA) is a lecturer at the Graduate School of Business and Leadership at the University of KwaZulu-Natal, South Africa. She has extensive experience in growing and developing businesses and people in blue-chip organisations and highly competitive industries.

Sabelo Wiseman Ndwandwe holds a Master of Arts in Philosophy from the University of Fort Hare, South Africa. His research area is human rights.

Azubike Onuora-Oguno (PhD) is a researcher at the Centre for Human Rights, University of Pretoria, South Africa, and a lecturer in the Faculty of Law, University of Ilorin, Nigeria. His research revolves around children's rights and international human rights law.

Matheanoga Fana Rabatoko is a music lecturer at Molepolole College of Education in Botswana. He collects, documents and publishes indigenous musical arts of Botswana.

Malatsi Seleka is a doctoral candidate (Africa studies: Peace and conflict in context) at the Centre for Africa Studies, University of Free State, South Africa. His research interests include sustainable development practices, indigenous knowledge systems, land management and conservation.

Sigrid Shaanika is a Counselling Psychology student at the University of Pretoria and an intern psychologist at Rahima Moosa Mother and Child Hospital in Johannesburg, both in South Africa. Her research focuses on children exposed to and affected by violence and trauma.

Pfunzo Sidogi is a lecturer in the Department of Fine and Applied Arts at the Tshwane University of Technology, South Africa. His research interests are South African visual culture, Post-Africanism and Afropolitanism.

Dunia Prince Zongwe (PhD) is a lecturer in the Faculty of Law at the University of Namibia. He specialises in international finance and human rights, focusing on Africa and, in particular, Southern Africa.

Index